Culture(s) and Authenticity

CULTURES IN TRANSLATION
INTERDISCIPLINARY STUDIES IN LANGUAGE, TRANSLATION, CULTURE AND LITERATURE

Edited by
Elżbieta Muskat-Tabakowska and Agnieszka Pantuchowicz

VOLUME 1

Zu Qualitätssicherung und Peer Review der vorliegenden Publikation

Die Qualität der in dieser Reihe erscheinenden Arbeiten wird vor der Publikation durch einen externen, von der Herausgeberschaft benannten Gutachter im Double Blind Verfahren geprüft. Dabei ist der Autor der Arbeit dem Gutachter während der Prüfung namentlich nicht bekannt; der Gutachter bleibt anonym.

Notes on the quality assurance and peer review of this publication

Prior to publication, the quality of the work published in this series is double blind reviewed by an external referee appointed by the editorship. The referee is not aware of the author's name when performing the review; the referee's name is not disclosed.

Agnieszka Pantuchowicz / Anna Warso (eds.)

Culture(s) and Authenticity

The Politics of Translation
and the Poetics of Imitation

PETER LANG

**Bibliographic Information published
by the Deutsche Nationalbibliothek**
The Deutsche Nationalbibliothek lists this publication in
the Deutsche Nationalbibliografie; detailed bibliographic
data is available in the internet at http://dnb.d-nb.de.

Library of Congress Cataloging-in-Publication Data
A CIP catalog record for this book has been applied for
at the Library of Congress

This publication was financially supported by the
SWPS University of Social Sciences and Humanities.

Cover image: © Bartosz Szymański, Uniwersytet SWPS

Printed by CPI books GmbH, Leck

ISSN 2511-879X
ISBN 978-3-631-73239-7 (Print)
E-ISBN 978-3-631-73240-3 (E-Book)
E-ISBN 978-3-631-73241-0 (EPUB)
E-ISBN 978-3-631-73242-7 (MOBI)
DOI 10.3726/b11652

© Peter Lang GmbH
Internationaler Verlag der Wissenschaften
Berlin 2017
All rights reserved.

Peter Lang – Berlin · Bern · Bruxelles ·
New York · Oxford · Warszawa · Wien

All parts of this publication are protected by copyright. Any
utilisation outside the strict limits of the copyright law, without
the permission of the publisher, is forbidden and liable to
prosecution. This applies in particular to reproductions,
translations, microfilming, and storage and processing in
electronic retrieval systems.

This publication has been peer reviewed.

www.peterlang.com

Contents

Foreword 7

Eriko Sato
Translation across Cultures: Domesticating/Foreignizing Cultural
Transplantation 15

Said Faiq
Imitation, Representation… or the Master Discourse of Translation 23

Lada Kolomiyets
The Untranslatable Ethnic: Always an Outsider? A Brief Review of
Ukrainian-to-English Literary Translation Practices 41

Wojciech Kozak
Authenticity Reexamined: Muriel Spark's *The Public Image* 57

Piotr Skurowski
White-to-Black: Racechange and Authenticity, from John Howard
Griffin to Rachel Dolezal 69

Jerzy Sobieraj
Inversion, Conversion, and Reversion in Ellen Glasgow's *The Deliverance* 87

Agnieszka Podruczna
But Who Does Live? Postcolonial Identities, Authenticity, and Artificial
Intelligence in Darryl A. Smith's "The Pretended" 97

Jacek Wiśniewski
Editorial Revision and Recovery: Authenticity and Imitation in
John Clare's Early Poetry 105

Eliza Borkowska
The Birth of the Poet: The Role of S. T. Coleridge in the Making of
"William Wordsworth" 119

Natalia Kamovnikova
Identity Blurred: The Use of Interlinear Trots for Translations of Poetry
in the Soviet Union 133

Hanna C. Rückl
Imitation and Creativity: Ernst Jandl's Writing in Translation and Completion 143

Joanna Gładyga
The Birth of the Editor: On Authenticity in Raymond Carver's Writing and Editing 153

Nafize Sibel Güzel, Abdullah Küçük
A Non-Existent Source, A Successful Translation: Nihal Yeğinobalı's *Genç Kızlar* 161

Yulia Nanyak
Language Personality: Problems and Opportunities in Translation (Based on the Characters from the Tragedy *Faust* by Johann Wolfgang von Goethe and its Ukrainian and Anglophone Translations) 173

Debora Biancheri
Representations of Identity in Italian Translations of Seamus Heaney: Rewriting Poetry "True to Life" 183

Mark Ó Fionnáin
"The Future's Bright, the Future's Orange!" On the Translation of the Colour *Orange* into Irish 197

Contributors' Notes 207

Foreword

> Textual production may be initiated and guided by the producer, but it puts to work various linguistic and cultural materials which make the text discontinuous, despite any appearance of unity, and which create an unconscious, a set of unacknowledged conditions that are both personal and social, psychological and ideological. (Venuti, 24)

Authenticity seems to be an unquestionably positive category. In his reading of Sartre and Heidegger as thinkers obsessively calling us to be authentic, Roger Waterhouse looks at authenticity both as an object for which we struggle, and as the struggle itself – an effort whose ardor is opposed to "the tempting surrender to inauthenticity" (22). In fact we struggle with ourselves against the temptation of passively, or perhaps, lazily, accept what we are. Authenticity, unlike inauthenticity, is not easy and it requires from us a certain renunciation of passivity which is also a gesture of accepting the given whose "givenness" is always susceptible to being imposed. The work of authentication is thus tantamount to being independent from others, to an absolute kind of individuality or uniqueness which is also absolutely self-centered, so absolutely, in fact, that any identification with others, is a denial of my autonomy and integrity: "I am both a subject and an object, but only my subjectivity is freedom: my objectivity is unfreedom, the vehicle of inauthenticity, the interference of society with my autonomy and my integrity" (26).

The papers included in this volume address not so much the vehicle of inauthenticity as its mirror image – the vehicle of authenticity – the vehicle which Waterhouse does not mention by the name in his critique of the pursuit of authenticity, though which he implicitly finds at work in the construction of the negativity of the inauthentic. This negativity, at least in absolute terms, has become strongly weakened in more recent critical approaches to the question of the authentic through bringing the inauthentic itself to the sphere of interest and critical care. The effect of weakening the positive power of the original has been achieved, at least partly, through the deconstructive acceptance of the other as constitutive of the center. The Derridean principle of constitutive outside in which the contamination of the authentic is the inevitable effect of any writing has brought attention to the workings of any inscription, including the inscription of the authentic "itself", as a vehicle of constructing authenticity within the realm of iteration, of partial repetition which does not fully replicate, which does not duplicate, but allows for the entrance of others into the processes of production and creation. This weakening is also, an among others, the effect of bringing translation to the study of culture, of listening to it and seeing it with the ear of the other and noticing that translation, as Mark Wigley remarks in his essay on Babel and Derrida, "constitutes the original it is added to" (8), the addition, or surplus being the only possible and thinkable end or limit of the authentic. It is from the position of the other, the inauthentic "not-me," that the "me" can be spoken, and, as Derrida phrases it in *The Ear of the Other*, "[t]he ear of the other says me to me and constitutes the autos of my autobiography" (51). The perception of the authentic seems to be a projection of my authenticity, of the kernel of me which, as in Sartre and Heidegger, must remain untouched, even untouchable – a phantasm which is reflected in the idea of translation in which "we must translate ourselves into [the other language] and not make it come into our language" (115). Hence the ideal of what Lawrence Venuti calls "fluent translation", the translation in which the foreign does not speak – "the regime of fluent translating" in which "the translator works to make his or her work 'invisible,' producing the illusory effect of transparency that simultaneously masks its status as an illusion: the translated text seems "natural," i.e., not translated" (5).

The essays included in this volume speak about those and numerous other paradoxes of authenticity, the ways in which the authentic is searched for, staged, admired, dismissed, replicated or simply taken for granted. What seems to be at work in such discursive practices is a poetics of imitation, a paradoxical kind of poetics which renounces the authenticity of the created text for the sake of its semi-religius offering to the origin figuring somewhere else, in the sphere of a "there" in which the "here"of the translated text is subjected to the otherwise sovereign rule of the Authentic. Translation figures as an advertised imitation, an imitation which announces its inauthenticity so as to avoid any suspicion of thievery, of the appropriation of what does not really belong to the translator. What is at stake is also a divination of the Authentic which translates the poetics of imitation into a poetics of idolatry governed by a suspicion of its being iconoclastic, the suspicion which Kenneth Gross analyses as a complex dialectic of attacking the false and the simultaneous attempt to construct its "true" expression, to conclude that "idolatry is itself iconoclastic" (160). What the essays also address is the unity of the effects of textual/cultural production which Venuti (in the epigram above) finds to be illusory, their imaginary unity, singularity and oneness being crucial, though seemingly immobile, vehicles of authenticity.

The first three essays investigate translation as a space of intercultural encounter as well as the forces and tensions that impact its shape. To discuss the transformation of proper names in English translations of Japanese literary works, Eriko

Sato complements the categories of domestication and foreignization with the category of cultural transplantation, borrowed from Hervey and Higgins, and analyzes its consequences for what she calls the cultural identity of the text. In her essay, Sato emphasizes the danger of incongruence resulting potentially from such a process of transplantation, regardless whether it is oriented toward domestication or foreignization. Meanwhile, drawing on examples of translation from Arabic into English, Faiq investigates the evolution of master discourses rooted in systems of norms that regulate the production and consumption of meanings in specific cultural contexts, noting that "translation yields sites for examining a plethora of issues: race, gender, (post-) colonialism, publishing policies, censorship, and otherness, whereby all parties involved in the translation enterprise … tend to be highly influenced by their own *culguage* and the way it sees the *culguage* they are translating from." The sites of encounters between the Arabic and Western languages, recent transformations of master discourses, and their cultural and political ramifications, present a particularly fertile ground for analysis especially after the events of September 2001. Finally, Lada Kolomiyets, commenting on the growing interest of the Western European, American and Canadian publishers, editors, and translators mainly in contemporary Ukrainian literature, points to the key presence and role of Taras Shevchenko's translations against the context of the 2013–2014 events in Ukraine and its international echoes. In her text, Kolomiyets stresses the gap between what she terms as "insider's" and "outsider's" translation strategies, resulting from the (un)familiarity of the translator with the rich Ukrainian vernacular (and by extension, ethnic Ukrainian culture), one much different from its normative variety fixed in the Soviet era dictionaries, and earlier, by the tsarist Russia's policies.

Wojciech Kozak's essay on Muriel Spark's *The Public Image* offers yet another perspective on the highly complex relationship between the sides of representation, and on the problematic status of "the source" which becomes subject to translation and reenactment. Spark's heroine, a young English actress stationed in Italy, struggles to negotiate the boundary between the private and the public spheres. Undergoing several transformations under the pressure of her *skopos*-driven producer, Annabel creates several desirable versions of herself for the needs of the public. And yet, it is largely the "unfaithfulness" or "inauthenticity" of these copies that "facilitates [the protagonist's] rise to individuality and independence", observes Kozak: eventually, Spark's Annabel manages to reclaim and consciously put to use her public persona(s) in a gesture of self-determination.

Kozak's discussion of the reappropriations of images may well be read alongside Piotr Skurowski's reflections on the issue of "racechange" and passing in the

American context. Spark's protagonist comes to terms and regains several versions of her "self" coming from a position largely devoid of power, the process takes place in an environment largely unmarked by the notion of race – the environment where the notions of race are heavily disguised or repressed. Skurowski's analysis concerns enactments not only of racialized subjectivity but also of that performed by actors occupying a privileged social position. Although the intent behind the "racechanges" performed and described by John Howard Griffin and Grace Halsell may arguably be viewed as noble, the status of the actors clearly remains an important factor and continues to play a role in the reception of their experiments. As Skurowski notices, "Griffin elaborates on the fact that, ironically, it was his whiteness, and not the adopted blackness, which authenticated the book in the eyes of his white readers." It seems that while the translations of race reveal and document dimensions of violence, both literal and symbolic, directed against the racialized Other, they are also a poignant testimony to the power relations, historical and present, influencing the process itself and potentially perpetuating violence, the problem many translators are more than familiar with today.

The issues of authenticity, subjectivity, identity, class and power resurface also in Agnieszka Podruczna's essay on Darryl A. Smith's short story "The Pretended" and Jerzy Sobieraj's discussion of the patterns of inversion and reversion in Ellen Glasgow's *The Deliverance*. Sobieraj focuses on various presentations of the post-Civil War South reality found in Glasgow's novel and their relation to the imagery of the "good old times", one infused with a nostalgic longing for the vanished, idealized (or perhaps even imagined) *antebellum* order; Podruczna analyzes the status of Mnemosyne, a female android whose appearance and behavior are meant to replicate those of African-Americans in a world where the African-American minority has been annihilated. Podruczna begins her investigation with a commentary on the problematic attitude to race found in the older, mainstream SF texts – these often served as an extension of the imperialist, colonial narrative of expansion and conquest against which postcolonial SF emerged as a "counter-discursive reaction" – and proceeds with an analysis of Mnemosyne's resistance to being domesticated into the categories and concepts of the hegemonic power structure. Podruczna poignantly notes that the android's rebellion against the desires of dominating narratives "becomes a 'malfunction' to be eradicated" and that Mnemosyne's strangeness is rejected and effectively silenced by a system of binaries reluctant to be reconfigured and receptive only to elements pre-fabricated to fit its structures.

The essays by Jacek Wiśniewski, and Eliza Borkowska offer an overview of editorial practices and their impact on the writings of, respectively, John Clare and

William Wordsworth. The extent, number as well as the historical and political context of the thoroughly examined instances of revision, rewriting, alteration, altercation and censorship, in some instances ostensibly self-induced, in other – ostensibly external, provide an intriguing frame of reference for a reflection on the origins and complexities of the "authorial voice". By extension, they also reflect on the production of subjectivity whose locus, as some believe, lies precisely in the voice. It seems that the typical attributes of style or attitudes represented by the discussed authors prove to be exactly that: qualities attributed rather than intrinsic, acquired and/or co-produced rather than inborn, and always marked by the ghost presences, both malignant and amicable, of the editors, proof-readers, fellow authors and publishers. As such, the resulting texts, in their diverse interconnected variations, unfold like a fan and resound with a polyphony of voices, far from a monolithic ideal, where the voice attributed to the author is less discernible than we were once willing to admit.

Commenting on the prevalence of domesticating strategies involved in the process of translating poetry from interlinear trots, Natalia Kamovnikova emphasizes its political and historical context, as the Soviet publishing houses demanded conformity of translations to the requirements of clarity and Socialist Realism. Popularity of the practice produced an abundance of intriguing material which allows Kamovnikova to analyze the economic, cultural and literary contexts of translation in the Soviet Union as well as numerous instances of what Andrey Fedorov termed "hybrid creativity", "individual creative work based on the impulse coming from the foreign source." Creative aspects of translation are explored further in Hanna C. Rückl's presentation of "gedichte zum fertigstellen" (poems to be completed) by experimental Austrian poet Ernst Jandl encouraging the readers of poetry to become writers. Rückl notes several correspondences between the procedures of translation and completion, and following, among others, Perteghella & Loffredo, places translation firmly within the scope of creative writing.

The intricacies of influence and co-authorship, discussed by Kamovnikova and Rückl, are problematized also in Joanna Gładyga's investigation of the scope and consequences of the editorial amputations inflicted on Raymond Carver's prose by Gordon Lish. Declared a "great minimalist" after the publication of his first collection of short stories, Carver is presented initially as an author struggling for his "authentic" voice to be heard among the ghostly choir of the editor's corrections and revisions. However, following Roland Barthes, Gładyga grows increasingly aware that "no one utters" the written sentence as "the true locus of writing is reading," which further complicates the concepts of the "source" and "origin" in relation to texts.

Considering Barthes's assertion that the birth of the reader is only made possible by the death of the author, we have found it proper to follow Gładyga's analysis with an essay on pseudotranslations, or, in Toury's words, "texts which have been presented as translations with no corresponding source texts in other languages ever having existed." Disguised as translation, *Genç Kızlar* (Young Girls) offered Nihal Yeğinobalı a chance to talk about subjects considered taboo in Turkey in the 1950s but also to open the national literary canon to the chick-lit genre. Passing as a male English author "with an aristocratic look" (for which she used a photograph cut out of a French fashion magazine) Yeğinobalı performs an act of cultural intervention and innovation but also reveals, yet again, as translations are predisposed to do, the invisible power structures regulating who is allowed to speak and when, and what they are allowed to say.

The essay by Yulia Nanyak is devoted to the issues of authenticity and theatrical stage as well as to the place and role of the translator acting as a part of the staging process. Nanyak analyzes Goethe's *Faust* in translation using a model of "speech personality", as proposed by Karaulov, and the difficulties to render it in translation related to what she identifies as the cognitive level of text highlighting several dimensions of the text's signification variously pronounced and sometimes entirely absent from the presented translations.

The sometimes divergent re-significations in poems, sometimes quite distant from what triggered their conception and yet inevitably remaining influenced by their original dynamics are also the subject of Debora Biancheri's discussion of representations of identity in Italian translations of Seamus Heaney. When she writes about the Italian versions of the poet's work as a "complex mosaic of the elements constituting Heaney's profile in Italy", Biancheri creates an interesting visual parallel to the situation of translations' co-existence with the translated texts, one where certain elements become more distinct depending on the location of the viewing eye but nonetheless build together a constantly transforming whole.

The volume concludes with Mark Ó Fionnáin's zesty commentary on the translations of the word "orange" into Irish, its history and cultural significance, providing a closing pop of color to the presented collection along with the idea that even the authenticity of colors, at least in some contexts, need not be taken for granted.

Papers included in this volume have been written by scholars for whom, in most of the cases, English is a "foreign" language. Though this aspect of academic writing is usually dealt with by various methodologies of EFL studies, writing in a language which is not one's own might be an interesting issue to be taken up by translation studies as well. What translation does is in fact a certain, and inevitable, foreignization of authenticity, the theme which is both implicitly and explicitly recurring in what follows.

References

Derrida, Jacques. *The Ear of the Other. Otobiography, Transference, Translation*. Trans. Peggy Kamuf. New York: Schocken Books, 1985.

Gross, Kenneth. *Spenserian Poetics: Idolatry, Iconoclasm, and Magic*. Ithaca: Cornell University Press, 1985.

Waterhouse, Roger. "A Critique of Authenticity." *Radical Philosophy* No. 20 (Summer 1978): 22–26.

Venuti, Lawrence. *The Translator's Invisibility. A History of Translation*. London and New York: Routledge, 1995.

Wigley, Mark, "The Translation of Architecture, the Production of Babel." *Assemblage*, No. 8, (1989): 6–21.

Eriko Sato

Translation across Cultures: Domesticating/Foreignizing Cultural Transplantation

Abstract: This paper examines two kinds of cultural transplantation of proper names: one is directed toward domestication and the other is directed toward foreignization. The qualitative study of English translations of two Japanese literary texts shows that cultural transplantation of proper names can seriously ruin not only the text's pragmatic integrity, but also the major authorial theme.

Keywords: domestication, foreignization, proper names, cultural transplantation, Japanese

The dichotomy between "fidelity" and "freedom" has frequently recurred with different labels in the history of translation studies: Nida's *formal equivalence* and *dynamic equivalence*; Newmark's *semantic translation* and *communicative translation*; House's *overt translation* and *covert translation*. However, the fidelity-freedom dichotomy dissolves once a theory of translation is relativized according to the function as proposed by Vermeer and others. On the other hand, the fidelity-freedom dichotomy is viewed as an ethical issue by Venuti, who distinguishes *domestication* and *foreignization*, where domestication is "an ethnocentric reduction of the foreign text to target-language cultural values, bringing the author back home" and foreignization is "an ethnodeviant pressure on [cultural] values to register the linguistic and cultural difference of the foreign text, sending the reader abroad" (Venuti 1995, 20). Venuti recognizes unbalanced relationships between the dominant culture and the marginal culture in the context of translation:

> This relationship points to the violence that resides in the very purpose and activity of translation: the reconstitution of the foreign text in accordance with values, beliefs and representations that preexist it in the target language, always configured in hierarchies of dominance and marginality, always determining the production, circulation, and reception of texts. (Venuti 1995, 18)

On the other hand, Venuti (2010) tries to present a unified theory of translation that can account for the form, meaning, and effect in all translation types regardless of whether it is a technical translation or literary translation.

> On the materialist assumption that language is creation thickly mediated by linguistic and cultural determinants, the hermeneutic model treats translation as an interpretation of

the source text, whose form, meaning, and effect are seen as variable, subject to inevitable transformation during the translating process. (Venuti 2010, 5–6)

In the translation theory based on the hermeneutic model, the interpretation of the source text is expected to vary. Similarly, the representations of each of the interpretations can also vary (ibid, 6). While this model provides a uniform account of all kinds of translations, it potentially diminishes the significance of the source text. Because such a translation theory has no restrictiveness based on equivalence, the fate of the cultural identity of the text is contingent upon the translator's consciousness regardless of whether the text is domesticated or foreignized. An interesting question is what effect an extreme form of domestication or foreignization can impose on the message of a text after the text's cultural identity is radically shifted through the process of translation.

To examine the consequences of cultural shift caused by translation, this paper examines two cases of cultural transplantation of proper names identified in English translations of Japanese literary works, of which one is directed toward domestication and the other is directed toward foreignization. The reason why proper names are the focus of this study is because they are the most powerful tools for shifting the text's cultural identity due to their referential nature. The first section reviews the state of proper names in a translational context. The second section presents a case of domesticating cultural transplantation, and the third section presents a case of foreignizing cultural transplantation. The fourth section is the conclusion of the findings of this paper.

Proper Names

Following Mill's view where the meaning of a proper name is only its referent, Sciarone and Vendler consider names to be inherently untranslatable. For them, phonological/orthographical adjustments as well as equivalent names (e.g. the English name, *Vienna*, for the German name, *Wien*) are not translations, but are versions, which can simply be added to the stock of proper names in the given language. Similarly. Newmark claims that names should not be translated unless a single object's or a person's name already has an accepted translation (Newmark 1981, 70). Hervey and Higgins also claim that the names can be either unchanged or can be adapted to conform to the phonic/graphic conventions of the receiving culture (32).

However, the complexity of rendering proper names in a translational context crucially depends on their context and their identity. In literary translation we cannot ignore connotative meanings of proper names. Names are "dense with information" (Tymoczko, 223) and can serve as a "rigid designator" of the textual context (Lyotard, 319). Translators also consider "recognizability and memorizability" (Tymoczko, 225) as well as auditory preference and familiarity. Christiane Nord states "translators do all sorts of things with proper names" (182). If a name is non-fictional, referring to a real place, person, or object, it most rigidly and clearly designates the text's cultural identity while fictional names may have more flexibility.

A number of strategies for rendering names have been identified, labeled, and discussed in the field of translation studies (Aixelá; Davies; Fernandes; Hasegawa, Hervey and Higgins; Jaleniauskienė and Čičelytė, Newmark, 1981, 1988; Nord; Tymoczko; Vermes; Zauberga, among others). They include direct transfer (repetition), transliteration, transcription, substitution, modification, semantic translation, addition, omission, globalization, and cultural transposition (localization) although there are some variations on how to label them among scholars. The most domesticating strategy of rendering proper names is called *cultural transplantation* by Hervey and Higgins, where "SL names are replaced by indigenous TL names that are not their conventional or literal equivalents, but have similar cultural connotations" (33). Hervey and Higgins state that the French translation of *Harry Potter* presents clever cultural transplantation of names (33) such as: *Ravenclaw > Serdaigle; Hufflepuff > Poufsouffle; Scabbers > Croûtard; Malfoy > Malefoy; Neville Longbottom > Neville Longdubat*. Hervey and Higgins also illustrate cultural transplantation with the fictional characters in Hergé's book *Titin*, where the French names *Dupond et Dupont* are rendered as *Thomson and Thompson* in their English translation, maintaining the commonness of the names and the playfulness of their spellings (33). Hervey and Higgins warns that cultural transplantation must be done "with care," avoiding the creation of inconsistency. However, cultural translation should not be limited to domestication. It may be directed toward the culture of the source language, thus being oriented toward foreignization.

Domesticating Cultural Transplantation

Sato shows a case where a real place name in Japan in a Japanese poem is rendered as a real place name in America in one of its English translations. Kōtarō Takamura (1883–1956) was one of the pioneers of modern Japanese poetry written in free verse in the vernacular. Takamura published *Chieko-sho*, a collection of poems about his wife, Chieko, in 1941. One of the poems in this collection, entitled "Hito ni (To a Person)," was written before his marriage to Chieko. In this poem, Takamura expresses his strong opposition to the arranged marriage offered to Chieko by her family in her hometown. The following is a part of the fourth stanza of this poem:

まるでさうチシアンが描いた絵が鶴巻町に買い物に出るのです
<Literal translation>
It is just like a painting by Titian goes to Tsurumaki Town for shopping.

Two English translations that I identified keep the referent of *Tsurumaki Town*; however, one translation shifts its referent, rendering *Tsurumaki Town* as *Times Square*, as in *"like a Titian out shopping in Times Square"* (Takamura and Furuta).

This is an instance of domesticating cultural transplantation of a place name. As the place reference changes, the text identity also shifts from Japan to America. However, unlike Times Square, Tsurumaki Town is not a well-known city even inside of Japanese. Furthermore, unlike Times Square, Tsurumaki Town is not an entertainment district, but is a university town, which was in the author's neighborhood. Accordingly, the change of *Tsurumaki Town* to *Times Square* significantly alters the connotative meaning and the effect of the text. For Takamura, Tsurumaki Town could have been "a common town" or "a neighborhood town," but Times Square would imply a world-renowned crowded exotic entertainment center. Furthermore, this cultural transplantation causes an incongruous effect because the poem is a part of *Chieko-sho*, a collection of poems for Chieko, which remains as a Japanese name. The translator must have interpreted the source text in the Japanese context, but tried to deconstruct it and reconstruct it in an American context. However, the result was only partial, impairing the text's coherence and puzzling the readers in the target language culture. If we are to complete cultural transplantation to gain consistency and cohesion, the Japanese name, *Chieko*, must also be changed to a Western name in every poem in this collection; however, it will obviously efface the main theme and the purpose of the collection. If we hypothetically do change Chieko's name, then we also would have to change all other Japanese icons that appear in this collection, including Japanese food items, Japanese measurement units, Japanese currency units, and all other proper names including the names of mountains and coasts.

Foreignizing Cultural Transplantation

Sato also shows a case where European names of characters that appear in a Japanese novel are transformed into Japanese names in one of its English translations. *Ginga Tetsudō no Yoru* (Night of the Galactic Railway) was written around 1927 by Kenji Miyazawa (1896–1933), and was discovered and published in 1934, one year after his death. The story is about a schoolboy named *Giovanni* and his surreal train trip through the stars on one summer night, after which he hears about the drowning of his best friend in a river.

This novel is unique in that it contains no Japanese place names although the story is obviously based in the author's hometown, Hamamaki, and the nearby river, Kitakami River, in Japan. By contrast, the novel includes a number of non-Japanese place names, some of which are real names such as *Connecticut*, *Lancashire*, *Colorado*, and *Pacific*, while others are fictional names that do not sound

Japanese. Another unique aspect of this novel is that the main characters, who are obviously Japanese, have European names. Their names are written in katakana characters, indicating that they are foreign names:[1]

ジョバンニ [Jobanni] < Giovanni (the protagonist)
カムパネルラ [Kamupanerura] < Campanella (the protagonist's best friend)
ザネリ [Zaneri] < Zanelli (the protagonist's schoolmate who constantly ridicules him)
マルソ [maruso] < Marceau (the protagonist's schoolmate)

By contrast, two supporting characters, who are apparently Christians and victims of the shipwreck, which is clearly based on the tragedy of the Titanic that sank in the North Atlantic in 1912 (Miyazawa 1991, 107), have Japanese names:

かおる [Kaoru] (a Christian girl who was one of the victims in the shipwreck)
タダシ [Tadashi] (Kaoru's younger brother)

Although the ethnicity of the names of main characters and supporting characters are counterintuitive, five English translations of this novel that I have identified keep the ethnicity of these names. However, one English translation transform the main characters' European names into common Japanese names:

ジョバンニ [Jobanni] < Giovanni → Kenji
カムパネルラ [Kamupanerura] < Campanella → Minoru
ザネリ [Zaneri] < Zanelli → Akira
マルソ [Maruso] <Marceau → Masaru (Miyazawa 1996)

The translators, Sigrist and Stroud, state in their introduction that they have changed the main characters' names to "eliminate any confusion caused by Japanese characters in a Japanese setting having European names" (Miyazawa 1996, 11). This is a case of foreignizing cultural transplantation and their book cover states "translated and adapted from Japanese."

The hermeneutic model of translation can fully account for their strategy: the translators have interpreted the source text as a story in a Japanese context, and then reconstructed it as a Japanese story for the audience in the target language culture according to their interpretation of the source text and according to their choice for recontextualization. However, if this is the case, they should have changed the Japanese names of the obviously European children from the shipwreck, but they did not. This incomplete cultural transplantation ruins the integrity found in the original story.

In addition, this cultural transplantation seems to fail to maintain the hidden text message. It appears that the ethnically mismatching name assignments

---

1   The specifications provided in angle brackets are Romanized specifications of Japanese names.

were deliberately and purposely done by the original author. Strong states that Miyazawa is cleverly challenging the conventional distinction between "familiar and foreign" (Miyazawa 1991, 84). Pulver states that it is not only to achieve universalism, but also to represent the author's "social model, the kind of ideal society that he envisaged for the human race, where boundaries are not even earthly, but cosmic." This proves why Miyazawa has included only non-Japanese place names and flipped ethnicity of characters' names. In addition, it explains why this novel mixes items from different cultures, different eras, different languages, and different knowledge areas such as agriculture, biology, mineralogy, geology, music, religion, and cosmology. If this is the case, cultural transplantation performed by Sigrist and Stroud in Miyazawa (1996) is effacing the author's original theme of the entire novel. The next question is how the readers of the target language culture perceive the translation. Minh-ha Trinh states that her perception of this novel was significantly different when she read two different translations:

> In the first version I read of his novel Milky Way Railroad, the translators had taken the liberty of changing the characters' names into Japanese names, under the pretext that it would "eliminate any confusion caused by Japanese characters in a Japanese setting having European names." Since I usually prefer (at first) to enter a text directly and to follow the writer's thought process afresh, without the mediation of an introduction, at the end of the book I was deceptively left with a feeling of wonder for what I considered to be a harmlessly charming story of coming to terms with death, a story "typically Japanese," as my prejudices dictated. It was only a year later, when a Japanese friend offered me another translated version of the novel, that I realized with awe and utter excitement the scope of Miyazawa's experimental and cosmopolitan mind. In this translation, not only do the main characters' names, Giovanni (Jovanni) and Campanella (Kanpanera), appear as originally intended, but a whole complex tapestry of foreign-sounding names of people and places emerges from the story, as if by magic. Suppressed in the first adapted version I read, these Italian, French, English, and American names, coexisting with Japanese names, make all the difference. Here the politics of naming takes on an inventive role of its own. (Trinh, 7)

This shows that two translations, one with cultural transplantation and the other without it, yield a significant difference for the perception of the authorial theme. Sigrist and Stroud's cultural transplantation was undone in their later edition published in 2009 (Miyazawa 2009).

Conclusion

The theory based on the hermeneutic model of translation is also based on the affirmation of variants that arise in all phases of the process of translation. It also foregrounds the subjectivity of translation described by Naoki Sakai, who states, "the translator is both an addressee and not an addressee at the same time" (11).

We have observed that the hermeneutic model of translation theory successfully accounts for the two instances of cultural transplantation regardless of whether it is oriented toward domestication or foreignization. However, we have also observed that these cases have produced an incongruous effect that result from the incompleteness of cultural transplantation. In addition, we observed that they caused the change of connotative meanings hidden in names to the extent that the authorial theme of the text is effaced. These empirical facts show the potential danger of cultural transplantation and the significance of proper names as expressive tools in a translational context.

Works Cited

Aixelá, Javier Franco. "Culture-Specific Items in Translation." *Translation, Power, Subversion* (Topics in Translation 8). Ed. Román Álvarez and M. Carment-África Vidal. Clevedon: Multilingual Matters, 1996. 52–78.

Davies, Eirlys E. "A Goblin or a Dirty Nose?" *The Translator: Studies in Intercultural Communication* 9 (2003): 65–100.

Fernandes, Lincoln. "Translation of Names in Children's Fantasy Literature: Bringing the Young Reader into Play." *New Voices in Translation Studies* 2 (2006): 44–57.

Hasegawa, Yoko. *The Routledge Course in Japanese Translation*. Milton Park, Abingdon, Oxon: Routledge, 2012.

Hervey, Sándor, and Ian Higgins. *Thinking French Translation: A Course in Translation Method: French to English* (2nd edition). London: Routledge, 2002.

House, Juliane. "Text and Context in Translation." *Journal of Pragmatics* 38 (2006): 338–358.

Jaleniauskienė, Evelina, and Vilma Čičelytė. "The Strategies for Translating Proper Names in Children's Literature." *Studies about Languages* 15 (2009): 31–42.

Lyotard, Jean-François. "Universal History and Cultural Differences." The Lyotard Reader. Ed. Andrew Benjamin. Cambridge: Blackwell, 1989. 314–323.

Mill, John Stuart. *A System of Logic, Ratiocinative and Inductive*. London: Longmans, Green and Company, 1843/1956. Page references are to 8th edition published in 1956.

Miyazawa, Kenji. *Night of the Milky Way Railway*. Trans. Sarah Strong. Armonk, N.Y: M.E. Sharpe, 1991.

Miyazawa, Kenji. *Milky Way Railroad*. Translated and adapted by Joseph Sigrist & D. M. Stroud. Berkeley, CA: Stone Bridge Press, 1996.

Miyazawa, Kenji. *Milky Way Railroad* (2nd edition). Trans. Joseph Sigrist & D. M. Stroud. Berkeley, CA: Stone Bridge Press, 2009.

Newmark, Peter. *Approaches to Translation*. Oxford: Pergamon Press, 1981.

—. *A Textbook of Translation*. New York: Prentice Hall International, 1988.

Nida, Eugene. *Toward a Science of Translating with Special Reference to Principles and Procedures Involved in Bible Translating*. Leiden: Brill, 1964.

Nord, Christiane. "Proper Names in Translations for Children: Alice in Wonderland as a Case in Point." *Meta: Translators' Journal* 48 (2003): 182–196.

Pulvers, Roger. "Miyazawa Kenji's Prophetic Green Vision: Japan's Great Writer/Poet on The 80th Anniversary of His Death." *The Asia-Pacific Journal* 11. 44. 2. 4 Nov. 2013. 30 Sept. 2015 <http://japanfocus.org/-Roger-Pulvers/4021/article.html>.

Sato, Eriko. "Proper Names in Translational Contexts." To appear in *Theory and Practice in Language Studies 6*.

Sakai, Naoki. *Translation and Subjectivity: On Japan and Cultural Nationalism*. Minneapolis: University of Minnesota Press, 1997.

Sciarone, Bondi. "Proper Names and Meaning." *Studia Linguistica* 21 (1967): 73–86.

Takamura, Kotaro, and Soichi Furuta. *Chieko's Sky*. Tokyo: Kodansha international, 1978.

Trinh, Minh-ha T. *D-Passage: The Digital Way*. Durham: Duke University Press, 2013.

Tymoczko, Maria. *Translation in a Postcolonial Context*. Manchester, UK: St Jerome, 1999.

Vendler, Zeno. "Singular Terms." *Semantics: An Interdisciplinary Reader in Philosophy, Linguistics and Psychology*. Eds. Danny D. Steinberg and Leon A. Jakobovits. Cambridge: Cambridge University Press, 1971. 115–133.

Venuti, Lawrence. *The Translator's Invisibility*. London: Routledge, 1995.

—. "Genealogies of Translation Theory: Jerome." *Boundary* 2 (2010): 5–28.

Vermeer, Hans-Josef. *A Skopos Theory of Translation: (Some Arguments For and Against)*. Heidelberg: TEXTconTEXT Verlag, 1996.

Vermes, Albert. "Proper Names in Translation: A Relevance-Theoretic Analysis." Diss. University of Debrecen, 2001.

Zauberga, Ieva. "Translation as Discursive Import: Changes in the Transfer of Proper Nouns in Latvian." *Sociocultural Aspects of Translating And Interpreting*. Eds. Anthony Pym, Miriam Shlesinger and Zuzana Jettmarová. Amsterdam: John Benjamins, 2006. 143–150.

Said Faiq

Imitation, Representation… or the Master Discourse of Translation

Abstract: The contribution explores how a culturally defined *master discourse* affects imitation and representation of texts produced by others through translation. How do constraints and disciplinary demands of a *master discourse* animate imitation and representation, leading along the way to the construction of images that defy the conventional definitions of both?

Keywords: master discourse, representation, imitation, translation

Introduction

Across the different approaches/models and their associated strategies, the primary objective of translation is to achieve the same informational and emotive effects contained in and realized by the source texts in the target ones (translations). Opposition and conflict between the different labels and terms used have been norm in translation studies.

> Much of the academic discourse on translation and interpreting has been articulated more or less explicitly in terms of conflict. Whilst some authors have focused on the tensions that are inherent in the process of translation (source texts versus target text, adequacy versus acceptability, literal translation versus free translation, semantic translation versus communicative translation, and formal correspondence versus dynamic equivalence, to name but a few dichotomies and constructed oppositions that underpin discussions of translation and classification of approaches and strategies), others have represented translation as an aggressive act. (Salama-Carr, 31)

The *Authenticity and Imitation in Translation and Culture* conference organized by the University of Social Sciences and Humanities in Warsaw in May 2015 addressed the thorny questions of the interface between culture, identity, language, and intercultural communication through translation. The call for papers illustrates the way the theme and its thematic steams framed the conference.

> … What is connoted by the word "imitation" is first of all a kind of copying, repetition and/or substitution of that which, otherwise, may be modified by the adjective "authentic", applicable to nouns ranging from "life" and "feeling" to "signature", "document" and, of course, "text"…. Since culture, and especially Western culture, may be read as a kind of discourse which "is born of translation and in translation", as Henri Meschonnic phrased it, the triad of authenticity, imitation and translation offers an array of issues which seem

to be worth an insight and a discussion as a perspective offering ways of rethinking the role of translation in the perception of culture and everyday practices at the time of fluctuation of meanings, an almost omnipresent absence of authenticity and its imitative replacement by all sorts of simulacra.

... What reverberates ... is not only the old question of constructing graven images and their worship, but also much more recently posited questions of the death of the author and the birth of the reader, of loss and gain in translation, of the invisibility of the translator, of estrangement and defamiliarization, of domesticity and foreignness, of, more generally, a certain politics and poetics of imitation in which authenticity looms large as a constitutive outside to which we inevitably, though sometimes highly critically, relate.

This passage from the conference call for papers indicates a plethora of issues that all relate to the problematics inherent in the role of translation and translators, and the corollary power and/or disempowerment dynamics that animates the spaces of transcultural encounters. Central to the conference, and to this contribution, is the relationship between language and culture. On this Kiely & Rea-Dickens (1) write:

> The notion of language and culture represents the communities and institutions which house and frame both language learning and language use. . . . [This notion] provides opportunities for engagement with issues of language use, language form, language learning, language pedagogy and language assessment which inform on the construction of identity and on the social and cultural contexts where identity is profiled.

In this context, translation demonstrates the complexity inherent in the process of intercultural communication. This complexity stems from the carrying-over of specific cultural products (texts) to receivers with specific systems that regulate imitation and representation in/of/through translation. These systems are based on particular norms for the production and consumption of meanings (texts), and ultimately evolve into master discourses through which imitation and representation are negotiated and realized (mediated).

Drawing on instances of translation from Arabic, the purpose here is to explore how imitation and/or representation reflect a culturally defined master discourse: How do constraints and disciplinary demands of a master discourse animate imitation and representation as translation, leading along the way to the construction of images that defy conventional and ethical definitions of both?

Imitation, Representation...

Translation usually refers to the handling of written texts; leaving spoken texts to the realm of interpreting, oral translation. Furthermore, translation is taken to refer to the process of translating, to the product (the target text), and to the reception of this product. As such, it covers a broad range of concepts and denotes as well as connotes different meanings.

Axiomatically, the primary objective of translation is to achieve the same informational and emotive effects of the source texts in the translations. The main theoretical basis for doing so has centred on the concept of equivalence. The search for equivalence in translation has often led theorists and translators alike to focus on aspects of either the form or content (manner or matter). But this polarization of what translation involves ignores the simple fact that any text produced in a given language is the product of a unique union between both manner and matter, and that the production and reception of texts are embedded in specific cultural contexts.

From the start, the study of what translation is and what it entails has centered on producing prototypes in a binary fashion (recall Salama-Carr). Different terms have been used, often with different meanings, to explain translation as both process and product. Imitation is one of these terms. According to Robinson (111), imitation comes with two meanings that often cause confusion.

> In ordinary English, imitation means slavish copying, mimicking, miming. Through a strange linguistic history, however, the word has come to mean almost the exact opposite in translation theory: doing something totally different from the original author, wandering too far and too freely from the words and sense of the SL [source text] text. In fact, imitation has come to be virtually synonymous with [free translation].

> Imitation is the Classical Latin translation of the Greek word mimesis, which was used in literary theory from Plato and Aristotle onward to describe the writer's imitation of reality; pedagogically it was used for revision exercises, in which students were taught to write or orate by rewriting or respeaking classic texts—changing them in some significant way, choosing new words for saying the same thing.

Dryden, for example, posited three types of translation (metaphrase or literal translation, paraphrase or translation with a latitude, and imitation or free translation that involves taking liberties with the source text). Although not his favorite strategy, Dryden found imitation to provide creativity through translation, leading to inventiveness and appropriation of the source, almost like procreation (cf. Bimberg). But, imitation has not always had good publicity. The translations of stream-of consciousness novels in China, for example, indicate "the difficulty of integrating imitations into a general history of translation" (Chan, 682).

Imitation is not that different from the concept of representation, which weighs heavily on the study of translation. Often translation is seen as both being and standing-for representation. Tymoczko, who sees translation as an instance of representation, writes:

> Representation is a large and capacious concept, and, thus, a full discussion of the issues pertaining to representation and translation is far beyond the scope of this book. Nonetheless, any consideration of the nature of translation must include representation, if only in a cursory manner, for almost all translations are representations: translation as a category is by and large a subset of representation and most individual translations fall within the larger category representation. (111-12)

Tymoczko further provides the following dictionary meanings of representation from the *Oxford English Dictionary*, and concludes that the definitions show "the broad scope of the concept."

> ... an image, likeness, or reproduction in some manner of a thing;
> ... the action or fact of exhibiting in some visible image or form;
> ... the fact of expressing or denoting by means of a figure or symbol; symbolic action or exhibition;
> ... a statement or account, esp. one intended to convey a particular view or impression of a matter in order to influence opinion or action;
> ... a formal and serious statement of facts, reasons, or arguments, made with a view to effecting some change, preventing some action, etc.; hence a remonstrance, protest, expostulation;
> ... a clearly-conceived idea or concept;
> ... the operation of the mind in forming a clear image or concept;
> ... the fact of standing for, or in place of, some other thing or person, esp. with a right or authority to act on their account; substitution of one thing or person for another ... (112)

When applied to translation, these definitions indicate the existence of an interventionist dimension similar to that envisioned for imitation by Dryden. Whether through imitation or representation, the product (translation) becomes "a statement intended to convey a particular aspect of a subject so as to influence its receptors" (112). Whether seen as imitation or representation, translation and translating involve much more, as Sukanta (94) puts it:

> The 'faithful' and the 'creative' translation can be one and the same, if the intention is merely to translate. But the urge to translate is inevitably combined with other redactive agenda, producing a displacement beyond that of language. It cannot disavow those other agenda insofar as language cannot disavow its social and epistemic environment, nor its contingent specificities of form. There is no 'mere' translation: it always incorporates the total process of textual generation.

In the main and except for specific samples, texts cannot be accurately, faithfully and neatly translated into others and be the same as their originals. There are linguistic difficulties (vocabulary, idioms, grammar, collocations, etc) and cultural difficulties (perceptions, experiences, values, religions, histories, etc.) The Romans, for example, imitated, in the orthodox sense of the term, Greek literary texts on the basis of a void that they wished to fill in their culture; they had it all -economic and political might, but lacked a literary tradition, (cf. Bassnett 2002). Likewise and based on their cultural context, medieval Arab translators managed to transform the medieval Arab into a global player. The decision to translate did not spring from a genuine interest in Greek or any other culture of the day, but was rather prompted by their urgent need to satisfy the necessities of a young nation. Culturally, medieval Arab translation was the tool for an interactive dialogue between the medieval Arabs and other cultures, but most importantly, it was seen as the means for the transformation of a group into a nation through the appropriation (imitation and representation) of the intellectual heritage (cultural goods) of other nations (cf. Faiq 2000a).

The Master Discourse of Translation

From imitation *à la* Dryden or representation *à la* Tymoczko, translation studies has, since 1980s, been extended to consider different and challenging issues. In particular, the view of culture-modelling through translation has ushered in questions that cannot be adequately answered by the conventionalized notions of equivalence, accuracy, fidelity, or 'sourceer vs. targeteer' approaches to translation and translating. The focus has shifted from (un)translatability to the cultural, political and economic ramifications of translation; away from concerns with translated texts toward treating translation as social, cultural and political acts taking place within and attached to global and local relations of power and dominance.

The infusions of ideas and paradigms from a basket of disciplines (cultural, post-colonial, gender, conflict studies, to name but a few) in translation has contributed a great deal to the issues of the formation of cultural identities and/or representation of foreign cultures, what Lefevere (1999) named 'composing the other' through translation. On this conceptualization of translation, Salama-Carr (32) appropriately argues:

> From within the discipline itself, the traditional issue of mediation linked with the increased visibility of the translator and the interpreter as agents, a shift of perspective promoted in great part by the so-called 'cultural turn' in translation and interpreting studies, followed and complemented by a 'sociological' engagement has paved the way for the growing interest in the role and responsibilities of translators and interpreters in

relating and formulating conflict, and in issues of trust and testimony that often arise in that context of shifting power differentials.

Fundamentally, under the umbrella of translation the issues of composition, reception and semiotic intertextuality interrelate in an intricate fashion within a context of ideological power struggle.

> With the spread of deconstruction and cultural studies in the academy, the subject of ideology, and more specifically the ideology of power relations, became an important area of study, and claims about ideology proliferate in many fields, though they are not always well substantiated. The field of translation studies presents no exception to this general trend. (Fawcet, 106)

Imitation and/or representation are instances of ideological power in action, whereby they become motivating factors for "additions, deletions, compression, zero translation, and other – major departures from the source text" (Tymoczko, 114–5).

In intercultural communication, translation should perhaps most appropriately be explored as involving interaction (communication) between and across different cultures through the languages of these cultures. This communication means that those carrying out the acts of translating bring with them prior knowledge (culture) learned through their own (usually mother or first) language. In any communicative act (even between people of the same group), culture and language are so intertwined that it is difficult to conceive of one without the other as it would be impossible to "take language out of culture or culture out of language" (Bassnett 1998, 81). Extending this relationship to include translation, Emig (203–4) maintains that:

> Culture itself is shown to be the result of translations, and these translations are depicted not so much as inevitable forces of history, but as individual acts that rely on their interplay with social and political contexts. Inside these contexts they often fail, and the consequences of these failures can indeed be fatal. But equally fatal is the attempt to ignore or even abandon translation as a crucial prerequisite of the formation of identity, be it personal, national or indeed cultural.

A culture seeks to tell its members what to expect from life, and so it reduces confusion and helps them predict the future, often on the basis of a past or even *pasts*. Cultural theorists generally agree that the very basic elements of any culture include history, religion, values, social organization, and language itself. The first four elements are interrelated and are all animated and expressed by language. Through its language, a culture is shared and learned behaviour that is transmitted across generations for the purposes of promoting individual and group survival, growth and development as well as the demarcation of itself and its group vis-à-vis other cultures and their respective members (Faiq 2014).

A very basic definition of language is that it is no more than the combination of a good grammar book and a good dictionary. But these two do not refer to what users actually do with the grammar rules and the words neatly listed in dictionaries. The grammar rules and the words in the dictionary mean what their users make and want them to mean. So use depends very much on the user, and language as a whole assumes its importance as the mirror of the ways a culture perceives reality, identity, self, and others.

It follows then that translating involves the transporting (carrying-over) of languages and their associated cultures to and recuperated by specific target reading constituencies. These constituencies have at their disposal established systems of representation, with norms and conventions for the production and consumption of meanings vis-à-vis people, objects and events. These systems ultimately yield a master discourse through which identity and difference are marked and within which translating is carried out (Faiq 2007).   Because it brings culture and language together, translation means transporting (causing to travel) texts (languages and their associated cultures) to become other texts (in other languages and their associated cultures). The culture of the others usually has an established system of representation that helps define this culture to its members, but more importantly it helps these members to define those (languages and cultures) they are translating from vis-à-vis their own through a master discourse that indicates different degrees of otherness vis-à-vis this self (cf. Bakhtin).

Whether treated as imitation or representation, as discourse, translation is by necessity a cultural act (Lefevere 1998). As such, translation has a culture (politics, ideology, poetics) that precedes the actual act of translating. Culture *A* views culture *B* in particular ways and vice versa. These particular ways of view affect the way culture *A* translates from culture *B* and vice versa; in the same way people tend to transfer ideas and concepts into other languages and cultures with significant effects and meanings from their own languages and cultures. To express this union between culture and language, perhaps one can restate the statement in the following way: Translation means transporting texts from a *culguage A* into a *culguage B*, where *culguage*, the blend from culture and language, is intended to capture the intrinsic relationship between the two.

So, in translation the norms of producing, interpreting and circulating texts in one *culguage* tend to remain in force when approaching texts transplanted through translation from another *culguage*. As with native texts, the reception process of translated ones is determined more by the shared knowledge of the translating community than by what these texts themselves contain. This is in cahoots with the view of Bassnett & Trivedi (2):

> ...translation does not happen in a vacuum, but in a continuum; it is not an isolated act, it is part of an ongoing process of intercultural transfer. Moreover, translation is a highly manipulative activity that involves all kinds of stages in the process of transfer across linguistic and cultural boundaries. Translation is not an innocent, transparent activity but is highly charged with signification at every stage; it rarely, if ever, involves a relationship of equality between texts, authors or systems.

The representation of others through translation is a powerful strategy of exclusion used by a particular *culguage* as normal and even moral (Said 1995; Venuti 1998). This exclusion is also accompanied by an inclusion process of some accepted members from the other *culguage* as long as these accepted members (foreigners) adopt and adapt to the norms of the *culguage* that is accepting them (the examples of some Maghrebi writers in French and some Indian and Arab writers in English are cases in point [cf. Faiq 2007]).

Approached from this perspective, translation yields sites for examining a plethora of issues: race, gender, (post-) colonialism, publishing policies, censorship, and otherness, whereby all parties involved in the translation enterprise (from choosing texts for translation to linguistic decisions) tend to be highly influenced by their own *culguage* and the way it sees the *culguage* they are translating from. The interface between different *culguages* through translation produces '... strategies of containment. By employing certain modes of representing the other—which it thereby also brings into being—translation reinforces "hegemonic versions of the colonized" (Niranjana, 3).

Naming it violence, Venuti (1996, 196) succinctly sums up the nature of translation as a particular instance of writing within the Anglo-American tradition:

> The violence of translation resides in its very purpose and activity: the reconstitution of the foreign text in accordance with values, beliefs and representations that pre-exist it in the target language, always configured in hierarchies of dominance and marginality....

Venuti (1998; 1995) further attempts to exorcise the ideological in the process of representation through translation. Injecting the old/new terms of domestication and foreignization with some of his own zest, Venuti argues how over the last three centuries the Anglo-American (by extension Western) translation theory and practice have had normalising and neutralising effects. The ultimate aim of such effects has been to subdue the dynamics of texts and realities of indigenous societies and to represent them in terms of what is familiar and unchallenging to the Western culture —the master discourse as labelled here.

The Case of Translation from Arabic

Almost a decade before the events of 9/11/2001, Barber posited two futures for the human race: One future is dictated by the forces of globalisation and the other future is driven by what he calls 'tribalism' and is seen as the complete extreme opposite of the former.

> [T]he onrush of economic and ecological forces that demand integration and uniformity and that mesmerize the world with fast music, fast computers, and fast food – with MTV, Macintosh, and McDonald's pressing nations into one commercially homogeneous global network: one McWorld tied together by technology, ecology, communications and commerce. . . . [A] retribalization of large swaths of humankind by war and bloodshed: a threatened Lebanonization of national states in which culture is pitted against culture, people against people, tribe against tribe – a Jihad in the name of a hundred narrowly conceived faiths against every kind of interdependence, every kind of artificial social cooperation and civic mutuality

The choice here of the words *Jihad* and *tribe* to describe the dangerous future for humanity immediately conjures up images of Arabs and Islam as the main causes of destructive nationalisms (tribalisms) that threaten the ways of life of the 'civilised' West. This representation is not new, however. On the contrary, it even preceded the spread of colonialism in the Arab/Islamic lands. Colonialism furthered this view and added to it elites from the natives to act as apologists and/or guardians of its order and system of representation during and after colonial rule (cf. Faiq 2000b).

The caricatures depicting Prophet Mohammed in a Danish newspaper, George W. Bush's use of 'shit' to describe the July 2007 war in the Middle East, the many mistranslations (misrepresentations) of concepts such as *jihad* and *fatwa* into fixed meanings and references that deform their native meanings and references, are further examples of authoritarian relationships between a *culguage* (Western) and how it represents –translates– the Arab/Islamic source *culguage* (although not translations as such, transliterations represent powerful strategies of fixing and popularizing in the target *culguage* particular connotations that sustain cultural conflicts and stereotyping).

Translation from Arabic into Western *culguages*, mostly into English and French, has followed representational strategies within an established framework of institutions with its own lexis and norms (Faiq 2004; Said 1993), recall Barber cited above. In a global context, translation, aided by the media and its technologies, yields "enormous power in constructing representations of foreign cultures" (Venuti 1998, 97). Given this situation, cultural encounters between Arabic, and by extension all that relates to Islam, through translation into mainstream Western languages, have been characterized by strategies of manipulation, subversion and appropriation, with cultural conflicts being the ultimate outcome. Such strategies have become 'nastier' and dangerously *topoied* since the events of September 2001. The media have played a major role in the rapid diffusion of subverted translations and coverage of this world – suffocating the diversity and heterogeneity of the different Arab and Muslim cultures; portraying them instead as a monolith and a homogeneous group that forms a specific cultural identity, and an otherness of absolute strangers, who need to be isolated, avoided and even abominated.

While seemingly both the West and the Arab/Islamic Worlds have decided to block themselves in their own towers, media coverage has created more reasons for cultural misunderstandings. Representations –translations from– of Arabic and its associated culture(s) are carried out through lenses that fall within a situation aptly described by Sayyed (1) as follows:

> Ghosts are the remains of the dead. They are echoes of former times and former lives: those who have died but still remain, hovering between erasure of the past and the indelibility of the present – creatures out of time. Muslims [including Arab societies] too, it seems, are often thought to be out of time: throwbacks to medieval civilizations who are caught in the grind and glow of 'our' modern culture. It is sometimes said that Muslims belong to cultures and societies that are moribund and have no vitality – no life of their own. Like ghosts they remain with us, haunting the present.

Translation from Arabic has generally been conditioned by its master discourse that not only distorts original texts, but also leads to the influencing of target readers. Carbonell, for example, reports that in his comments on Burton's translation of the *Arabian Nights*, Byron Farwell wrote:

> The great charm of Burton's translation, viewed as literature, lies in the veil of romance and exoticism he cast over the entire work. He tried hard to retain the flavour of oriental quaintness and naivete of the medieval Arab by writing as the Arab would have written in English. (Qtd. in Carbonell, 80)

These views of translation, and by extension of readers, lead to translations that imply the production of subverted texts at all levels, "not only the source text, but also the target context experience the alteration infused by the translation process when their deeper implications are thus revealed" (Ibid., 93). This alteration ultimately leads to manipulations of the target text through the process of translation, thus, regulating and/or satisfying and agreeing with the expected response of and/or sought by/from the receivers of the translations. The pressures of the master discourse, through which Arab and Islamic *culguage(s)* are imitated or represented, exists prior to the translation activity itself. Here, translation

... becomes a significant site for raising questions of representation, power, and historicity. The context is one of contested stories attempting to account for, to recount, the asymmetry and inequality of relations between peoples, races, languages. (Niranjana, 1)

In this framework of relations of power and knowledge, the West, satisfied and content with its own representations, has not tried, in an honest intercultural fashion, to appreciate and know fully, through translation, the literatures and respective *culguages* (with their differences and heterogeneity) of Arabs and Muslims (there are, of course, exceptions but they do not affect mainstream trends). Reporting on personal experience of translating contemporary Arabic literature into English, Clark (109) writes:

> I wanted ... to translate a volume of contemporary Syrian literature. I ... thought the work of 'Abd al-Salam al-'Ujaili was very good and well worth putting into English. 'Ujaili is a doctor in his seventies who has written poetry, criticism, novels and short stories. In particular his short stories are outstanding. Many are located in the Euphrates valley and depict the tensions of individuals coping with politicisation and the omnipotent state.... I proposed to my British publisher a volume of 'Ujaili's short stories. The editor said, "There are three things wrong with the idea. He's male. He's old and he writes short stories. Can you find a young female novelist?" Well, I looked into women's literature and did translate a novel by a woman writer even though she was and is in her eighties.

Clark's experience is not incidental; it still applies today. His account shows that translation from Arabic into mainstream Western languages is essentially still seen as an exotic voyage carried out through a weighty component of representation in the target *culguage*, in which the objective knowledge of the source *culguage* is substantially altered by a dialectic of attraction and repulsion. The *Arabian Nights* (a title preferred for its exotic and salacious resonance to the original *A Thousand and One Nights*), for instance, is more famous in the West than in the Arab East. The exotic, and often distorted, view of the Arab and Islamic worlds has led to a situation where the proportion of books written about this world in Western languages is greatly disproportionate to the small number of books translated from Arabic.

Based on data provided in Venuti (1995), table 1 shows the numbers of translations from Arabic, Spanish, Hungarian, and Classical Greek and Latin into English for the years 1982, 1983 and 1984 respectively. One can easily notice the insignificance of the number of translations from Arabic —a language of a culture that affected and still affects humanity in many ways.

Table 1. Translations from Arabic in the United States (1982–84)

Year	Translations from Arabic	Translations from Spanish, Hungarian, and old Greek and Latin
1982	298	715-847-839
1983	322	703-665-679
1984	536	839-1116-1035
Total	1156	2257-2628-2553

In an extensive survey of literary translation from Arabic in the UK and Ireland, Büchler & Guthrie (21) provide the following statistics for 20 years (1990–2010) as shown by table 2.

Table 2. Translations from Arabic in The UK and Ireland (1990–2010)

Fiction (novel)	Memoir	Miscellaneous	Poetry	Short Fiction	Plays
192	11	1	37	65	3

The numbers shown in table 2 provide a yearly average of literary translations from Arabic into English in the UK and Ireland of some 15 titles (translations). This old/current situation prompted Said (1995, 97) to aptly conclude:

> For all the major world literatures, Arabic remains relatively unknown and unread in the West, for reasons that are unique, even remarkable, at a time when tastes here for the non-European are more developed than ever before and, even more compelling, contemporary Arabic literature is at a particularly interesting juncture.

The Western centric assumptions about others return time and again to haunt the production, reception and circulation of Arabic texts, and in turn complicate the issue of translation. Thomas (104–5), for example, examines the relationship between the Arab World and the West, in general, and the politics behind the awarding of the Nobel Prize in literature to Naguib Mahfouz (an author with the lion share of translations from Arabic):

> In this regard it is interesting to consider Naguib Mahfoudh – the only Arab writer to have been given the full western seal of approval through his winning of the Nobel Prize. He worked as a censor throughout the Nasser and Sadat eras, eras not noted for liberal attitudes to the arts or critical awareness. . . . Despite what one may think of the literary merits of his work . . . the fact remains that nearly all of his work has been translated, which compares very favourably with translations of other Arab writers who have been much more critical of the West.

Still and despite interesting junctures, despite a Nobel Prize in literature and despite the current almost hysterical attention given to Arabs and Islam, translation from Arabic still proceeds along a familiar and established master discourse whereby

> ... stereotyping, strategies of signification and power: the network in which a culture is fashioned does appear as a texture of signs linked by endless connotations and denotations, a meaning system of inextricable complexity that is reflected, developed and recorded in the multifarious act of writing. (Carbonell, 81)

In his translation of Naguib Mahfouz's novel *Yawma qutila z-za'iim* (The Day the Leader was Killed/Assassinated) into French, André Miquel, for example, explains in his foreword that he kept footnotes to the very minimum (Mahfouz, 1989). Yet, Jacquemond (1992) counted 54 footnotes in a translation of 77 pages. What transpires is that the translator-cum-orientalist expert assumes total ignorance on the part of readers, and proceeds to guide them through assumed authoritative knowledge of an unfathomable world where backwardness and the assassination of peacemakers are the norms. But this would be acceptable compared with Edward Fitzgerald's infamous comment on the liberties he had allowed himself to take with his version of *The Rubaiyat of Omar Khayam*, "really need a little art to shape them" (Bassnett 1998, 78). The master discourse rules supreme, and fits the authoritarian dimension of translation as representation along Bakhtin's view:

> It is not a free appropriation and assimilation of the word itself that authoritative discourse seeks to elicit from us; rather, it demands our unconditional allegiance. Therefore authoritative discourse permits no play with the context framing it, no play with its borders, no gradual and flexible transitions, no spontaneously creative stylizing variants on it. (343)

Language choices are not the issue here, but the prior-translation master discourse that controls all involved. A case in point here is the novel *Girls of Riyadh* by Rajaa Al-Sanea, translated into English by Marilyn Booth, apparently with considerable help from the author (Sanea 2007). The translator claims to have opted for a foreignizing translation to let the source shine through, but when the translation appeared, Booth found it unacceptable; leading to the situation whereby such a translation is "[e]nforced by the prevailing practices of marketing, reading and evaluating translations" (Emmerich, 200). If Booth's translation was modified, then the modifications were prompted by the requirements of a particular master discourse, presumably forced into and onto the English text by those working for the publishers, editors, for example with little or no knowledge of Arabic. In the words of Lefevere (1992, 41), such a situation comes about as a result of:

> Two factors basically determine the image of a work of literature as projected by a translation. These two factors are, in order of importance, the translator's ideology (whether he/she willingly embraces it, or whether it is imposed on him/her as a constraint by some form of patronage, and the poetics dominant in the receiving literature at the time of the translation.

In the English translation of *Girls of Riyadh*, for example, a date given in Arabic (Sanea, 2005, 22) as "20/2/2004" becomes "February 20, 2004" (Sanea 2007, 14)! Why opt for such a representation? Is it too difficult for US readers to interpret the Arabic as a day of a month of a year! In the same Arabic text (Sanea 2005, 23), a passage that literally translates into English as, "Lamees sat in the passenger seat, while the rest of the girls, five in total, sat in the back seats. They all sang along with the loud music from the CD player and moved as if they were dancing," is given in the published English translation as: "Lamees took her place next to Michelle while Sadeem and Gamrah climbed into the backseats. The CD player was on full blast. The girls sang along and swayed their *abaya-clad* shoulders as if they were dancing on the seats" (Sanea 2007, 16). One can easily notice that facts are changed (where is the number five), and why add, "their abaya-clad"? The only viable reason was perhaps to consolidate the view of how these little Muslim girls dress! This is perhaps why the reviews of the English translation were firmly couched in the requirements of the master discourse of translating from Arabic into English. Without a single exception, the excerpts that appear on the back cover of the English translation all invoke ideas about "most repressive society," "a rare glimpse," "secretive/closed society," recall the idea of the *harem*, the charm of Burton, Fitzgerald's views, Clark's experience, and so on.

Through adherence to the requirements and pressures of a master discourse, translation from Arabic becomes situated into ways of representation ingrained in the shared experience and institutional norms of the translating community or communities (self, selves, us). Source texts and their associated peoples are transformed from certain specific signs into signs whose typifications translators and others involved in the translation enterprise claim to know (knowledge is power). Historically, the other and otherness have been feared more than appreciated (with the exception perhaps of the phenomenon of exoticism, where the other, though often misunderstood and misrepresented, is perceived as strange, but at the same time somehow attractive, like fruits from Asia to European consumers). On this link between ideology (master discourse) and translation, Tymoczko (114), writes:

> Ideological representation *per se* is sometimes the primary goal of translations, and it can be an overt aspect of a translator's decision-making process as well; in such transla-

tions the image cast of the source material can be demonstrated to be the controlling determinant of particular translation decisions and strategies, as well as the shape of the entire translated text. The result can be seen in colonialist and anticolonialist translations alike, but the tendency is also clear in contemporary translations of advertisements, for example.

Although representations of weak cultures by powerful ones—mostly assumed to be Western cultures—in negative terms have been part of the scheme of history, no culture has been misrepresented and deformed by the West like the Arab/Islamic one (the term 'West' is used here to refer to intellectual framings, frames of reference, and a body of knowledge rather than necessarily to geographical places or dimensions).

Conclusion

Translation does not exist; it becomes. This becoming is realized through a complex process that should be explored in a cross-cultural site of interaction. Currently, globalization is the term used to refer to this site where intercultural communication through translation-becoming takes place. Here, information is communicated as translation that forms or further consolidates an existing body of knowledge of the translating *culguage* about the translated one (Cronin).

Notwithstanding the complexities of intercultural communication, the ethics of translation, at least in theory, postulates that it should lead to a rapprochement between the *au-delà* (Bhabha, 1), the Arab/Muslim World for our purpose here, and the Western World, as the translator of this *au-delà*. And, since it covers the *betwixtness* (the space-between *culguages*), translation could render encounters less painful, less conflictual, less antagonistic, and less bloody. Whether seen as imitation or representation translation cannot escape the constraints of its master discourse. Perhaps, what might help intercultural encounters would be a critical understanding and appreciating of the ways in which discourses operate, with the aim of establishing some efficient self-monitoring on the part of producers of master discourses. This could be achieved through a cross-cultural appraisal of the discourses underlying translation and translating with a view to better understanding the issues of identity (self and other), translation enterprise (patronage, agencies, translators) and norms of representation (master discourse).

But current practices of translation indicate that this aim is almost untenable. Arabic literary texts, for example, are rarely chosen for translation for their innovative approaches or for their socio-political perspectives. Rather, texts chosen are recognizable as conforming to the master discourse of writing about and representing Arabs, Arab culture and Islam. The complex historiography of translation indicates that the culture of translation (master discourse) ultimately guides and regulates the translation of culture, call it imitation or representation, it is the master discourse.

Works Cited

Bakhtin, Mikhail. *The Dialogic Imagination*. Trans. Caryl, Emerson, and Michael, Holquist. Austin: University of Texas Press, 1981.

Barber, Benjamin. "Jihad vs. McWorld." *The Atlantic Monthly* 3 (1992): 53.

Bhabha, Homi. *The Location of Culture*. London: Routledge, 1994.

Bassnett, Susan. "Translating Across Cultures." *Language at Work*. Ed. Susan Hunston. Clevedon: Multilingual Matters, 1998, 72–85.

—. *Translation Studies*. London & New York: Routledge, 2002.

Bassnett, Susan, and Harish Trivedi. "Introduction: of colonies, cannibals and vernaculars." *Post-Colonial Translation*. Ed. Susan Bassnett and Harish Trivedi. London: Routledge, 1999. 1–18.

Bimberg, Christiane. "Poetry as Procreation: John Dryden's Creative Concept of Poetry and Imitation." Connotations, vol. 8.3 (1998/99): 304–18.

Büchler, Alexandra, and Guthrie, Alice. *Literary Translation from Arabic into English in the United Kingdom and Ireland, 1990-2010*. Mercator Institute: Aberystwyth University, Wales, UK, 2011.

Carbonell, Ovidi. "The Exotic Space of Cultural Translation." *Translation, Power, Subversion*. Ed. Roma Alvarez and Carmen Vidal. Clevedon: Multilingual Matters, 1996. 79–98.

Chan, Leo, Tak-Hung. "First Imitate, then Translate: Histories of the Introduction of Stream- of-Consciousness Fiction to China." *Meta*, vol. 49, n° 3, 2004. 681–91.

Clark, Peter. "Contemporary Arabic Literature in English. Why is so little translated? Do Arabs prefer it this way?" *The Linguist* 364 (1997): 108–110.

Cronin, Michael. "Globalization and translation." *Handbook of Translation Studies*, Vol. 4. Ed. Yves Gambier and Luc van Doorslaer. Amsterdam: John Benjamins, 2013. 134–40.

Emig, Rainer. "All Others Translate: W.H. Auden's Poetic Dislocations of Self, Nation, and Culture." *Translation and Nation: Towards a Cultural Politics of Englishness*. Ed. Roger Ellis and Liz Oakley-Brown. Clevedon: Multilingual Matters, 2001. 167–204.

Emmerich, Karen. "Visibility (and invisibility)." *Handbook of Translation Studies*, Vol. 4. Eds. Yves Gambier and Luc van Doorslaer. Amsterdam: John Benjamins, 2013. 200–06.

Faiq, Said. "Culture, language and translation from Arabic." *Culguage in/of Translation from Arabic*. Ed. Said Faiq, Ovidi Carbonell and Ali Almanna. Muenchen: Lincom, 2014. 1–13.

—. *Trans-Lated: Translation and Cultural Manipulation*. Lanham & Oxford: Rowan & Littlefield, 2007.

—. "The cultural encounter in translating from Arabic." *Cultural Encounters in Arabic Translation*. Ed. Said, Faiq. Clevedon & New York: Multilingual Matters, 2004. 1–13.

—. "Arabic translation: A glorious past but a meek present." *Translation Perspectives XI: Beyond the Western Tradition*. Ed. Marilyn Gaddis Rose. Binghamton: State University of New York at Binghamton, 2000a. 83–99.

—. "Back to the original: Translating Maghrebi French literature into Arabic." *Translating French Film and Literature II*. Ed. Myriam, Salama-Carr. Amsterdam and Atlanta: Rodopi, 2000b. 201–17.

Fawcet, Peter. "Ideology and translation." *Routledge Encyclopedia of Translation Studies*. Ed. Mona, Baker. London & New York: Routledge, 1998. 106–11.

Jacquemond, Richard. "Translation and cultural hegemony: The case of French-Arabic translation." *Rethinking Translation*. Ed. Lawrence Venuti. London: Routledge, 1992. 139–58.

Kiely, Richard, and Pauline, Rea-Dickins. "Introduction". *Language, Culture and Identity in Applied Linguistics*. Ed. Richard Kiely, Pauline Rea-Dickins, Helen Woodfield and Gerlad Clibbon. London: Equinox, 2006. 1–16.

Lefevere, Andre. "Composing the other." *Post-Colonial Translation*. Ed. Susan Bassnett and Harish Trivedi. London & New York: Routledge, 1999. 75–94.

—. "Chinese and Western thinking on translation." *Constructing Cultures*. Ed. Susan Bassnett and Andre Lefevere. Clevedon, UK & New York: Multilingual Matters, 1998. 12–24.

—. *Translating Literature*. New York: Modern Language Association of America, 1992.

Mahfouz, Naguib. *Le Jour de l'Assassinat du Leader*. Trans. André Miquel. Paris: Sindbad, 1989.

Niranjana, Tejaswini. *Siting Translation: History, Poststructuralism and the Colonial Context*. Berkeley: University of California Press, 1992.

Robinson, Douglas. "Imitation." *Routledge Encyclopedia of Translation Studies*. Ed. Mona, Baker. London & New York: Routledge, 1998. 111–12.

Said, Edward. "Embargoed Literature." *Between Languages and Cultures*. Ed. In Anuradha Dingwaney and Carol Maier. Pittsburgh: University of Pittsburgh Press, 1995. 97–102.

—. *Culture and Imperialism*. London: Chatto & Windus, 1993.

Salama-Carr, Myriam. "Conflict and translation". *Handbook of Translation Studies*, Vol. 4. Ed. Yves Gambier and Luc, van Doorslaer. Amsterdam: John Benjamins, 2013.

Sanea, Rajaa, al. *Girls of Riyadh* (Trans. Marilyn, Booth). New York: Penguin Press, 2007.

—. *Banaatu r-Ryiaadh* (Girls of Riyadh). London: Saqi Books, 2005.

Sayyed, Bobby. *A Fundamental Fear*. London: Zed Books, 1997.

Sukanta, Chaudhuri. "Translation and displacement." *Translation: Reflections, Refractions, Transformations* Ed. Paul St-Pierre and Prafulla Kar. Amsterdam & Philadelphia: John Benjamins, 2007. 87–94.

Thomas, Stephen. "Translating as intercultural conflict." *Language at Work [British Studies in Applied Linguistics 13]*. Ed. Susan, Hunston. Clevedon: Multilingual Matters, 1998. 98–108.

Tymoczko, Maria. *Enlarging Translation, Empowering Translators*. Manchester: St Jerome, 2007/2010.

Venuti, Lawrence. *The Scandals of Translation*. London: Routledge, 1998.

—. "Translation as a Social Practice." *Translation Perspectives 9* (1996): 195–213.

—. *The Translator's Invisibility*. London: Routledge, 1995.

Lada Kolomiyets

The Untranslatable Ethnic: Always an Outsider? A Brief Review of Ukrainian-to-English Literary Translation Practices

Abstract: This essay focuses on the potential difficulties of rendering vernacularity in the works of classical Ukrainian authors such as Taras Shevchenko into modern English. It discusses the non-dictionary spoken forms and evanescent meanings of colloquial phrases, which not infrequently pose a problem for contemporary translators, threatening the accuracy of literary expression. The discussion notes how translating from a secondary language into a dominant one seems to have authorized literalness in place of the translator's cognizance of the source language writer's cultural experience and the unique purport of what is actually said in the source text.

Keywords: colloquial Ukrainian, Taras Shevchenko, poetry in translation, rendering vernacularity

Notwithstanding a distinct interest in Ukrainian literature in the West, it has been and still is considered a "minority literature" by English-speaking academic communities because of its history as an oppressed part of the former Tsarist and then Soviet Russian empires from 1654, when the Ukrainian people had fallen victim to a tergiversating treaty with Moscow, up to 1991, when the majority of citizens of the Ukrainian Soviet Socialist Republic voted in a referendum for the independence of Ukraine as a nation.

An extensive bibliography of Ukrainian literature in English from 1840 to 1989 (including books and pamphlets, articles in journals and collections), as well as selected articles in journals and collections published since 2000, with this section being in progress, is provided in the annotated bibliography of Canadian researcher Marta Tarnawsky, held at the *Electronic Library of Ukrainian Literature* website of the Canadian Institute of Ukrainian Studies.[1] A much smaller but nevertheless important contribution to the study of Ukrainian literature-in-translation and

---

1 *Ukrainian Literature in English:* An Annotated Bibliography by Marta Tarnawsky. – Electronic Library of Ukrainian Literature. Accessed 09 Aug. 2015. <http://www.utoronto.ca/elul/English/ULE/>.

translation markets in English-speaking countries from 1991 till 2013 was made in a prefaced bibliography compiled by Ukrainian scholar Nadiya Polischuk.[2]

In the introduction to her recent overview of the perception of Ukrainian literature in English-speaking countries "Strategies for Popularizing Ukrainian Literature in Translation", Olha Luchuk, a co-editor of several literary anthologies in Ukrainian-to-English translation, poses the following question: "… can we state that this literature, translated into English, comprises a constituent component of North American culture?" (Luchuk, 111) And she immediately provides the answer: "Unfortunately the answer is "no" – at least not at this time". But at the same time Luchuk rightly observes that "although Ukrainian literature for the time being is not particularly well known in the United States or in other English-speaking countries, a cultural dialogue has been taking place" (112). Luchuk traces back the main roadmap in Ukrainian-American literary contacts of the late 20th-early 21st century and comes to the conclusion that there is an orientation toward contemporary Ukrainian literature. Even more so, she ventures upon an exact date, observing that

> The breakthrough of contemporary Ukrainian literature onto the English literary scene happened in 1996 and afterward when, simultaneously, in various American and Canadian publishing houses, books that reflected the Ukrainian literary process of the 1980s and 1990s appeared, with little time-lag between publication of the originals and translations. (114–15)

In combination with those of Olha Luchuk, my personal observations also attest to the fact that West European, American and Canadian publishers, editors, and translators become more and more interested in contemporaneous Ukrainian literature, whereas the 19th-century Ukrainian classics would have been almost devoid of attention on the part of Anglophone audiences if not for one important date: the bicentennial of the greatest Ukrainian Romantic poet Taras Shevchenko on 9 March 2014.

In an unusual but logical way — in the sense that history has its own logic — the image of Shevchenko most actively participated in the late 2013 – early 2014 political events in Ukraine, since many a native Ukrainian began to call their national emblem and idealized prophet "Our Father Taras." The tradition was so

---

2 *Translations from Ukrainian into English Language between 1991 and 2012*: A study by the Next Page Foundation in the framework of the Book Platform project. Conducted by Nadiya Polischuk, translated into English by Anna Ivanchenko. February 2013. 09 Aug. 2015. <www.bookplatform.org/…/ukrainianenglish_translationsstudy_en1.doc>.

strong in the Soviet Ukraine that the official regime was willing to support the myth of Shevchenko as the "Father of Nation" rather than fight it (Єкельчик, 185). The *EuroMaidan* movement and the *Revolution of Dignity* events, which this movement developed into, were accompanied by Shevchenko portraits and his poetry on banners. One may consider a particularly telling example of the producer Serhiy Proskurnia. When he was working on the film project *Є люди* (There are people) for the 200th Anniversary of Shevchenko's birth in December 2013, he managed at that time to record video footage of the Armenian-Ukrainian *Euromaidan* activist Serhiy Nigoyan (who was born and grew up in Ukraine) reciting a fragment from Shevchenko's poem "The Caucasus" against a background of barricades.[3]

The celebration of the bicentennial anniversary of Shevchenko — a milestone of Ukrainian poetic heritage and of the poet himself, seen as the founder of the updated Ukrainian literary language based on vernacular speech,[4] turned into a nationwide commemoration, both ceremonial (with many festivities planned beforehand) and spontaneous: people gathering and folklore performances, recitations of Shevchenko's poetry organized in public squares of major Ukrainian cities and towns on those days.

Shevchenko's poetry, having influenced Ukrainian self-identification through the 19th and 20th centuries, once again was focused upon as a tool to consolidate the Ukrainian people in the early 21st century, and it was addressed not only to those who customarily speak Ukrainian, but also to those who habitually speak Russian or Crimean Tatar or any other language of the native population of Ukraine (because Shevchenko, the poet-Romanticist, had a great dream of a world of equal people, of a world which was freed from tyranny).

The 2014 bicentennial anniversary of Shevchenko, therefore, caused significant interest and a significant number of commemorative activities both in Ukraine and abroad including involvement by the Ukrainian diaspora and émigré communities in English-speaking countries, especially in view of the fact that it coincided with the *EuroMaidan* and *Revolution of Dignity* events in Ukraine. The main Ukraine-focused scholarly institutions in the English-speaking space, such

---

3   Serhiy Nigoyan (August 2, 1993 – January 22, 2014) was the first protester killed by shooting during the 2014 Hrushevsky Street riots where he was acting as a security person for the Maidan protesters. For more details see <en.wikipedia.org/wiki/Serhiy_Nigoyan>.

4   "Шевченко Тарас Григорович. Українська мова …" [Shevchenko Taras Hryhorovych. Ukrainian language]. *Ізборник*. 26 Apr. 2016. <litopys.org.ua/ukrmova/um145.htm>.

as the Shevchenko Scientific Society in New York, the Harvard Ukrainian Research Institute, and the Canadian Institute of Ukrainian Studies, as well as several of the Slavic-oriented publishing houses (including the recently emerged and highly productive joint British-Dutch Glagoslav Publishers in Amsterdam and London), have played a role in arranging a whole spectrum of commemorative events, including, but not limited to, book publications and presentations, poetry performances, art exhibitions, and gala concerts.

By examining authenticity and imitation concerns in translation, this article will focus on Shevchenko's poetic texts in jubilee English-language editions. And of this series, the most conspicuous publication was released in 2013 by the above-mentioned Glagoslav Publishers: a complete collection of Shevchenko's poems, both short and long, assembled in one volume under the name *The Kobzar* (the term *kobzar* meaning a wandering folk musician who sings to the accompaniment of the musical instrument called the *kobza*) in Peter Fedynsky's translation.

Although the first, almost complete, English edition of *The Kobzar* was published in Toronto as early as 1964, it was lacking two longer Russian-language poems, several shorter verses and the soldiers' dialogues in the poem "Гайдамаки" (The Haidamaks).[5] But even though this copious scholarly edition has served as a reference book and model of translation for at least two generations of university students and scholars, introducing Shevchenko's ideas to the English-speaking readership in a much better way than the previous translations, it nevertheless wasn't free from inaccuracies in semantic detail and deviational shifts of verse form. Although this book of translations resulted from a fruitful collaboration of the professional linguist Constantine Henry Andrusyshen (1907–1983), the son of Ukrainian immigrants who was the first Canadian-born Slavist, and the reputable Canadian poet-translator and scholar Watson Kirkconnell (1895–1977), the latter enjoyed much freedom in improving philological translations prepared for him by Andrusyshen.

The un-rhymed and non-metrical, concise and explicating translation of *The Kobzar* by Fedynsky, Ukrainian-American journalist and interpreter, may be read as committed to semantic accuracy. The translator grounds his content-based strategy in objective lexico-grammatical differences between the Ukrainian and English languages, with the former being regarded as melodious, lyrical, and the latter more laconic and business-like ("KOBZAR"). Contrary to the majority of preceding trans-

---

5   Shevchenko, Taras. *The Poetical Works of Taras Shevchenko: The Kobzar*. Translated from the Ukrainian by C.H. Andrusyshen and Watson Kirkconnell. Toronto: Published for the Ukrainian Canadian Committee by University of Toronto Press, 1964.

lators, Fedynsky defies Shevchenko's rule of vocalic quality and the overall idealistic endeavor to recreate the source text's vocal harmony ("KOBZAR").

Fedynsky completed his translation of the entire *Kobzar* in three years, starting from the moment when he was struck by the idea at the end of his assignment as the Voice of America bureau chief in Moscow. This decision was taken in such a short time thanks to the translator's overwhelming fascination with the images, thoughts and ideas of *The Kobzar* and to his confidence in the importance and relevance of Shevchenko's discourses to current life. With certainty and passion, he claims that "the very content of Shevchenko's *Kobzar* has no less power than the lyricism of his diction ("KOBZAR," translation mine). Fedynsky has personally travelled along the poet's life paths, including his journeys to St. Petersburg and Orenburg, as well as to the areas of Shevchenko's exile in the Urals where he was able to conduct bio-bibliographic research in archival repositories.

Michael Naydan, a prolific translator of Ukrainian literature in the USA, who has received several awards for his translations, most recently the George S.N. Luckyj Award in Ukrainian Literature Translation (2013) from the Canadian Foundation for Ukrainian Studies, has always aimed to reach a wide audience. Having already published 28 literary books either in his own translation or under his editorship, he still extensively translates and publishes anthologies of translations and writes essays on any successive editions of translated literature. The anthology of contemporary Ukrainian women prose writers entitled *Herstories* and released by Glagoslav Publishers in 2014, is noteworthy among his most recent publications as translation editor.

In his recently-published book of translations titled *The Essential Poetry of Taras Shevchenko*, which was released as a tribute on the bicentennial of the poet's birth in 2014 by Piramida Publishers in Lviv (a bilingual Ukrainian and English edition illustrated with linocuts by Ukrainian graphic artists Volodymyr and Lyudmyla Loboda produced during 1984–86), Naydan tends to construct his own idiosyncratic projection of the 19th-century Ukrainian ethnic world onto the cultural skyline familiar to the 21st century. Numerous markers of textual renovation as well as the narrative framing of the book testify to the translator's undisguised presence in Shevchenko's poetic discourses. For instance, he creates anew an important ethno-cultural reference to the term *moskal* by using the contemporary term and explaining this tactic in his "Note on the Translation":

> The word "moskal," which in Shevchenko's time was a pejorative term used by Ukrainians for Russians, and which particularly meant young Russian soldiers in his poetry, has been translated as "Russky," "Russky soldier boy," or "Russky boy." I have additionally used the word "Russkies" and on occasion the term "Muscovites" for the generic term for the plural "moskali." (Naydan)

With a communicative purpose in view, Naydan also introduces a simplified, transliterated version of the authentic Ukrainian term *Kozak*, "to differentiate the indigenous Ukrainian freedom fighters of the 16th to 18th centuries from Russian Cossack troops in the Tsarist army in later times" (Naydan).

Through such annotations and updates the translator manifests the need for new translations that would be able to counter the idea of Shevchenko's poetry collection, *The Kobzar*, as a museum of ethnographic artifacts and reveal its relevance to the present-day ethnical concerns of the Ukrainian people.

The black-and-white illustrations in *The Essential Poetry of Taras Shevchenko*, created in a minimalistic style, resemble primordial petroglyphs that symbolically depict in broad straight and curved lines the crude contours of squat human figures with surly faces. Those schematic pictographic images featuring the archetypally deprived – the blind, the forlorn, the betrayed, and the poet-martyr himself – represent the Lviv artists' self-reflection under Soviet rule and their associated projection of Shevchenko's poetry onto the Ukrainian world that they felt to be oppressed. This Ukrainian world may well have been destroyed by the Tsarist and Soviet Russian occupational regimes had there not been such a poet as Shevchenko, whose ethnic rootedness has never precluded his ethics from being UNIVERSALLY recognized. For instance, Professor of Slavic Studies at the University of Manitoba, Myroslav Shkandrij, in his talk opening the Shevchenko exhibition at the Manitoba Legislature, 15 July 2014, affirmed that

> [Shevchenko] was a great democrat in the European tradition. An anti-imperial and anti-colonial writer, he identified with the struggles of subjugated peoples and told their stories – long before postcolonial studies became popular in the last decades of the twentieth century. <…> This concern for all oppressed people places Shevchenko in the mainstream of European and international movements for popular sovereignty, national liberation, and the spread of humane, democratic values – movements that have over many generations shaped the thinking of enlightened and progressive societies. (Shkandrij)

Both American translators of *The Kobzar* – Fedynsky and Naydan – seem to share a belief that they cannot put their work into rhyme because American readers would not understand and appreciate rhymed poetry, due to the nature of the American free-verse literary tradition, exemplified by Walt Whitman's innovative, mostly un-rhymed poetic works, and therefore they focus their translations on the relevance of Shevchenko's ideas to contemporary life. They respectively focus on literalist strategies that prune away all ornamentation of traditional poetry. This is contrary to Ukrainian translators' adherence to regular meter and rhyme when dealing with traditional poetry, whose canons are well accepted and well reflected in the developments of the Ukrainian school of artistic translation in the

20th century, in particular in the works of such poet-translators as Mykola Zerov (1890–1937), Maksym Rylsky (1895–1964), and Hryhoriy Kochur (1908–1994).

However, literal translation can turn a proverbial colloquialism into a rather baffling statement. I would like to illustrate this kind of difficulty with a proverbial phrase (highlighted in bold) from Shevchenko's early poem "До Основ'яненка" (To Osnovyanenko): *Поборовся б і я, може, /Якби малось сили; /Заспівав би, –* ***був голосок, /Та позички з'їли*** (Шевченко, 52). In Naydan's literal rendering it is: "I would fight, perhaps, / If I had the strength; /I would sing, — **I had a voice, / And debts ate it up**" (52). The speaking persona alludes here to rhetorical parallelism by using, self-ironically, a colloquial antithetically constructed proverb *був голосок, та позички з'їли* which implies that he is no longer in the prime of life, as worrying has aged him prematurely. But the translator, apparently, does not notice the figurativeness of this set expression, even though one can find a whole range of colloquial Ukrainian proverbs, synonymic to the above-mentioned, with the same or similar syntactic patterns, such as *був кінь, та з'їздився; доконала Гнідка дорога негладка; були коралі, та пішли далі; були перли, та ся стерли; був колись горіх, та став свистуном; був лісничим, а став нічим* (Вирган, Пилинська, 449).

However different if translated literally, they all imply that someone is no longer in the prime of life and/or is of no account. And all of them distantly correspond to the archaic 16th-century English proverb "care killed a/the cat," which according to the 1894 newer and enlarged edition of E. Cobham Brewer's *Dictionary of Phrase and Fable* is based on a popular adage "a cat has nine lives," declaring that care would wear them all out. In present-day English, an approximate cultural correspondent to the above series of Ukrainian proverbs is "fretting cares make grey hairs." Thereby the contextually relevant meaning of Shevchenko's colloquial proverb *був голосок, та позички з'їли* extends far beyond its textual semantics and cannot be translated other than culturally. And accordingly, a cultural correspondent or its variation would be more appropriate here than literal wording. Consequently, literalness is particularly fraught with risk when applied to informal idiomatic speech.

I will further discuss colloquiality at greater length, as a particular linguistic zone of narrow translatability for any translator of Shevchenko and such work, within the hypotheses that, firstly, speech-related pitfalls can waylay even the most accurate translators for the reason that polysemy and/or idiomaticity of a vernacular locution do not lie on the surface, and therefore finding its proper meaning requires additional lexicographic and field research; and secondly, the discussion in this article dissociates common idioms of Ukrainian vernacular occurring in literary works from those extraordinary linguistic items that comprise the author's idiolect. While the writer's idiolect may be viewed as necessarily untranslatable and actually is being viewed as such, for instance by George Steiner, as Tim Parks observes (Parks 2007, 15), "the vernacular idiom may be found difficult to convey in translation if not properly understood outside the milieu in which the author was writing, but, in my perception, it is not untranslatable, albeit a question of how much linguistic work is required to express the hitherto inexpressible."

To better illustrate the subject matter discussed in this article, I will proceed to compare colloquial locutions from *The Kobzar* with their interpretation in recent English-language translations, bearing in mind the favorable mention of such a comparison of the original and translation, side by side, by the internationally recognized author, translator and essayist Tim Parks in the introductory chapter "Identifying an Original" in his book *Translating Style: A Literary Approach to Translation, A Translation Approach to Literature*:

> By looking at original and translation side by side and identifying those places where translation turned out to be especially difficult, we can arrive at a better appreciation of the original's qualities and, simultaneously of the two phenomena we call translation and literature. (*Ibid.* 14)

In those "places where translation turned out to be especially difficult" Parks sees a propulsive force both for those researching original sources and specialists in translation. Parks' broad juxtaposition of two phenomena — literature and translation — appeared to be conducive to a view of translation as a set of shifting operations, as is evident from his remark when he graphically describes the translator's task using the word "shifting" as a constituent feature of translation: "Imagine shifting the Tower of Pisa into downtown Manhattan and convincing everyone it's in the right place; that's the scale of the task" (Parks 2010).

Particularly if they deal with 19th-century Ukrainian authors, the translators cannot rely exclusively on dictionaries as their contemporary guides to the spoken forms encountered in vernacular writings, such as the colloquial register in Shevchenko that complicates the translator's task and discounts metaphoric representation of the translation process as a set of shifting operations.

The point is that although the Ukrainian language is not a non-familiar tongue to translators in the West, it remains known broadly and generally learned in its prescriptive part as was fixed by the Soviet-era dictionaries, having been largely diluted firstly by the tsarist Russia's imperialistic policies and then later by the Soviet regime's repression and censorship. The first universally-adopted native Ukrainian orthography, established at the International Orthographic Conference (which had been convened in Kharkiv, 1927), was eventually abolished by Stalin's government in 1933 as a "nationalist fallacy," and the steps were taken to bring the Ukrainian language orthography, its lexical and idiomatic stock substantially closer to Russian. Regarding this aspect, it will not be superfluous to look back to the 1920s and early 1930s in Ukraine which have gone down in history as a period of national revival after the centuries of persecution in tsarist Russia. Those years testify to the real renaissance in the scope of strengthening the living Ukrainian language through systematizing it in all forms of dictionaries and its use in all the domains of social, administrative, economic, scientific, and cultural life.[6] Suffice it to say that the Institute of Academic Ukrainian Language, which successfully functioned from 1921 to 1930 at the All-Ukrainian Academy of Science, worked for several years on the, unique in its kind, multi-volume *Dictionary of the Living Ukrainian Language,* which recorded a huge and invaluable collection of spoken-language material. But then, together with over fifty other general and specialised dictionaries, including Russian-Ukrainian dictionaries, compiled and edited by the Institute's team of linguists, with many practicing translators among them, all printed editions together with the printing matrix of this unique *Dictionary* were destroyed by Soviet regime officials in 1933, in what proved to be an irreparable loss of vernacular Ukrainian. This loss was increased by the spelling reform introduced the same year for the purpose of bringing its lexical and grammatical standards closer to Russian.

Amidst tremendous human and national devastation, as an aftermath of the Great Terror of the 1930s, the Great Artificial Famine (or Holodomor of 1932–33), the atrocities of World War II, and Post-War Soviet political repression, there was little chance of survival for the *living*, vernacular Ukrainian in the 20th century. Threatened with extinction, it nevertheless has been held up throughout the century by a few writers and – particularly – by translators because the ubiquitous censorship was relatively less harsh toward translated texts than the original works. Hence the diversity of Ukrainian vernacular has been comprehensively

---

6   In 1923, the All-Union Communist Party of Bolsheviks declared governmental support for the Ukrainian language and its usage in all domains of social, administrative, economic, scientific, and cultural life in the Ukrainian Socialist Soviet Republic by launching the "policy of Ukrainianization" of the Republic's bureaucratic apparatus and its major state-financed institutions, but actually keeping in mind a policy of strengthening their own power in Ukraine. The period of so-called "active Ukrainianization" lasted until 1929. Although aborted, the policy of Ukrainianization greatly influenced all areas of cultural life, and its positive consequences survived until the late 1930s in spite of the fact that the Bolsheviks eliminated the policy for maintenance of national languages in the late 1920s and early 1930s.

collected, for instance, in a great many translations of Western classics by Mykola Lukash (1919–1988) who suffered persecution during his lifetime, struggling to preserve the ethnic authenticity of the language of translation in the 20th century, but whose ethnically-biased School of Domesticating and Re-creative Translation has eventually become widely recognized in today's Ukraine.

Authentic colloquial Ukrainian, which is regarded as being rich in synonymic and dialect variation, has died out to a vast extent. And Ukrainian-to-English translators hardly seem cognizant of the uniqueness of native speaker's language experience and simply tend to pass over the liminal zone of purport when it is evidently considered, or felt, unworthy of the English reader's attention and non-truncated representation, and consequently remains elusive and untranslated, or even left out as untranslatable. This may be demonstrated by noting that literary Ukrainian language has substantially evolved from the living vernacular, so that cultivated and non-standard speech patterns often intermingle with each other and become inseparable. Such intermingling can pose a particular problem both for novice and experienced translators who in the first instance are bound to translate the source language text into a discourse, i.e. connected, purposeful, and mutually comprehensible communication that will enable them to make textually asymmetric decisions.

As stated earlier, the identification of ethnically-biased lexical units not infrequently requires supplementary lexicographic and field research. And in most such cases literalness would be the worst choice of all. As an example, I will consider Shevchenko's enactment of figurative meaning in an idiomatic phrase *приспати під серцем*, where the verb *приспати* means "to induce abortion," while the entire phrase *приспати під серцем* refers to killing an unborn child in its mother's womb (*під серцем*). And, in a figurative sense, it refers to preventing a bigger problem, or nipping it in the bud. In the poem "Розрита могила" (The Ransacked Grave) an anthropomorphized Ukraine bitterly blames her "unwise" son Bohdan (Hetman Bohdan Khmelnytsky), who in 1654 signed the Treaty of Pereyaslav with Muscovy that marked the beginning of Russian colonization of the lands formerly belonging to the Zaporizhian Cossacks. Ukraine the Mother despairingly addresses Hetman Khmelnytsky with striking words of maternal damnation: *Якби була знала, /У колисці б задушила, /Під серцем приспала* (Шевченко, 106). Naydan accurately translates: "If I had known, /I would have strangled you in the cradle, /Put you down under your heart" (106), though his version of the line *Під серцем приспала* as "Put you down under **your** heart" sounds nonsensical – it could have been the editor's misreading, anyway – since the line in question unambiguously implies "I would have killed you in **my** womb."

Further there follow several more cases of misinterpretation of source language colloquial phrases that happen to be unrecorded or indistinct in present-day dictionaries. Shevchenko's early romantic poem "Катерина" (Kateryna), which tells the story of the deceit and treachery of a chaste Ukrainian peasant girl Kateryna by a Russian military officer, who seduces her and leaves her with a child, is based on semantic oppositions both at the microstylistic (associational) and macrostylistic (ideational) levels. I will for instance refer to the scene when Kateryna is grievingly taking leave of her home, leaving for Muscovy for good. This scene reflects a centuries-old Ukrainian native tradition (from the Carpathian Mountains to that territory which is nowadays called the Donetsk and Luhansk region) to take a small amount of earth from your birthplace when embarking on a long journey so that this same earth may be put on your coffin if death overtakes you in foreign lands. And so Kateryna "went into the cherry orchard /And prayed to God, /She took some earth from under a cherry tree /And hung it on a cross: / She said: "I won't return!" /In a far-off land, /In a foreign land, foreign people / Will bury me" (23); further I will proceed in Ukrainian highlighting in bold the words in question:

А **своєї ся крихотка**
Надо мною ляже
Та про долю, моє горе,
Чужим людям скаже...(23)

The highlighted elliptical colloquialism *своєї ся крихотка* ("this ounce [of my native soil]") in the above fragment, where *крихотка* is a colloquial diminutive form of the noun *крихта* ("a very small amount"), happens to be ambiguously rendered by Naydan as "my little one" (this English idiom in back translation into Ukrainian in its proper sense sounds as *моя крихітка*), and hence the presupposed symbolic meaning of the highlighted phrase, namely a handful of earth from one's native land — in sharp opposition to the far-off /foreign land, becomes insufficiently clear in English:

And **my little one**
Will lie down over me
And will tell foreign people
About my fate and my grief... (23)

Further in the poem, Kateryna's parents — killed by sadness — did not hear the rumours that were spreading in the village after she had left: *Та не чули вже тих річей /Ні батько, ні мати...* (24). In Naydan's rendering: "And neither her father nor mother /Heard those things..." (24). The translator encounters here the genitive plural form *річей* (which is exclusively colloquial) of the polysemic noun *річ* in its colloquial meaning "speech /talk" that contextually means "rumours." But contrary to what the semantic context implies, he opts for the literary meaning of the noun *річ* ("thing") apparently taking no notice that the literary genitive plural form – *речей* (things) – is slightly but significantly different from its colloquial near-homonym *річей* (rumours). Would it not be more relevant to the context if the translator had similarly used here such words as "rumours" or "gossip"?

Finally, I will examine an excerpt from the Introduction to the poem "The Haidamaks," where the lyrical subject addresses the moon, which connotes with the masculine gender in Ukrainian. Subsequently, a masculine grammatical gender manifests itself both in the common noun *місяць* (the moon) and its standing epithet *білолиций* (pale-faced). Shevchenko follows the folklore tradition and figuratively uses the standing epithet *білолиций* in place of the noun to which it refers (highlighted in bold):

> А сонечко встане, як перше вставало,
> І зорі червоні, як перше плили,
> Попливуть і потім, і ти, **білолиций**,
> По синьому небу вийдеш погулять, (98)

Yet in translation, both the gender and the subject identity of the lyrical addressee are left undetermined; the translator simply shuns denomination, and the speaking persona addresses the moon (or is it no longer the moon?) as just "you":

> And the sun will rise, as it first had risen,
> And crimson stars floated off as though for the first time,
> They will float afterward, and **you**
> Will step out to dance along the blue sky. (98)

Further among other non-standard forms, from the literary language perspective, Shevchenko uses an informal verb pattern *сіять* (with the second syllable stressed: *сіять*) of the standard verb *сяяти* (first syllable stressed: *сяяти*), meaning "to shine," which in translation becomes transformed into the verb "to sow." Below follow the source excerpt and Naydan's rendering of it, with the erroneous substitution highlighted, which was made possible because the colloquial form *сіять* of the verb *сяяти* ("to shine"), and the colloquial form *сіять* (with the first syllable stressed) of the verb *сіяти*, meaning "to sow," are near-homonyms in Ukrainian:

> Вийдеш подивиться в жолобок, криницю
> І в море безкрає, і будеш **сіять**,
> Як над Вавилоном, над його садами
> І над тим, що буде з нашими синами. (98)

You step out to take a look at the gutter, the well,
And the boundless sea, and you will **sow**,
Like above Babylon, above its gardens,
And above what will be with our sons. (28)

Likewise, several cases of misinterpretation in Fedynsky's translation of *The Kobzar* poetry collection could have been avoided had the translator not placed too much confidence in the literal meaning and had he been sufficiently aware of the traps of colloquial words. I will analyze just one such case. The protagonist of Shevchenko's poem "Чернець" (The Monk) is the historical figure of Semen Paliy (1640–1710) – a colonel from the Ukrainian town of Fastiv. Hero of a social uprising, whom Russian Tsar Peter I exiled to Siberia, he later was released and fought on Russia's side against Hetman Ivan Mazepa at the battle of Poltava. He is shown on his way from the old central area in the city of Kyiv, Podil, to the Mezhyhirsky Monastery on the outskirts of Kyiv. Surrounded by his comrades, the Zaporizhian Cossacks, and he dances and sings all the way to the monastery. In this joyful manner Paliy says goodbye to the life of freedom, driving away gloomy thoughts and preparing himself for a vigil in the monastery. On his way, he dances to a popular Ukrainian humorous folk song with the refrain:

Дам лиха закаблукам,
Дам лиха закаблам,
Останеться й передам! (Shevchenko, 228)

In my loose translation: "I'll quicken my heels, / I'll make them knock faster, / And the front [of my boots] will take no rest [beating to the rhythm]." But the translator appears to be misled in the line *Останеться й передам* by the homoform *передам* [*peredam*], which is the 1st person singular, future tense, of the literary verb *передати* ("to hand over") and, simultaneously, the dative case of the colloquial plural noun *переди* ("the front part of the boots"), and as a result, he renders the sense of the whole refrain deviously:

I'll give my heels hell,
And if there's strength remaining,
I'll share it with another. (228)

Consequently, what may become confusing while translating from 19th-century Ukrainian, based on vernacular colloquial idioms, is the lack of distinction on the translator's part between the literary norm and those lexical and grammatical forms of the colloquial register that have not entered the present-day Ukrainian orthographic standards, yet remain functional in folklore or in speech only.

But before summarizing the difficulties of conveying vernacular locutions in literary translation, I would also like to briefly mention an apparent disregard on the translator's and/or editor's part for the elements of spoken language, which are well recorded in digitized and thus widely available dictionaries, such as the four-volume *Ukrainian Dictionary* (1907–09),[7] compiled and edited by prose writer, ethnographer, and educator Borys Hrinchenko (1863–1910), whose literary legacy was forbidden in the USSR, and the largest *Dictionary of the Ukrainian Language* in 11 volumes, compiled by the Institute of Linguistics at the Academy of Science of Ukraine from 1970–80.[8] An example follows: a colloquial set phrase *тілько мріє* in the poems "Перебендя" (Perebendya) and "Kateryna" with the meaning "(someone/something) is barely seen in the distance /pinpoints out of sight /hangs as an afterimage," which is mistaken in translation for a literary collocation *тільки мрії* ("just dreams") because of the 3rd person singular homoform *мріє* of the two different, but etymologically cognate Ukrainian verbs *мріти* (to be barely seen) and *мріяти* (to dream).

Consider the excerpts in question (the respective phrases highlighted): *За могилою могила, /А там – **тілько мріє*** ("Perebendya"). (My gloss: "Behind the grave another grave, /And anything further is barely seen"). Naydan's version: "Behind the grave another grave, /And there he **just dreams**" (Шевченко, 14). *Пішла… **тілько мріє*** ("Kateryna"). (My gloss: "And left… /Her figure became barely seen in the distance"). Naydan's version: "And left… **Just daydreaming**" (Шевченко, 24).

Of all the possible potential difficulties of rendering 19th century Ukrainian authors into modern English, the most problematic, therefore, is the abundance of vernacularity in their works, the peculiar obsolete and/or non-dictionary spoken forms, in addition to the evanescent meanings of colloquial phrases. Shevchenko's poetic diction in particular, which is characterized by a uniquely natural, easy-flowing, and passionate conversational style, gives the impression of being ostensibly perspicuous and plain, though it is virtually interspersed with vernacular colloquial meanings and idioms that not infrequently can pose a problem for contemporary translators, and mislead them, threatening the accuracy of literary expression.

---

7   Словарь української мови: в 4-х тт. / За ред. Б. Грінченка. Кіев, 1907–09. Online version: Грінченко. Словарь української мови – Укрліт.org. 12 Aug. 2015. <ukrlit.org/…/hrinchenko_slovar_ukrainskoi_movy>.

8   Словник української мови: в 11 тт. / АН УРСР. Інститут мовознавства; за ред. І. К. Білодіда. Київ: Наукова думка, 1970–80. Online version: Словник української мови в 11 томах (СУМ-11) – Укрліт.org. 12 Aug. 2015. <ukrlit.org/…/slovnyk_ukrainskoi_movy_v_11_tomak…>.

There seems to be a substantial incommensurability between the viewpoints of insiders and outsiders to ethnic Ukrainian culture, with the former's intention to preserve the authenticity of the *vernacular* language of translation and the latter's intention to preserve the authenticity of the translator's *unbiased* voice. Translating from a secondary language into a dominant one seems to have empowered literalness in place of the translator's cognizance of the source language writer's cultural experience and the unique purport of what is actually said in the source text. That is why any gap between the insider's and the outsider's translation strategies should not be underestimated. It underscores the reasons why a literalist approach to ethnically-biased classical Ukrainian poetry is being currently in use, and points to cases of *undertranslation,* or a tendency toward generalization and literal wording noticeable in 21st-century American translation practices and clearly observable even in the works of Fedynsky and Naydan, who both are highly skilled, professional translators from Ukrainian.

As in the expressive episode evoked in Willard Van Quine's book *Word and Object*,[9] when a bewildered but opinionated field linguist hearing an aboriginal utter "gavagai" just as a rabbit scuttles past, surmises that he understands the meaning of the native's utterance "gavagai," vernacular Ukrainian phrases, even in well-studied classical works, often represent something different from what the translators may suppose them to represent. Moreover, authentic colloquial Ukrainian, compared to its standardized written form, results in being a source of perplexity for even the best translators into English. Metaphorically speaking, vernacular informal expressions taken out of context can turn into something baffling like Quine's coined foreign word "gavagai" that became a powerful example of what can be referred to as indeterminacy of reference of a native speaker's utterances in isolation. In a sense, Quine's aboriginal informant on the meaning of "gavagai" extrapolated into a Ukrainian context largely remains an ethnic outsider for the English interpreters of Ukrainian literature.

Works Cited

"KOBZAR". У Нью-Йорку відбулася презентація першого повного англомовного перекладу *Кобзаря*… [A Presentation of the first complete English translation of the *Kobzar* took place in New York City]. An Interview

---

9   Quine, Willard Van Orman. "Chapter 2: Translation and meaning." *Word and Object.* Cambridge, MA: Massachusetts Institute of Technology Press, 1960. New ed. 2013. 23–72. Online version: Word and Object by Willard Van Orman Quine … – Questia. 13 Aug. 2015. <https://www.questia.com/library/94067342/word-and-object>.

with Peter Fedynsky, conducted by Kateryna Kindras'. *Ukrainian Weekly "Nova Gazeta"* 07 Nov. 2013. 12 Aug. 2015. <www.novagazeta.info/kobzar.html>.

Luchuk, Olha. "Strategies for popularizing Ukrainian Literature in Translation." *The Ukrainian Quarterly*, Vol. LXVII, No. 1–4, 2011: 111–21.

Naydan, Michael M. "A Note On the Translation." In Шевченко, Тарас. *Кобзар*. Переклад Михайла Найдана; за редакцією Алли Перміновоï. / *The Essential Poetry of Taras Shevchenko*. Trans. Michael M. Naydan; translations edited by Alla Perminova. Lviv: LA "PIRAMIDA", 2014: 9.

Parks, Tim. "Why translators deserve some credit." *The Guardian*. 25 Apr. 2010. 13 Aug. 2015. <www.theguardian.com › Culture › Books>.

—. *Translating Style: A Literary Approach to Translation, A Translation Approach to Literature*. 2nd ed. Manchester, UK & Kinderhook (NY), USA: St. Jerome Publishing, 2007.

Shevchenko, Taras. *The Complete Kobzar: The Poetry of Taras Shevchenko*. Translated from the Ukrainian by Peter Fedynsky. London: Glagoslav Publications, 2013.

Shkandrij, Myroslav. "Shevchenko's Relevance Today." A talk opening the Shevchenko exhibition at the Manitoba Legislature, 15 July 2014. 10 Jan. 2016. <www.ukrainianwinnipeg.ca › Blogs>.

Вирган І.О., Пилинська М.М. *Російсько-український словник сталих виразів*. [Russian- Ukrainian Dictionary of Set Expressions]. First printing Kyiv, 1959; reprinted Kharkiv, 2000. Online version. Text processing by Anatolii Yevpak. Last update 05 Jul. 2008. 12 Aug. 2015. <http://www.rosukrdic.ho.ua/>.

Єкельчик, Сергій [Yekelchyk, Serhy]. *Імперія пам'яті: російсько-українські стосунки в радянській історичній уяві* [*Stalin's Empire of Memory: Russian-Ukrainian Relations in the Soviet Historical Imagination*]. Revised edition with a new Introduction by the author. Toronto, Buffalo, and London: University of Toronto Press, 2004. Видавництво «Часопис "Критика"», Київ, 2008.

Шевченко, Тарас. *Кобзар*. Переклад Михайла Найдана; за редакцією Алли Перміновоï. / *The Essential Poetry of Taras Shevchenko*. Trans. Michael M. Naydan; translations edited by Alla Perminova. Lviv: LA "PIRAMIDA", 2014.

Wojciech Kozak

Authenticity Reexamined: Muriel Spark's *The Public Image*

Abstract: This article discusses Muriel Spark's novel in relation to the manipulative power of the media and their perpetuation of the cultural stereotypes of gender. Tracing the process of the "fall into inauthenticity," triggered off by the protagonist's cultivation of her public image, the article also points out the ambiguous treatment of the novel's central concept, which results in the author's questioning of the traditional opposition between the private/authentic and public/inauthentic self.

Keywords: authenticity, gender, media, public image

When Muriel Spark's novel *The Public Image* was published in 1968, she was already an important figure in the English-speaking literary world. She had written most of her best novels, including her masterpiece, *The Prime of Miss Jean Brodie*, and received wide critical acclaim both in Britain and America.[1] Flattered as she was by this attention, she felt far from comfortable about being a celebrity. Spark undoubtedly found her life in London and New York to be an attractive alternative to the provincialism of Edinburgh, where she had spent her childhood and adolescence.[2] Nonetheless, she also felt apprehensive about the dangers that the media's interest in her person might pose to her privacy and the possibility of being misrepresented to the general public.[3] Her moving to Rome in 1967, i.e. shortly before *The Public Image*

---

1 Among Spark's admirers were both famous writers and critics, such as Evelyn Waugh, Graham Greene, John Updike, Frank Kermode and Lionel Trilling, to name but a few.
2 Spark left Edinburgh in 1937, at the age of 19, and moved to live in Southern Rhodesia (now Zimbabwe) with her husband. After her return in 1944, she settled in London, from which she made a few trips to the USA, before she finally took up residence in Italy, first in Rome, and then in the Tuscan countryside, where she lived with her friend, Penelope Jardine, till her death in 2006. Despite occasional visits to her home town, where both her parents and son lived, the writer never considered the possibility of returning there for good, as Edinburgh was for her a place "where [she] could not hope to be understood" (Spark 2014, 64). On Spark's life see Stannard, whose study is the main source of biographical information given in this essay.
3 Stannard describes the author as an "intensely private person" (xxiii) and emphasizes her dislike for public speaking, as well as her strong refusal to bring her private matters to public attention (xvi, 238). As related by Lessing, Spark felt bitterly resentful at the

appeared on the market, could only exacerbate these fears, for this was a city that the writer saw as a hothouse of gossip and sensationalism. Spark's subsequent decision to leave Rome and to settle in a country house in Tuscany seemed to testify to her disillusionment with the great metropolis. This biographical information provides a relevant context for *The Public Image*,[4] since it is in the Rome of the 1960s that the story is set, and it is the tension between the private and the public life of the protagonist that lies at the core of the novel's structure.

The Public Image presents the life of Annabel Christopher, a young English actress on the threshold of a great career, who has progressed from playing minor parts in productions of moderate success at home to starring in box office hits in Italy. Initially given the roles of inconspicuous girls by English directors, Annabel undergoes a radical transformation when an Italian producer, Luigi Leopardi, decides she should be typecast as a "Lady-Tiger"[5] — a *femme fatale* character her audience finds to be irresistibly attractive. Meanwhile, with the help of Leopardi's secretary and agent, a young girl called Francesca, Annabel's public image as a loving wife and passionate lover is created, which she is determined to keep up until the last pages of the book, when she unexpectedly decides to leave the great world of cinema behind and embark on a plane to Greece with her baby son, Carl.

Most conspicuously, *The Public Image* voices Spark's concerns about the role the contemporary film industry, television and the press play in falsifying reality. As argued by Anna Walczuk, Rome, itself a cradle of Western civilisation, traditionally credited with creation and preservation of the fundamental values of the Western world, in the novel

> becomes a twentieth-century version of the empire of intrigue and manipulation dominated by uncontrollable forces of mass-media which are entirely committed to the fabrication of vulgar publicity not only in demand by pop-culture, but also continually coveted by uncritical public. (249–250).

Contrary to popular belief, Spark suggests it is Italy, rather than America that plays the central part in this specific manifestation of "media imperialism":

> To start in this setting was a good start. If the stories caught on at all they caught on well. Germany and France picked them up. In slow whispers and in more sophisticated

---

manipulation she fell victim to during one of her TV interviews (216). At the same time, she attached great importance to her appearance and her public image in general (Standard, 302; Whittaker, 34).

4   For a biographical reading of the novel see Stannard, esp. 353–356.
5   *The Public Image*, 420, *passim*. Hereafter abbreviated to *PI* and cited parenthetically in the text.

accents they seeped westward. It is a mistake to think that sensational publications start in America. They end there, in a somewhat tired form. But they start, classic, innocent, thoughtless and young, in Italy, the Motherland of Sensation. (*PI*, 433)

It is also in Italy that great careers in the world of film are launched, and the story of Annabel testifies to the power the media play in shaping the life of an individual once they become a celebrity. When seen in private, Annabel looks less than ordinary, "a puny little thing, . . . with a peaky face and mousey hair" (420), which makes her perfectly suitable for the roles she is initially given by English directors. Therefore, the first stage of her professional life closely corresponds to her true self, as she hardly needs to perform in the proper sense: "she only had to exist . . . she only had to be there in front of the camera" (423). Being herself either on or off the screen, however, is not likely to guarantee her international success, and when by "some deeper, more involved mystery" (421) Annabel is discovered by Leopardi, it becomes clear that she must leave her real, uninteresting self behind.

The fact that success and fame come with a price is already suggested at the beginning of the novel, when its protagonist, despite all the thrills that being a celebrity brings, intuitively fears the dangers that lie in wait: "She found it exciting. She found it frightening" (425). The glamour of Annabel's professional career is contrasted to and, to a large extent, responsible for the disappointing reality of her private life. She discovers that now she has "more money, more letters, more business, more to talk and think about" (425), but, in fact, she has less and less. The letters she receives from film producers or fans, only interested in her as a public figure, are unlike the letters she used to send to her friends, who are "now very few" (442), as she no longer has time to write to them. Her prosperity leads to the disintegration of her marriage, since it arouses obsessive envy in her husband, Frederick: a second-rate, jobless actor and a misogynist, who cannot approve of his wife's doing better in life than himself and eventually commits suicide. Most importantly, however, by choosing to be a film star, Annabel risks losing her authenticity, for her belief that she can draw the line between the public and the private aspects of her life turns out to be illusory.

Apparently, Annabel is "entirely aware of the image-making process in every phase" (435). She knows her worth as an actress and believes that she is in full control of the part of the loving wife she is playing. Subsequently, despite hating her husband, when taken to a mortuary to identify his dead body, she kisses his forehead, and, later on, in a statement to the press, fakes her grief over his suicide, insisting it was an accident. Similarly, although she doesn't approve of forgiveness, "I forgive her" (494) is what she says to the journalists when she goes to hospital to see a girl from a party arranged by Fredrick in order to tarnish his wife's public image. The bunch of flowers that Annabel takes with her for this occasion is, again, emblematic of the self-imposed theatricality of her performance, since she has instructed her agent that they should "look as if they've come out of someone's garden . . . not at all got up by a florist" (492).

Nonetheless, Annabel gradually identifies with her public image to such an extent that she becomes living proof of the aphorism attributed to Kurt Vonnegut: "Be careful what you pretend to, because you are what you pretend to be." The image of the door of her new flat "shift[ing] open as if by a slight breeze" (419) to be found on the novel's first page connotes an invasion of her private space by outsiders, i.e. people from the film company, journalists and neighbours — an invasion that leads to the blurring of the boundary between her authentic and inauthentic selves.[6]

As it turns out, the impact of Annabel's recent film is so great that even though the Christophers' marriage is falling apart, they decide to stay together, not so much because they have a public image to maintain but because their personal lives have become "a trailing extension of the film" (431). To quote Fontini Apostolou, "Annabel and Frederick are caught in their 'living parts,' an oxymoron used to reveal how the sudden and thorough invasion of the media into their lives has made them unable to distinguish between life and role, acting and being . . ." (60). This accounts for the fact that they desperately resume their sex life and explains the paradoxical nature of Annabel's feelings about Chris: "it was both inconceivable to her that Frederick should not continue to be her husband, and inconceivable that they could live on together" (*PI*, 442). In this way, *The Public Image* is illustrative of a typically Sparkian technique of ironic reversal, since it is not the Christophers' real life that gets distorted in the tabloid press but rather the entirely fictional story of their perfect marriage that forms the pattern of their actual existence.

Significantly enough, this inability to distinguish between reality and its fictitious counterpart also carries over to the general public, who despite being "on the safe side of the real" as members of the audience, start imitating the Christophers' life as gossip has it.[7] The description of their behaviour is one of the few examples of humour in the novel:

---

6   In her interpretation of the novel's opening scene, Susan Selter sees the Christophers' empty flat, which is to be soon furnished, as a metaphorical representation of Annabel's private self being gradually taken over by the public one (36).

7   The concept of gossip is transgressive, since as a secret generally known and believed to be true, it crosses the boundary between the private and the real on the one hand and the public and the fictitious on the other. This paradoxical quality of gossip is suggested

Authenticity Reexamined: Muriel Spark's *The Public Image* 61

> It was somehow felt that the typical Englishman, such as Frederick Christopher was, had always really concealed a foundry of smouldering sex beneath all that expressionless reserve. It was suggested in all the articles that cited the Christopher image, that this was a fact long known to the English themselves, but only now articulated. Later, even some English came to believe it, and certain English wives began to romp in bed far beyond the call of their husbands, or the capacities of their years, or of any of the realities of the situation. (436)

Following Jean Baudrillard's concept of the hyperreal, it can be argued that in Spark's novel "the world of the media has turned everything into a mere replica" (Apostolou 57). As Leopardi is looking at his friend, what he can see is "not Annabel, but her recordable image" (*PI* 486), which seems to have obliterated or replaced the original.

It is not accidental that driving home from the mortuary after she has identified Frederick's body, Annabel should think of life in terms of film, for her husband's suicide is not a spontaneous, desperate act of a man no longer capable of controlling his life but a perverse plan devised in order to ruin her career. By jumping from the scaffolding of St John's Basilica, Frederick casts himself in the role of a martyred husband, and in aid of this public image he writes letters to his family and friends, in which Annabel is presented as an unfaithful wife and uncaring mother. This sets in motion a vicious circle of inauthentic behaviour, since having discovered Frederick's letters, Annabel decides to defend herself by producing another false story of her husband's death, according to which he fell off the scaffolding by accident when, as a faithful husband, he was escaping from his female admirers. As a result, the Christophers' life becomes a bizarre performance "beyond the grave," in which even the death of one of the spouses does not put an end to the theatrical quality of their existence.

In Spark's "Websterian melodrama of deceit and counter-deceit" (Stannard, 353), the only character who has the courage to expose the falsehood of Annabel's public image is Gelda Tomassi, the young daughter of the Christophers' family doctor. Shortly before the press conference, after Annabel has prepared herself and her neighbours for the occasion "just as successfully as if the scene had been studied and rehearsed for weeks" (*PI*, 467), she is unexpectedly confronted by the Italian girl:

---

in Spark's novel when the narrator ironically implies how the public gaze penetrates behind the impenetrable aspect of Annabel's life: "Within a few weeks, throughout Italy and beyond, it was decidedly understood, thoroughly suggested, hinted and memorized, that in private, inaccessible to all possible survey, and particularly in bed, Annabel Christopher, the new star who played the passionate English governess, let rip" (435–436).

'It is what Frederick would have wanted,' Annabel said. 'I know he would have wanted me to carry on with my career.' . . . Then the lumpy, silent, little girl, who was there . . . said in Italian, 'If that's what he wanted why did he commit suicide and make a scandal for you?" (464).

This innocent character, very much like the truth-telling child from Andersen's "The Emperor's New Clothes," stands in the moral centre of the story and serves as a yardstick by which the author judges the false pretenses of the adult world.[8] Unlike in Andersen's tale, however, Gelda's words fall on deaf ears, and she is rebuked by her mother so that the show can go on.

Go on it does till the last pages of the novel when at the inquest into her husband's death, again rehearsed as if it was a film, Annabel unexpectedly produces his letters, which she has taken so much care to conceal from the public, and leaves the courtroom never to be seen again. The motives behind this startling decision[9] are not clear. It might be argued that Annabel is simply not willing to pay the exorbitant sum of blackmail money that is demanded of her by "the family friend," Billy O'Brien, who has copies of Frederick's letters. By disclosing the letters to the public, she might also engage in yet another power game against her enemies.[10] However, it seems more likely that she chooses to leave Italy because she is no longer able to cope with the strain that the never-ending denial of truth puts on her life. As she says to her lawyer, "I want to be free like my baby" (509). This has led many critics to assume that Annabel's boarding a plane to Greece[11] is an act of affirmation of her true

---

8 The only clearly positive adult character in *The Public Image* is Frederick's lover, a simple and unpretentious girl called Marina. Having received Frederick's megalomaniac letter, she is shocked by its perfidiousness and hands it to his wife despite having a reason to hate Annabel as her rival. Marina's keeping out of the letter intrigue points to her moral integrity and innocence. When asked by Leopardi whether the girl may have had Fredrick's letter photocopied in order to use it for blackmail, Annabel rules out the possibility by saying that she "probably doesn't know about photo-copies" (502). Thus, in a manner typical of her writing, Spark puts this peripheral character, who the general public regards as a "fallen woman," in the moral centre of the novel.
9 As aptly noted by Walczuk, Annabel's unexpected behaviour is anticipated on the first page of the novel, when it is suggested that her arrangements "would start moving anticlockwise at some point" (*PI*, 419, Walczuk, 260).
10 Similarly to Minister D– from Poe's "The Purloined Letter," Bill can only control Annabel as long as Fredrick' letters occupy the private space of her life. Once they are "employed" by him and become public property, all the power he exerts over Annabel is gone.
11 Annabel's journey south-east might connote her spiritual rebirth. Since she leaves Rome for Greece, her journey might also imply a movement towards authenticity, as Roman culture is to large extent a replica of the Greek one.

self, which offers hope for a better future. In Jennifer Randisi's opinion, "By moving from an association with dead art to one with the possibility of natural regeneration, Spark suggests that Annabel may become her own creator rather than the artifact of others' invention" (65). In a similar manner, Peter Kemp maintains that the novel's protagonist "undergoes a moral re-awakening," moving "back towards natural and spontaneous life, towards truth" because "she has grown in moral strength" (118–119).

Nonetheless, Spark is far from leading her readers to obvious conclusions. To read the novel only as a harsh criticism of the media world, which poses a threat to individuality and authenticity,[12] is to ignore its essentially ambiguous treatment of the very concept of the public image. It is hoped that a subsequent discussion of this ambivalence will serve as useful, if somewhat competing, supplement to the interpretation offered above.

The question "What is wrong with a public image?" which Annabel, in slightly different versions, keeps repeating throughout the novel does not simply imply that, as an obtuse character, she is incapable of seeing anything dangerous about the way she lives her life as a celebrity. Rather, by making this question a leitmotif of her novel, the author signals its rhetorical character and urges the reader to reconsider the implications of the concept in question. On second thoughts, it transpires that despite being critical of many aspects of her character's public image, Spark also speaks in defence of it.

Annabel's acute consciousness of her person as perceived by others brings to mind some aspects of Mikhail Bachtin's philosophy of dialogism, formulated in his *Problems of Dostoevsky's Poetics*, in which he postulates the heteronomous ontological status of the self:

> I am conscious of myself and become myself only while revealing myself for another, through another, and with the help of another. The most important acts constituting self-consciousness are determined by a relationship toward another consciousness. . . . everything internal gravitates not toward itself but is turned to the outside and dialogized, every internal experience ends up on the boundary, encounters another, and in this tension-filled encounter lies its entire essence. . . . I cannot manage without another, I cannot become myself without another." (287)

Similarly to the protagonists of Dostoevsky's fiction, characterised by "an intense sensitivity toward the anticipated words of others about them, and with other's reactions to their own words about themselves" (205), Annabel seems to be ob-

---

12 When interpreted as such, the novel must turn out to be disappointing. It is probably this kind of reading that has led Saul Maloff to dismiss *The Public Image*'s moral content as "both banal and thin-to-vanishing" (qtd in Stannard, 350).

sessed with her public image. Yet, it is impossible to conceive both of her private and public existence otherwise than in and for the gaze of others. If Annabel is "stupid" (*PI*, 422) she has also learnt to "circumvent" her stupidity (423) by taking the theatricality of her life at face value and handling it in a very professional manner. As an actress, she intuitively feels that if one has to perform under others' eyes, one should always try to perform well. Since as a human being she will inevitably be constructed by the gaze of another, this Bakhtinian "outsideness" of her existence calls into question the stability of the opposition between her private/authentic and public/inauthentic selves.[13]

This problem is brought to the reader's attention by Leopardi, whose words seem to represent the opinion of Spark herself:

> He was not all concerned or cynical about the difference between her private life and her public image; he did not recognize that any discrepancy existed. He said, 'What is personality but the effect one has on others? Life is all the achievement of an effect. Only the animals remain natural.' (440)

Although Leopardi goes on to explain that one's personality is different from one's character, he also adds that "even character could change over the years, depending on the habits one practised" and stresses that there is nothing hypocritical about Annabel living up to what the public thinks of her (440).

With the exception of Leopardi, the other characters do not seem to be aware that being natural is neither here nor there in the world of human relations. Dr Tomassi's wife, for instance, is outraged that Annabel should have invited journalists to her flat shortly after her husband's death: "This is ridiculous, for an actress to think of the public when there is a private tragedy. . . . It's unnatural for her to have a press conference at this moment" (463). Mrs. Tomassi's reaction apparently testifies to "common sense and moral candour" (Walczuk, 255) but, in fact, it is a manifestation of her naivety, if not hypocrisy. She is the first to "throw a stone" at her hostess minutes before she silences her daughter so that she does not upset the briefing. Tomassi's reaction makes one wonder whether it really would be more "natural" for Annabel to lock herself away from her neighbours and the press in order to mourn the death of a man she loathes.

It should also be noted that thanks to her public image Annabel does not only live for herself but also for others. Accordingly, despite having conceived a baby

---

[13] Alan Kennedy argues that Spark's writing is generally expressive of "the union of the private and the public" (155). Accordingly, he reads *The Public Image* as a manifestation of the novelist's conviction that "full integration of the self can only come with self-dramatisation" (197).

in order to impress the general public as an exemplary wife and mother, she soon becomes entirely devoted to her son. As it turns out, "it was not that the baby fitted the public image, it was rather that the image served the child so well" (*PI*, 439). The mother never breastfeeds her son and may occasionally use him as a "triumphant shield" (464) in confrontation with the public, but this does not change the fact that Carl is "the only reality of her life" (441) and that she goes a long way to protect him from the inquisitiveness of paparazzi, refusing to have any of his unauthorised photos published in the press.

Annabel's concern for Carl makes her essentially different from her selfish husband, who cuts himself off from the outside world and cultivates his own "private self-image" (431)[14]. His "monologic" attitude to life leads to the extinction of his personality, for, to quote Bakhtin, "separation, dissociation, and enclosure within the self [are] the main reason for the loss of one's self" (287). Unable to love his own son, and consumed by obsessive envy about his wife's professional success, Fredrick lives and dies for himself only, and his suicide at the place of St Paul's martyrdom serves as an ironic exposure of the wrong choices he has made both as an actor and as a man.

Finally, although Annabel's public image has been entirely invented for her by others, it paradoxically facilitates her rise to individuality and independence. Spark's novel can be read as a modern parody of the Cinderella story, in which continental "princes" of film industry miraculously save Annabel from the oppressive, authorial and narrow-minded English directors, who stifle her artistic potential by always giving her "the worst jobs" to do. By drawing this implicit analogy, Spark not only ridicules the stories of success as presented in tabloid press and TV programmes, but also, and more importantly, hints at the role the modern media, similarly to traditional Western fairy tales, play in upholding the traditional image of a woman in patriarchal society. The interest Annabel arouses in film producers comes from the fact that as an unremarkable female with limited intellectual capacity, she is likely to be manipulated and reinvented by men so as to fit the stereotype of femininity that the general public craves for.

Apart from being a Cinderella awaiting a prince to shape her destiny for her, Annabel also resembles Liza Doolittle from Shaw's *Pygmalion* — a simple, if not crude, girl who becomes "a lady" thanks to her male protectors and instructors. These men are in no doubt that were it not for them, Annabel would have no

---

14 This oxymoronic phrase points to the falsehood of Frederick's conception of himself, for any image of a person, is, in fact, public in the sense that it always arises from how others see us and what others think of us. As argued by Bakhtin, "a person's image is a path to the I of another" (294).

identity at all. The passage in which Frederick talks to his wife about the script he has written for her new film is reminiscent of Professor Higgins' disdain for his cockney student:

> He took the script from her hand with ominous care and consideration; then said in the tones of a phoneticist addressing an illiterate foreigner, 'Will you do me a favour, Annabel? ... Please do not talk of "significance", because you do not understand it. And that is because you are *in*significant yourself.'" (427)

Similarly, when in a conversation with Leopardi Annabel protests against being identified with her public image, she is immediately "put right" by her interlocutor: "Before I made you the Tiger-Lady, you didn't even look like a lady in public, never mind a tiger in private. It's what I began to make of you that you've partly become" (441).

However, despite being an object of male sexual desire constructed by the patriarchal gaze of the film camera, Annabel reciprocates this gaze, as implied by her mysteriously large eyes (421–22), which are the most striking aspect of her image. In confrontation with the individuality-stifling world of gossip and sensationalism, she makes the most of her resourcefulness and resilience, and the arrangements she makes for herself and her son in Rome bear witness to the aspect of her character that is ignored by her male adversaries. As "a strong woman, a sort of tiger at heart" (442), Annabel has enough courage to take the "film script" from the hands of its authors and place herself at the other side of the camera, becoming a director of her life.[15] Hence, it can be argued that the real reason why she persists in saving her public image is that by now she has stolen it from its original owners and made it her own. That is why she believes it is up to *her* to decide what to do with it and when to do it: "She did not expect this personal image to last long in the public mind, for she intended to play other parts than that of the suppressed tiger, now that she was becoming an established star" (435).

In the course of the novel, its protagonist has managed to transform herself from an image of a woman into a woman with an image. Although her transformation deserves recognition rather than condemnation, it is hardly surprising

---

15 A similar conclusion is reached by Apostolou, who writes that "the novel seems to be playing with the idea of the dominance of the active male gaze and the passivity of the female behind the camera. Annabel participates in the mythologies that are formed around her by her own free will" (60). In Page's opinion, "it is only by turning her back on this male world, ever ready to exploit her, that she can realise her selfhood" (67). Annabel's strength of character is also accentuated by Richmond (107).

that she gets none,[16] for her autonomy undermines the confidence of men who usurp the right to control her destiny. When Leopardi realises that, ironically enough, there is a substantial truth to Annabel's public image ("she was a lady-like, genteel sort of tiger; but still, indeed, a tiger," 486), he suggests replacing it with another one, in which she is supposed to "play wild, mad girls" (488). As can be expected, Annabel dismisses this suggestion because she sees it as another attempt at dominating her.[17]

With her main enemy dead and her reputation secured, time is ripe for Annabel's final decision to start anew — once she has become the owner of her public image, she can afford to shed it. This point in her life does not so much signify her "rebirth to authenticity" but rather a state, in which, having discarded one of her public selves, she is pondering the possibilities of "playing other parts" and shaping her life accordingly.

Unrecognised by other passengers at the airport despite not wearing her dark glasses, Annabel feels "both free and unfree," "pregnant with the baby, but not pregnant in fact," an "empty shell" that nonetheless contains "the echo and harking image of former and former seas" (510). The closing passage of *The Public Image* quoted above perfectly illustrates the "nevertheless principle" — one of the structural hallmarks of Spark's writing, which the author wrote about in her essay "What Images Return":

> I believe myself to be fairly indoctrinated by the habit of thought which calls for this ["nevertheless"] word. In fact I approve of the ceremonious accumulation of weather forecasts and barometer readings that pronounce for a fine day, before letting rip on the statement 'nevertheless, it's raining.' I find that much of my literary composition is based on the nevertheless idea. (64–65)

In accordance with the "nevertheless idea," many of Spark's novels and short stories question the ontological stability of such traditional oppositions as appearances vs. reality, truth vs. falsehood or the self vs. the other, which accounts for the essentially paradoxical and ironic quality of her writing.[18] Annabel Christopher may be "a screen upon which her author could project her nightmares and her endless curiosity, an

---

16 The only exception is Dr Tomassi, in whose words "You are very brave" (*PI*, 462) a kind of admiration can be sensed.
17 Similarly, despite having apparently agreed to her lawyer's plan to pay O'Brien, Annabel eventually rejects it as a decision made for her instead of by her — without having consulted her client, Tom Escon simply informs her that he has accepted the blackmailer's offer.
18 On an insightful study of this problem in Spark's fiction see Walczuk, who, nonetheless, does not consider it in relation to *The Public Image*.

image, perhaps, of what Muriel might have become had she been weaker" (Stannard, 354). Nevertheless, this character also illustrates her creator's awareness that, whether she liked it or not, her public image was too important to be ignored altogether.

Works Cited

Apostolou, Fontini E. *Seduction and Death in Muriel Spark's Fiction*. Westport, CT – London: Greenwood, 2001. Contributions to the Study of World Literature. No. 107.

Bakhtin, Mikhail. *Problems of Dostoevsky's Poetics*. Ed. and trans. Caryl Emerson. 1984. Theory and History of Literature. Ed. Wlad Godzich and Jochen Schulte-Sasse. Vol. 8 Minneapolis: University of Minnesota P, 1999.

Kennedy, Allan. "Cannibals, Okapis and Self-Slaughter in the Novels of Muriel Spark." *The Protean Self. Dramatic Action in Contemporary Fiction*. London: Macmillan, 1974. 151–211.

Kemp, Peter. *Muriel Spark*. Novelists and Their World. Ed. Graham Hough. London: Elek, 1974.

Lessing Doris. "Now You See Her, Now You Don't." *Hidden Possibilities: Essays in Honour of Muriel Spark*. Ed. Robert E. Hosmer, Jr. Notre Dame, IN: University of Notre Dame P, 2014. 212–219.

Page, Norman. *Muriel Spark*. London: Macmillan, 1990. Macmillan Modern Novelists. Ed. Norman Page.

Randisi, Jennifer Lynn. *On Her Way Rejoicing. The Fiction of Muriel Spark*. Washington, D. C.: The Catholic University of America P, 1991.

Richmond, Velma Bourgeois. *Muriel Spark*. New York: Frederick Ungar, 1984.

Sellers, Susan. "*Tales of Love*: Narcissism and Idealization in *The Public Image*." *Theorizing Muriel Spark: Gender, Race, Deconstruction*. Ed. Martin McQuillan. London: Palgrave Macmillan, 2002. 35–48.

Stannard, Martin. *Muriel Spark. The Biography*. London: Weidenfeld, 2009.

Spark, Muriel. *The Public Image*. 1968. *Muriel Spark Omnibus 4*. London: Constable, 1997. 417–510.

—. "What Images Return." *The Golden Fleece. Essays*. Ed. Penelope Jardine. Manchester: Carcanet, 2014. 63–65.

Walczuk, Anna. *Irony as a Mode of Perception and Principle of Ordering Reality in the Novels of Muriel Spark*. Kraków: Universitas, 2005.

Whittaker, Ruth. *The Faith and Fiction of Muriel Spark*. New York: St Martin's, 1982.

Piotr Skurowski

White-to-Black: Racechange and Authenticity, from John Howard Griffin to Rachel Dolezal

Abstract: This article deals with the challenges posed by transgressing racial boundaries, where the perceptions and evaluations of such acts as "(in)authentic" provide a highly important dimension. Autobiographical texts by John Howard Griffin and Grace Halsell are examined, in an effort to show the effect of the racial "passing" experience on subjectivity.

Keywords: authenticity, racial cross-dressing, passing, whiteness, blackness

Among the leading 2015 news stories bearing on the race relations in the U.S. was the case of Rachel Dolezal, a naturally blonde and pale-skinned white person with no apparent black roots, who for years claimed black descent until she was finally "unmasked" as a fraud. In her defense, Dolezal argued that she came to identify herself as black, as she had a black husband and a biracial child; she also adopted a black child. Modifying her argument somewhat for a TV interview, Dolezal explained that, at least, she was not white: "Well, I definitely am not white. Nothing about being white describes who I am." (Johnson, Perez-Pena and Eligon).

It soon turned out Dolezal was a notorious liar with a long record of lying about her life; at some point she even claimed one of her black friends was her biological father (Johnson, Perez-Pena and Eligon).[1] Yet, regardless of the psychological aspect of Dolezal's masquerade, one can't fail to notice how her "blackness" evidently helped her to strengthen her professional credentials in, for example, her work as instructor at North Idaho College and at Eastern Washington University, where she worked in the Africana studies program and became an adviser to black student groups and a NAACP activist (serving as president of the Spokane, Wash., chapter of the NAACP).

Needless to say, Dolezal's unmasking followed by her arguments used in self-defense (why can't one legitimately identify as black, non-white, or at least "transracial" despite white parentage) caused an outburst of angry comments from the

---

[1] In her answer to a reporter's question "Have you done something to darken your complexion?" she responded, "I certainly don't stay out of the sun." She turned out to be "a standing customer of Palm Beach Tan in Spokane and was a fan of Mystic Tan…a brand of spray tan." (Blow)

black community. The *New York Times* columnist Charles Blow's opinion in this matter seems to be representative of this wave of critical opinion. Blow believes that, all along, Dolezal was cashing in on her status as a white person, or "white privilege:" "Dolezal was able to convincingly present and perform blackness as a lightskinned black woman is a form of one-directional privilege that simply isn't available to a black person starting at the other end of the melanin spectrum." Blow insists that "Dolezal wasn't passing in the traditional sense of the word, she was merely commandeering and concocting a biography of burden to obscure the shift and lay claim to authenticity," blaming her of being a fraud and causing insult to the African-American community. Another commentator, Jonathan Capehart in *The Washington Post*, also denied authenticity to Dolezal's 'act':

> There is nothing wrong white people identifying strongly with African Americans and African American culture. I personally know three such people who are so down with the cause that I often have to remind myself that they are not indeed a person of color. Their cultural fluency and commitment to understanding impresses us and makes them "one of us," as we affectionately say. Not pretending to be African American or denying being white makes my friends powerful civil rights allies. They are authentically themselves."

Had Dolezal, in this view, "simply identified as African American and not denied her white parents and lineage or fabricated her story to seem more authentically black, there would have been no controversy.[2]

Shocking, or perhaps ridiculous as Dolezal's conduct may appear, it nonetheless addresses a number of relevant issues stemming from the white-non-white racial relations in the U.S. and parallels, even though perhaps in a distorted, caricature-like way, sets of behaviors firmly present in American social and cultural history. The phenomenon I'm referring to is known as racial 'passing,' which, to be sure, has attracted a lot of attention from the cultural historians and literary scholars.[3]

"Passing", or crossing the color-line, has mostly been effected by those who sought a social or economic advantage, which, in the context of American realities (white hegemony and oppression of the 'non-white races'), usually meant that a 'colored person' would affect being white. The objectives of such a racial impersonation were perfectly clear and understandable, as the minority group members used that means to seek inclusion into the American Dream, otherwise

---

2 See also, for example, Osamundia James, "What Rachel Dolezal doesn't understand: being black is about more than just how you look." *The Washington Post* (June 12, 2015).
3 Most recently, this complex history has received an excellent treatment in Allyson Hobbs, *A Chosen Exile. A History of Racial Passing in American Life* (Cambridge, Mass. and London: Harvard University Press, 2014).

not truly available to them.[4] 'Passing' was obviously motivated by the specificity of American racial practices and ascriptions (consistent with the one-drop rule which made a person with even a very remote 'black' ancestry and sometimes with a perfectly 'white' look being considered legally 'colored'). Needless to say, the commonly accepted racial divisions have always been inconsistent and easily open to revision/deconstruction. Based on myth as they were, they nonetheless constituted a brutal social reality that caused many light-skinned mulattos attempt to cross the color-line dividing the oppressed from their masters. The practice of black-to-white passing, nowadays basically defunct, continued for a remarkably long period of time, including the 1940s and 1950s, and left a strong imprint in American culture. As late as the 1940s and 50s, a noted New York times literary critic Anatole Broyard, born 'colored', was passing for a white person, evidently in fear of being 'unmasked' and thus losing his high professional status. The cost of such race performances must have been tremendous (in the case of Broyard, we have the testimony of his daughter, who painfully reminisces being denied knowledge of her father's true racial identity and of her family past; one can only surmise the amount of tension and stress that must have been suffered by the critic himself, who did not reveal his racial identity even on his deathbed).[5] Perhaps the most suggestive accounts of the sufferings related to passing can be found in now classic literary sources, from William Wells Brown and Charles Chesnutt to James Weldon Johnson, Nella Larsen, Claude McKay and, more recently, Toni Morrison. The second world war and the years immediately following it showed a strengthening of the white liberal sensibility, which found its expression in an outcropping of "tolerance" novels and films, condemning the racial prejudice and oppression and showing empathy for the oppressed racial minority. In particular, the "tragic mulatta" theme gained a visible presence in such Hollywood movies as *Pinky* (1949), *An Imitation of Life* (1959).

The incipient cultural radicalism symbolized by Norman Mailer's celebrated essay "The White Negro" (1957) attempted even to idolize the black urban male as a prototype of the hipster. In fact, Mailer's gesture may be seen as a cross-racial masquerade becoming increasingly common in the postwar years. In her book *Racechanges,* Susan Gubar observes that for whites crossing the color line

---

4   See Jennifer L. Hochschild, *Facing Up to the American Dream. Race, Class and the Soul of the Nation.* Princeton, NJ: Princeton University Press, 1995.

5   See Anatole Broyard's daughter's testimony in Henry Louis Gates's excellent TV documentary, *The African Americans: Many Rivers to Cross* (2013), PBS, Part I. The same documentary features some highly revealing confessions about "passing" by a number of African-Americans.

was merely a pose, while for blacks it remained a strategy of survival. The black impersonations, so commonly to be found in American popular culture, were once even staged by the African-Americans themselves, acting in blackface along with white performers to reinforce the stereotypical racial imagery hungered for by the white audiences of mass culture spectacles. In Gubar's words, "blackface in the movies, blackface on the black faces of African-American Broadway entertainers, and various aesthetic transmutations of blackface flirt with even as they defend against the black Other, who becomes a kind of commodity fetish for white people" (45). Gubar devoted her book to a study of the cultural and psychological complexities involved in the widespread twentieth-century practice of white people's blackface performances of "blackness", from the white minstrels' depictions of African Americans to more complex and sophisticated renderings of 'blackness' by the contemporary artists and writers like Robert Mapplethorpe, Norman Mailer, Saul Bellow or John Berryman. As she stated, both in popular culture and in "elite art forms," „racial masquerade and racechange appeared to play a crucial role for white men and women" (xv).

Much has been written on the "Africanization" of American popular culture, which goes back at least to the rise of ragtime, jazz and blues in the early 20th century. One immediately thinks of the *Jazz Singer*, Hollywood's first sound movie, whose most famous scene has the Jewish-American performer, Al Jolson, appear in blackface.[6] Gubar refers to such interaction between white performers and African-American tradition (symbolized by, among others, Benny Goodman's swing, Elvis Presley's rock 'n' roll, or Vanilla Ice's rap) as acts of "racial crossover and ventriloquism" (10). In time, the phenomenon of white artists' adopting and imitating "black" cultural idiom and styles became a striking feature of contemporary American popular culture. This trend was going to gather speed in the course of the 60s, 70s and 80s, leading to the phenomenon Cornel West recently called "the Afro-Americanization of white youth" (Gubar, 121).

Yet in the real world – the world of work, business, residential patterns, a white person claiming a black social identity would long remain an anomaly – little surprise, perhaps, in view of the brutal facts of American life allowing the continued oppression of the black minority, to which, in the postwar years, was soon added

---

6   See, for example, Jeffrey Melnick's *A Right to Sing the Blues. African Americans, Jews, and American Popular Song* (Harvard University Press, 1999). Melnick writes that "(i)n a variety of ways, music industry figures such as Irving Berlin, George Gershwin, Harold Arlen, Al Jolson, and the Witmark brothers established Jewish agility at expressing and disseminating Black sounds and themes as a product of Jewish suffering and as a variant of Jewish cultural nationalism" (12).

the exclusion of African Americans from the newly expanding suburbs, the latter quickly becoming the target of the "white flight" from central cities.

Such a rather fantastic scenario – of a white man adopting a black social identity – was the subject matter of the 1947 Sinclair Lewis's social protest novel (and a scathing satire on whiteness), *Kingsblood Royal*. It is a story about a model white suburbanite, citizen of the proud town of Grand Republic, who discovers he is 1/32 black (one of his grandmothers was an octoroon, or 1/8 black) and decides to proclaim himself a "Negro," which leads to disastrous consequences. The plot of the novel was criticized as absurd, unrealistic and overly sentimental, even though some leaders of the black community regarded the novel as profoundly perceptive. In this argument, *Kingsblood Royal* is a cultural text raising important questions undermining the authenticity of racial subjectivities and legitimacy of racial ascriptions. It shows a radical bent in Sinclair Lewis's social satire, whose purpose seems to have been to de-authenticate, and de-legitimate, the racial categories and boundaries, to subvert the logic of the "one-drop rule" and of racism, in general. The text appears to be representative of a new climate of opinion among America's white liberal elites, showing a greater sensitivity and empathy toward African-Americans and a tendency to condemn, in principle if not in practice, the racial prejudice still visibly present in everyday life.

Some twelve years after the publication of Lewis's book – in the autumn of 1959, a 39-year-old white Texan named John Howard Griffin, decided to sneak across the color line through a brave act of racial cross-dressing, to find out how it "really" felt to be black in a racist society.

Prior to setting out on a 6-week ramble across the Deep South, posing for a black man, Griffin submitted himself to a skin-darkening treatment which allowed him to easily pass for a black person. The result of that experience was going to come out first in a series of articles, and then in the form of a diary, titled *Black Like Me* (1961), which became an instant bestseller.

By the time Griffin, in blackface, took to the road, the Civil Rights Movement was in full swing. What had happened along the way, was, among else, the Brown v. Board (1954); the Rosa Parks incident and the Montgomery bus strike (1955); the desegregation of Little Rock High (1957). Soon, the "freedom riders", black and white, were going to take to the road and try to desegregate railroad and bus stations throughout the South. People followed with keen interest the news from the race front. There was a big demand for "authentic" material on racial issues, and *Black Like Me* – a first-hand account of white Southern racism by a white man posing for a black was perfectly situated to reach a vast audience.

Griffin was a Texan, but in no way a typical white Southerner. Though he grew up in Dallas, he went to school in France (lycée) and spent several years in Paris studying medicine (focusing in psychiatry) before the outbreak of the second world war. Upon his return to the U.S. he enlisted in the Navy and was sent to the Pacific, from where he returned as a legally blind person (as a result of a bomb attack on his base in Guadalcanal). It'd take 10 years for him to suddenly regain his eyesight, which he would most certainly regard as a sign of God's grace – Griffin was a deeply religious person, a Protestant converted to Roman Catholicism, steeped in the philosophy of Jacques Maritain. While still blind, he became a writer and published his first novel, *The Devil Rides Outside* (1952), which turned out a moderate success.

However, it was his idea to pass for a Southern Negro and in that capacity to find out what it felt like to be black in the South that made him really famous. The 1962 book which is the outcome of a 6-weeks odyssey that took him from New Orleans to Atlanta, became an instant bestseller not only in the United States but throughout the world. In France alone, some 2 million copies were sold. Signet brought out the paperback edition in late 1962, and it would sell over five million copies during the decade (Bonazzi, 144–145).

The book, preceded by a series of installments for *Sepia Magazine*, takes the form of a first-person journal narration in the past tense, based on notes made by Griffin during his stint as a Southern Negro. Having originated as an ethnographic project Griffin's journal ultimately expanded beyond the original plan, registering not only the 'findings' but also many private thoughts and reflections. As he explained in the Preface, "This began as a scientific research study of the Negro in the South, with careful compilation of data for analysis. But I filed the data, and here publish the journal of my own experience living as a Negro. I offer it in all its crudity and rawness. It traces the changes that occur to heart and body and intelligence when a so called first-class citizen is cast on the junkheap of second-class citizenship."

The approach taken by Griffin was unusual, though reminiscent of the methods used by some ethnographers ("going native') and such writers as Jack London and Nels Anderson, passing for hobos and writing autobiographical accounts based on their experience of being "down and out".[7]

---

[7] What comes to mind in the first place is, of course, the work of Bronisław Malinowski. As far as the explorations of the life of the urban underclass, see the classic first-hand accounts by Jack London, *The People of the Abyss* (1903) and Nels Anderson, *The Hobo. The Sociology of the Homeless Man* (1923).

> Under the direction of a New Orleans dermatologist, Griffin had taken medication orally and had exposed his entire body to the ultraviolet rays of a sun lamp. For about a week, up to fifteen hours each day, he had stretched out on a couch under the glare of the lamp. His eyes had been protected by cotton pads when he faced the lamp, and he had worn sunglasses when turned away from its rays. (Bonazzi, 37)

At last, in the privacy of his hotel room in New Orleans, away from home, Griffin applied the last touches to his metamorphosis, applying layers of black paste to his shaved skull. Then, looking in the mirror, he experienced a shock of non-recognition:

> In the flood of light against white tile, the face and shoulders of a stranger— a fierce, bald, very dark Negro— glared at me from the glass. He in no way resembled me. The transformation was total and shocking. I had expected to see myself disguised, but this was something else. I was imprisoned in the flesh of an utter stranger, an unsympathetic one with whom I felt no kinship. All traces of the John Griffin I had been were wiped from existence. Even the senses underwent a change so profound it filled me with distress. I looked into the mirror and saw reflected nothing of the white John Griffin's past. No, the reflections led back to Africa, back to the shanty and the ghetto, back to the fruitless struggles against the mark of blackness. Suddenly, almost with no mental preparation, no advance hint, it became clear and it permeated my whole being. My inclination was to fight against it. I had gone too far. (*Black*, 11)

Griffin's shock and disgust at his mirror reflection obviously loans itself to a psychoanalytical reading pointing to deep psychological structure of affect linked to this projection of an internalized racial Other. Inevitably, they reveal the emotional ambiguities inherent in Griffin's blackface performance. At the same time, Griffin's reracing act raises questions about the legitimacy of racial ascriptions and about the performativity of race.

In his account, his authenticity went entirely unquestioned, despite his earlier fears. From his first appearance in the streets of New Orleans until the last 'performances' in Atlanta, Griffin successfully poses as a 'Negro,' without being recognized and exposed as a fraud, by whites and blacks alike. What obviously helped was that Griffin was a sophisticated performer: native born, with a good ear for local accents and excellent command of the idiom, but also someone with a natural ethnographer's and psychologist's intuition, strengthened by a long foreign experience. Regardless of this, he keeps learning while 'on the job,' conducting what is both an ethnographic/psychological experiment and a moral mission; and even though the methodology and the ethics of this experiment would obviously disqualify his project as "scientific" in the strict sense of the word, the insights gained into the psychology of race prejudice are very revealing.

Someone's racial "authenticity," for that matter, is predicated on a common practice psychologists call "selective inattention", leading to stereotypization. At first, Griffin believed he can only 'fool' the whites but was afraid that he would be quickly unmasked as 'illegitimate' by the blacks who know more about the black 'type' – only to learn, in the process of his experiment, that his fears stemmed from "white" thinking. In reality, there is no 'black type,' but instead different individuals. A black person may or may not speak with a certain accent, he or she may have blue eyes, for example – usually perceived as the mark of whiteness. The 'black' thinking could be equally misleading, though: in his lectures, given already after the publication of the book, Griffin claimed that even when he confessed to his black hosts that he was white, they wouldn't trust him: "The looks of pain and distress in the eyes of my hosts told me clearly what they were too courteous to say in words. Their looks said: 'Who is this black man who thinks he's white? " (Bonazzi, 39–40)

The book's purpose was obviously to reveal the brutal facts about everyday life of the oppressed blacks in order to shock the white liberal opinion. Life of blacks, as described by Griffin, was, in the words of Margaret M. Russell, "a tale of degradation and cruelty", and the portrait of life in the South "almost unremittingly somber and bleak" (271). As Griffin explained it in *Black Like Me*, white-dominated culture "destroys the Negro's sense of personal value, degrades his human dignity, deadens the fibers of his being . . . . Existence becomes a grinding effort" (48).

Among the things that wearing a black mask allowed Griffin to learn was the silent language of white hate. The object of one early lesson was the hate look. In a poignant passage, Griffin described how his presence at a bus station in New Orleans elicited hate stares from a white woman selling tickets and an anonymous white man in the "white" waiting room. "Nothing can describe the withering horror of this," he confessed. This shock of "unmasked hatred" was "so new" to Griffin that he could not take his "eyes from the man's face" (54).

All along, Griffin keeps finding out about the sexual undertones and innuendos of seemingly "harmless" actions, when blacks interact with whites. Giving up a seat on a bus to a white woman – an instinctive gesture, one might say, for someone brought up as a 'Southern gentleman' – has potentially dangerous consequences. It is not a 'black' thing to do, as Griffin finds out from other black passengers on the bus – and from the insulting comments from the woman who regards his courtesy as a sexual advance. Indeed, an intriguing part of *Black Like Me* has Griffin find out about black man's role as a sex fetish to the whites. This is prominently present in the episodes in which Griffin, hitchhiking in the Deep South, is confronted with unexpected displays of curiosity about black sexuality.

> All but two (drivers) – he writes – picked me up the way they would pick up a pornographic photograph or book—except that this was verbal pornography. With a Negro, they assumed they need give no semblance of self-respect or respectability. The visual element entered into it. In a car at night visibility is reduced. A man will reveal himself in the dark, which gives an illusion of anonymity, more than he will in the bright light. Some were shamelessly open, some shamelessly subtle. All showed morbid curiosity about the sexual life of the Negro, and all had, at base, the same stereotyped image of the Negro as an inexhaustible sex-machine with oversized genitals and a vast store of experiences, immensely varied. They appeared to think that the Negro has done all of those "special" things they themselves have never dared to do. They carried the conversation into the depths of depravity. . . . In one case, a young white driver ended up wanting me to expose myself to him, saying he had never seen a Negro naked. (91)

Evidently those fragments of Griffin's narrative pushed Eric Lott to the conclusion that Griffin's "disguise" is nothing more— and nothing less— than an "externalization" of the "sexualized racial unconscious of American whiteness" and Elaine Ginsberg to a statement that they stand for "white masculinity's repressed libidinal investment in black masculinity" (Ginsberg loc. 3187).

Inevitably perhaps, Griffin's book abounds in inconsistencies, subverting and deconstructing the text. His persona, in fact, keeps switching between black and white. Despite the initial shock stemming from his changed identity (the mirror scene in a New Orleans hotel), Griffin renews the experience several times during his relatively short stint as a 'Southern Negro,' switching back and forth between his 'white' and 'black' identities. Thus he removes the dye when he decides to 'pass for white' and starts putting it back on when he decides to reassume a 'black' identity. This seems to partly de-authenticate Griffin's claim of having undergone a deep psychological transformation.

Acting in blackface does not prevent Griffin from reverting to 'whiteness'. This can be seen in the scopophilic aspect of his observations, where the grim realism and corresponding empathy coexist with something of a 'prurient interest' in the racial other: in Griffin's comments on the ghetto, we can find a perspective that seems, after all, more 'white' than 'black,' despite allegations to the contrary:

> It was the ghetto. I had seen them before from the high altitude of one who could look down and pity. Now I belonged here and the view was different. A first glance told it all. Here it was pennies and clutter and spittle on the curb. Here people walked fast to juggle the dimes, to make a deal, to find cheap liver or a tomato that was overripe. Here was the indefinable stink of despair. Here modesty was the luxury. People struggled for it. I saw it as I passed, looking for food. A young, slick-haired man screamed loud obscenities to an

older woman on the sidewalk. She laughed and threw them back in his face. They raged. Others passed them, hearing, looking down, pursing lips, struggling not to notice. . . . Here sensuality was escape, proof of manhood for people who could prove it no other way. Here at noon, jazz blared from juke boxes and dark holes issued forth the cool odors of beer, wine and flesh into the sunlight. Here hips drew the eye and flirted with the eye and caused the eye to lust or laugh. It was better to look at hips than at the ghetto. (*Black*,19)

Griffin's gaze in this fragment is evidently fetishistic, even though he himself (posing as a black man) – as we have seen, becomes the object of other white men's fetishism (compare the above comments on Griffin's hitchhiking experiences).

Griffin may seem inconsistent about his switching between sentimentalized essentialism and his proclaimed universalism, prominently expressed in the Preface:

> The Negro. The South. These are details. The real story is the universal one of men who destroy the souls and bodies of other men (and in the process destroy themselves) for reasons neither really understands. It is the story of the persecuted, the defrauded, the feared and detested. I could have been a Jew in Germany, a Mexican in a number of states, or a member of any "inferior" group. Only the details would have differed. The story would be the same. (n. pag.).

Black Like Me obviously raises many questions about the authenticity and legitimacy of Griffin's project. In his preface to *Black Like Me* Griffin responds to criticisms of his observations from "(s)ome Whites" that "this is the white man's experience as a Negro in the South, not the Negro's" (n. pag.). Griffin promptly dismisses such accusations, though, rejecting them on the grounds of the relevance of his topic: "But this is picayunish, and we no longer have time for that. We no longer have time to atomize principles and beg the question. We fill too many gutters while we argue unimportant points and confuse issues" n.pag.).

In his later book, *Prison of Culture: Beyond Black Like Me*, Griffin elaborates on the fact that, ironically, it was his whiteness, and not the adopted blackness, which authenticated the book in the eyes of his white readers, allowing him to better convey the message to them. "But because I was white once again, I could tell the truth without antagonizing the whites. If a black person said exactly the same words, no matter how tactfully he or she might put it, white leaders would be offended and the attempt at communication would turn into anger, with whites referring to blacks as arrogant or rude" (69).

Griffin evidently felt uneasy about that proof of trust. In the epilogue to the 1977 edition of *Black Like Me*, he writes that in the years following the book's publication, "it was my embarrassing task to sit in on meetings of whites and blacks, to serve one ridiculous but necessary function. I knew, and every black man there knew, that I, as a man now white again, could say the things that needed saying but would be rejected if black men said them." As he also admitted, "Often in the presence of local black men whites would ask me questions that should have been addressed to the black men present. They knew the community, I didn't. Always this was an affront to black men, one of the many affronts that white men apparently could not perceive" (Ginsberg loc. 3175).

New Americanist critics, Eric Lott and Elaine Ginsberg, unequivocally place Griffin in the mainstream of "white liberal" sensibility which they, needless to say, reject. Elaine Ginsberg seems to be going pretty far, arguing *Black Like Me* embodies a "mimetic desire" and a wish "to appropriate black experience without compromising a presumed white entitlement to speak for this experience, one that wants to lose itself in the 'other' without losing control" (loc. 3194).

Griffin couldn't read those comments, made in the 1990s, from a different time perspective and from a conceptually and ideologically different point of view. But by 1971, that is the 10th anniversary of the first edition of his book, he obviously realized the perspective on his book, particularly of its black readers, dramatically changed. Within a few years, his experiment, as well as his book, seemed to have lost much of its legitimacy. The authenticity of his "blackness", from a later perspective, appeared questionable, at least to the black readers who were no longer willing to hear their case pleaded by a white man. In the epilogue to the 1971 edition of *Black Like Me*, Griffin partly distanced himself from his book, writing that "The day was past when black people wanted any advice from white men" (Browder, 216).

In one of his later essays, he empathizes with "black people (who) resent not only the overt bigot but are learning to resent even more deeply what in the old days were called 'good whites'— the good whites, on whom so many black people counted, have not understood in sufficient numbers the core problems of the *intrinsic Other* and the *System* and have, therefore, failed to repudiate them and their deadly effects on the black community" (*Prison*, 61). Who but the white liberal are those words referring to? And in 1977, in "A Time to be human," he writes that "(t)he deepest shock I experienced as a black man was the realization that *everything* is utterly different when one is a victim of racism" (*Ibid*. 68), This sounds pretty radical, for a "white liberal." On a number of occasions, Griffin was supportive of the Black Power movement, even though he remained dedicated to the non-violent philosophy of Martin Luther King.

Even if one goes along with the view expressed by E. Ginsberg about the white liberalism and its pitfalls being reflected in the work of John Howard Griffin, this judgment ought to be qualified by the recognition of Griffin's display of the courage of his convictions. After the publication of his series titled "Journey into Shame" published in *Sepia Magazine* (April-October 1960) (which was the basis for *Black Like Me*) he was being terrorized by the white racists in his Texas home town of Mansfield. He was lynched in effigy, and castration threats were issued against him. As a result, he evacuated his home and moved his family to Mexico, where he was finally able to feel safe and complete the writing of *Black Like Me*. There's undoubtedly a heroic aspect to Griffin's life and work, regardless of what we may think today about the advisability and good judgment of white men acting in blackface, even for a noble purpose.

Griffin's famous blackface act was one of the important 'race gestures' of the 1960s and his book, *Black Like Me*, produced a significant resonance. Significantly, Laura Browder recently called it "the *ur*-text of the genre of postwar blackface" (213). Gayle Wald, who criticized Griffin for his assumption "that he could speak for black people," still notes "the extraordinary popularity of a book that became a staple in junior high and high school classrooms" (154). The five million copies of the book sold within a decade of the first edition[8] demonstrate that Griffin's narrative of his imitative blackface performance was widely received as a genuine cultural text enriching the ongoing racial debates and, in some cases, eliciting a film adaptation (directed by Carl Lerner and featuring James Whitmore in the main role, 1964) and a number of imitations and spoofs.

Among the early spoofs was the 1965 sketch by the black comedian Dick Gregory, "White Like You", with Gregory dressed up in patched up overalls and two watermelons in his hands (stereotypical "blackface" representation mocking Southern blacks), but with his face crudely painted white – Gregory's parody was obviously meant to question the authenticity of Griffin's 'race act'.[9] A similar *a rebours* masquerade was performed by Eddie Murphy in a 1989 *Saturday Night Live* episode, in which Murphy – a black 'researcher' in whiteface was trying to discover 'how it really feels' to be white among other whites. (By then, of course, the practice of 'passing' for a white person was already extinct; Murphy, in his comic number, was, instead, ridiculing the blackface tradition once so common in American popular culture.)[10] While talking about the seeds of *Black Like Me* in American popular culture, one should not fail to

---

8   The Polish edition, published by Iskry, came out in 1962.
9   See the photograph by Jerry Yushman in Dick Gregory's *What's Happening* (Dutton 1965), reprinted in Gubar (36). In fact, Griffin and Dick Gregory were soon to became close partners in the Civil Rights Movement (Bonazzi 146). Years later, in a 2011 TV documentary *Uncommon Vision: The Life and Times of John Howard Griffin* (<https://www.youtube.com/watch?v=DPP_n6cE_TA>), Dick Gregory appeared as one of the film's narrators, testifying to the authenticity of the vision of John Griffin.
10   See Murphy's now classic performance at <https://www.youtube.com/watch?v=l_LeJfn_qW0>.

mention the 1970 comedy *Watermelon Man* by Melvin Van Peebles (made one year prior to Van Peebles's famous Blaxploitation classic, *Sweet Sweet Badasss Song*), in which a white man (played by a black actor) waked up one day to discover he turned into a black man. One should also take note of a 1986 comedy directed by Steve Miner, *The Soul Man*, doubtless also relating to Griffin's widely known re-racing act. Its protagonist, a white man named Mark Watson, wins a scholarship to Harvard Law School by darkening his skin color as a result of overdosing tanning pills. The film is clearly the product of the post-Bakke era, marked by protests stirred by the affirmative action policies in university enrollments (quotas and scholarships for minority students).

More importantly, Griffin's boldness spawned a number of imitators. Among the latest of them was Joshua Solomon, a white male student at University of Maryland in the early 1990s, who described his experiences while posing for black in an article written for *The Washington Post* in 1994 and appeared twice on Opera Winfrey's shows in 1995 and 2011, which inevitably contained reminiscences of John Griffin.[11]

The most significant follower of John Griffin was Grace Halsell, author of the best-selling *Soul Sister. The Journal of a White Woman Who Turned Herself Black and Went to Live and Work in Harlem and Mississippi* (1969). Halsell (incidentally, like her mentor, a native of Fort Worth, Texas) was strongly impressed by *Black Like Me*, which she discovered some 9 years after its publication and immediately decided to repeat the experiment, hoping to find out how much change has taken place in the racial relations within a decade. She met with Griffin several times, asking him for advice and learning from his experience how to survive as a 'black' person. Griffin strongly supported her in her resolution, in his belief that as a woman she was better positioned to see the racial discrimination from a black woman's point of view (Halsell, 15–16). In contrast with Griffin, who had planned his masquerade to take place in his native South, Halsell decided to spend the first half of her experiment in Harlem, before she finally proceeded to the heart of Dixie – Mississippi.

Both Harlem and Mississippi, seen from the perspective of Halsell (who had undergone a tanning process largely along the same lines as her mentor), emerge as nightmarish race-scapes. The descriptions of Harlem (in the words of the author, situated beyond "the invisible but nevertheless real wall that separates the ghetto from the other world," [95]) in particular, are full of naturalistic detail authenticating the writer's experience:

---

11 See her *Race in America* program, aired on 17.01.2011.

> Now, walk the streets with me . . . You see streets littered with garbage, children chasing balls amid the cars; the drunks, the whores, the junkies, pushers, gamblers, pimps, the big, ugly black scar on your white existence; you don't want to think, you look away. . . . Climb the steps [of one of the dilapidated brownstones], go into the dark corridors. See the mass of slum dwellers living out their existence with the rats, the bed-bugs, and the empty liquor stores. Squeeze into one of the tiny rooms, not living quarters so much as a cell, a cell worse than you'd get if you were sentenced to jail – and you're supposed to pay twenty-five dollars a week for that! (66–67)

The experience described by Halsell largely overlaps with Griffin's: both books sympathetically portray the oppressed black community, valiantly struggling for survival against overwhelming odds posed by both official, and unofficial racism. Both authors learn to perceive 'their' (white) people and their institutions, including the economic system and the police, through the lenses of the oppressed, and both bitterly comment on the hypocrisy of the alleged 'race-blind' society. Both come to better appreciate African-Americans as warm, affectionate and righteous human beings, contrasting on many occasions with their cold-bloodied, calculating and bigoted white fellow citizens. Both obviously aim at authenticity, despite the fact that racial cross-dressing (or role-playing) lay at the core of their experience.[12] It was precisely due to their role-playing that they were better able to access what would otherwise be inaccessible to a white person.

Both accounts contain striking passages describing the psychic effects of being transformed into a person of another race. Both describe the pain of being reintegrated with the white society and shedding the temporarily acquired 'black' identity. One may, of course, ponder on the authenticity of Halsell's outburst that comes during her short-lived immersion in the social world of Harlem:

> I begin to feel that I belong here, that I was born here, that I will never leave Harlem. And, almost at once, the other feeling: would I want to leave? . . . Yes, I love you Harlem because I have to love you. . . . And unless I say I love you, then these streets, your people (and the city is the people, not all these buildings, all these businesses that whitey owns) would be ugly to me, and you are my people;" as well as one that stems from her aversion towards 'her own' people: "It was hell to get into the ghetto, but now it seems that hell is outside – awaiting me, that place across the line, over on the other side of the black curtain – where I'm not supposed to go. Into whitey's world! (120)

Like Griffin's, Halsell's account contains passages dealing with white sexual responses to blackness, in both cases 'verifying' the efficacy of the black masks worn

---

12 Dolezal, in contrast with Griffin, revealed the truth about her 'whiteness' to most of her black collaborators and hosts – emphasizing the authenticity of the experience, as opposed to the inauthenticity of her 'blackness'.

by them. While, though, Griffin's presence elicits white men's prurient interest in black sexuality, Halsell barely gets away from a rape attempt by her white employer in Mississippi; that event apparently terminated her blackface 'act' and sent her back home to her upper-middle class neighborhood in Washington, DC. The attempted rape came last in a long series of episodes where Grace Halsell learned about the black woman's perspective on racial relations, as well as her problem with black men, including their attraction to the lighter skin colors among their female partners.

Along the way, Grace gets to know and befriends a number of black women, like Mrs. Tubbs from Mississippi, whom she admires as a woman: "How close I felt to her, how rare and wonderful it is when two women have that warm, intimate, confiding kinship.... Here, women are stronger than men. And everything mostly done is women" (177–180). In contrast with the strong black women, Halsell discovers, the black men in Mississippi have not yet managed to overcome their complex toward the white men and need to regain their masculinity: „The black man's got to start wearing *pants*, he's got to put some starch in them. Start being *a man*" (164).

With the feminine gaze present in Halsell's book, her account occasionally reads differently from Griffin's, yet, as far as the 'white liberal' gaze the two books share a common perspective, the two authors being equally involved in the Civil Rights struggle. One other strikingly similar trait shared by the two was their cosmopolitan perspective, acquired through a long stay abroad. It seems that the occasional comparisons of the racial oppression in the U.S. to the world outside serve as another strategy 'objectifying' and thus further authenticating the accounts. For her part, Halsell was able to compare the racial situation in the U.S. with what she saw in Latin America and Europe, where she lived for extended periods of time: "The difficulties of daily living in Harlem or Manaus can be roughly comparable. But I was not prepared for the isolation, the separateness, of Harlem. Let no one think *apartheid* is a South African monopoly; legally, yes, but socially, spiritually, psychologically, no. The Berlin Wall is *papier-mâché* compared to the barriers surrounding Harlem" (207). In another passage, which begins with her sneaky passage to a courthouse in Carthage, Mississippi, under the scrutinizing stare of the KKK members, Halsell draws a comparison with the totalitarianism of the Communist countries: "I remember that I've walked in Communist Yugoslavia when almost no Americans went there, and in communist East Berlin, knowing that back of some drawn curtains eyes peered at me. I've been among those 'Reds' in Russia, living alone in a hotel, wondering if my phone was bugged, if my mail was read, if strange, armed men followed my every step. And yet none of those experiences prepared me for this march to the Carthage courthouse" (157).

Fast forward to the times of Rachel Dolezal. There's the obvious time gap, between her case and the publication of *Black Like Me, Soul Sister* and even the much later exploits of Joshua Solomon. Much has happened since then on the race front (besides Obama, of course), though many things stayed the same – witness the recent occurrences in places like Ferguson, Baltimore, Staten Island, North Charleston and Cleveland. If anything, the case of Rachel Dolezal provides a recent life-added epilogue to the story of John Griffin, and tests the authenticity of reracing attempts.

Works Cited

Blanks, Jonathan. "Rachel Dolezal's historical fraud." *The Washington Post Online* June 16, 2015.

Blow, Charles M. "The delusions of Rachel Dolezal." *The New York Times Online* June 17, 2015.

Bonazzi, Robert. *Man in the Mirror. John Howard Griffin and the Story of Black Like Me*. Maryknoll, New York: Orbis Books, 1997.

Browder, Laura. *Slippery Characters. Ethnic Impersonators and American Identities*. Chapel Hill and London: The University of North Carolina Press, 2000.

Capehart, Jonathan. "Caitlyn Jenner and Rachel Dolezal: Clash of identity and authenticity." *The Washington Post Online* June 15, 2015.

Delton, Jennifer. "Before the White Negro: Sin and Salvation in *Kingsblood Royal*."

American Literary History, 15 (Spring 2003): 311–333.

Griffin, John Howard. *Black Like Me*. Boston; Houghton Mifflin, The Riverside Press, 1960.

—. *Prison of Culture. Beyond 'Black Like Me'*. Ed. Robert Bonazzi. San Antonio, TX: Wings Press, 2011.

Gubar, Susan. *Racechanges: White Skin, Black Face in American Culture*. New York, Oxford: Oxford University Press, 1997.

Halsell, Grace. *Soul Sister*. Washington, D.C.: Crossroads International Publishing, 1999.

Hobbs, Allyson. *A Chosen Exile. A History of Racial Passing in American Life*. Cambridge, Mass. and London: Harvard University Press, 2014.

Hochschild, Jennifer L. *Facing Up to the American Dream. Race, Class and the Soul of the Nation*. Princeton, NJ: Princeton University Press, 1995.

James, Osamudia. "What Rachel Dolezal doesn't understand: being black is about more than just how you look." *The Washington Post Online* June 12, 2015.

Johnson, Kirk, Richard Perez-Pena and John Eligon. "Rachel Dolezal, in Center of Storm, Is Defiant: 'I Identify as Black.'" *The New York Times Online* 15 June 16 2015.

Lewis, Sinclair. *Kingsblood Royal*. 1947. A Project Gutenberg of Australia eBook, 2002.

Melnick, Jeffrey. *A Right to Sing the Blues. African Americans, Jews, and American Popular Song*. Cambridge, Mass. and London: Harvard University Press, 1999.

Newlyn, Andrea Kelsey. "Undergoing Racial 'Reassignment': The Politics of Crossing in Sinclair Lewis's *Kingsblood Royal*." MFS *Modern Fiction Studies* 48.4 (2002): 1041–1074.

Russell, Margaret M. "Race and the Dominant Gaze: Narratives of Law and Inequality in Popular Film". *Critical White Studies. Looking Behind the Mirror*. Eds. Richard Delgado and Jean Stefancic. Philadelphia: Temple University Press, 1997. 267–272.

Solomon, Joshua. "Skin Deep: Reliving 'Black Like Me': My Own Journey into the Heart of Race-Conscious America." *Washington Post Online* 30 October 1994.

Wald, Gayle. "'A Most Disagreeable Mirror': Reflections on White Identity in *Black Like Me*." Ed. Elaine K. Ginsberg. *Passing and the Fictions of Identity*. Durham and London: Duke University Press, 1996. Kindle Book. Loc. 2737–3236.

Jerzy Sobieraj

Inversion, Conversion, and Reversion in Ellen Glasgow's *The Deliverance*

Abstract: After the Civil War the world of the white man often lies in chaos reflecting destruction of the so-called Southern tradition. Glasgow shows this by inverting the *antebellum* social order. The ex-owner of the plantation, Christopher Blake, cheated by his ex-overseer, Bill Fletcher, now lives in a small house that once was inhabited by his employee, whereas the latter occupies Blake's mansion, which he purchased virtually illegally. The strategy to restore the traditional order is executed in three stages: the inversion of the property's original ownership, the conversion of Christopher Blake from the one who hates to the one who tries to overcome this feeling, and the reversion of the property to its "authentic" owner.

Keywords: Southern fiction, post-Civil War South, Reconstruction, Southern plantation

Fair is foul, and foul is fair
William Shakespeare

Not a word of the Past! It has perished,
Gone down in its beauty and bloom:
Yet because it so proudly was cherished,
Shall we sigh out our years at its tomb?
Margaret J. Preston

The post-Civil War reality was a challenge for almost every white Southerner. The war was lost, the *antebellum* order vanished, the world so comfortable to many was destroyed. It was as if one woke up from a Rip Van Winkle type of dream and found his habitat strange, as if falsified by some terrible power. The world of the planter was hit especially hard; slavery was gone and many plantations were destroyed. The planters used to the old system felt lost in the demands of the post-war economy. Though "the majority of the planter families managed to retain control of their land … war, emancipation, and Reconstruction fundamentally altered the planters' world and their own role in it" (Foner, 173). The owner of the best cotton plantation in South Carolina wrote in 1874 to a former Governor: "my life has been absorbed in trying to keep my head above water. The effect has been crushing" (qtd. in Foner, 173). Many plantations changed owners for different reasons; for instance, in 1881 no more than one third of the Mississippi Valley cotton plantations were held by the planters who owned them towards the end of the Civil War (Woodward, 179). In this harsh reality men fought for some new acceptable place and the best possible position. Ex-slaves were learning to live in the America of equality for all citizens; ex-slave owners were learning how to organize their farms, if they had not lost them already, to make them profitable in the *post-bellum* economic reality; poor whites, overseers, and slave traders of the old times were looking for new opportunities to survive, sometimes applying illegal or quasi-legal means to gain an attractive job, a favorable position or to obtain some wealth, which was easier to do in the chaos and turmoil of Reconstruction and the New South period.

American, especially Southern, literary fiction of the post-Civil War decades focused on these changes, signified by the so-called Lost Cause; the old pre-war times were defined by order, the *post-bellum* reality was marked by chaos and phoniness, especially if compared to the slave-based agrarian civilization. E. Stanley Godbold remarked that "[t]he ten years between 1895 and 1905, an era of social ferment in the South that recalled some problems of Reconstruction, coincided with a kind of renaissance in Southern letters" (99). Ellen Glasgow, a Virginian born in the Reconstruction era, knew the reality of the post-Civil War decades, and at the turn of the 19th century, in the period Godbold refers to, she started writing fiction often alluding to her home, Virginia.

One of the novels that focused on the *post-bellum* Virginia was her 1904 *The Deliverance: A Romance of the Virginia Tobacco Fields*. One of its significant themes, the social aspect of both *antebellum* and *post-bellum* South, is signaled on the first page of the novel: "A casual observer might have classified him (Mr. Carraway) as one of the Virginian landowners, impoverished by the war; in reality, he was a successful lawyer in a neighbouring town, who … had risen into a provincial prominence" (Glasgow, 3–4). The war is seen as the machine turning the old order into a new, often dissatisfying one. Inversion of social class and standing is its result; those once rich and eminent are turned poor and insignificant, those once not that rich and important become men of wealth and sometimes recognition. Some can only remember the past grandeur, some want to have it now, but one cannot fully possess what is strange, unfamiliar, and undeserved, the one who is not of the land and of the place.

The setting is a tobacco plantation, and "tobaccy's king down here,"(6) as one of the characters clearly states. The most popular name in the area is Blake, the name of the pre-war owner of the plantation, his family, and his slaves. The Blakes, Southern aristocrats, founders and owners of the plantation, unfortunately, lost their land and mansion. Christopher Blake, the inheritor of the place, instead of running the plantation business is reduced to a menial laborer, who lives now with his family in a cottage once occupied by his overseer, Bill Fletcher. Fletcher, conversely, lives in the Blake Hall, since he purchased the estate in a tricky and semi-legal way: 'old Bill Fletcher, stole his [Christopher's] house an' his land an' his money, law or now law…"(8).

This inversion of roles and property is shown in the novel with numerous references to spatial aspects. The greatness and significance of the Blake Hall, especially its past look, is commented upon in a pompous style:

> The Blake Hall rose gradually into fuller view, its great oaks browned by the approaching twilight…. [T]he house presented a cheerful spaciousness of front – a surety of light and air – produced in part by the clean, white Doric columns…. For more than two hundred years Blake Hall had stood as the one great house in the county – a manifestation in brick and mortar of the hereditary greatness of the Blakes. (15)

The pomposity of the language is achieved not only by the appropriate lexicon, but also by the intensive application of the sound [r], which, on the onomatopoeic level, produces that sense of greatness and importance, referring to both notions. The interior of the mansion, now owned by Christopher's ex-employee, does not even resemble the old grandeur. Mr Carraway, the lawyer, who pays Bill Fletcher a visit, notices

> [a] crudely furnished room, which gave back to his troubled fancy the face of a pitiable, dishonoured corpse the soul of it was gone forever – that peculiar spirit of place which makes every old house the guardian of an inner life – the keeper of a family's ghost. What remained was but the outer husk, the disfigured frame, upon which the newer imprint seemed only a passing insult. (16)

This image of dead glamour, expressed by such phrases as "dishonoured corpse," and "gone forever," is only intensified by further description of the dwelling, "the dust-marked squares where the Blake portraits had once hung …" (16). Not only is the house left by its legitimate owners, but the family portraits set against the "dust-marked squares," are a distant reminder of the living people inhabiting the place in the past, the place now filled with a sort of spiritual emptiness. Further details reveal the phoniness and falsification of the interior "[a] massive mahogany sofa … purchased perhaps at a general sale of the old furniture… . [L]ater additions were uniformly cheap and ill-chosen…"(16). Fletcher, a new inhabitant of the house, appears here as a false Southern aristocrat, an imperfect imitator. He is an imitator, but not in Burke's understanding of the term (36). He does not imitate to learn. His reason for imitating is vanity. The imitator Fletcher cannot become the authentic owner of the mansion, Christopher Blake. As a person who appears to be someone he is not, Fletcher functions in the novel as a kind of a *poseur*. He is a usurper who by illegal means takes over Christopher's place, but one cannot learn nobility, whether of blood or character. Thus it is impossible for him to follow the model in any way. As Edgar Allan Poe suggests in "The Philosophy of Composition," "The people *will* imitate the nobles, and the result is a thorough diffusion of the proper feeling" (462). The proper feeling is something Fletcher absolutely lacks. An immensely imperfect imitation is what characterizes the interior of the house as inhabited by Fletcher. The original interior, which displays Blake's genuinely elegant taste, becomes a parody of itself and once again reveals the clash between authenticity and imitation. This clash becomes a feature of the post-Civil War social scene, so well reflected in Glasgow's novel.

Money does not buy Fletcher taste and an aptitude for decoration. As Poe stated, commenting on the lack of gustatory qualities of his contemporaries, "How this happens, it is not difficult to see. We have no aristocracy of blood, and having therefore as a natural, and indeed as an inevitable thing, fashioned for ourselves an aristocracy of dollars…" (462). Fletcher, an unrefined *nouveau riche*, cannot even spend his money wisely. He does not care for the mansion's past. He is unable to furnish this place neither with appropriate decorations nor even with costly objects. Even two paper books and the Bible, traditional carriers of memory and family past seem to be forgotten by Fletcher; they may fit the room but they do not fit Fletcher. As Yi-Fu Tuan emphasizes, citing pseudonymous Aristides, "A book in one's own library … is in a sense a brick in the building of one's being, carrying with it memories, a small block of one's personal intellectual history, associations unsortable in their profusion'" (187).

A sense of one's own place is an important part of what we call tradition, a significant element of the myth of the South, and of even an individual family history. Here the loss of the plantation, destructively affects the myth, since it is the microcosm in which the myth can be shaped; "the plantation … [is] the breeding ground for heroes" (MacKethan, 48). To Fletcher, the Hall, though familiar, is empty, artificial, devoid of that "inner spirit" known best to the Blakes. As Maria, Bill Fletcher's granddaughter, remarks, "[Blake Hall] has not suited us, and we have only disfigured a beauty into which we did not fit" (Glasgow, 407). Time affects place; "[s]ense of time affects sense of place" (186). As Tuan states, "We are what we have … friends, relatives, ancestors; … To strengthen our sense of self the past needs to be rescued and made accessible" (186–187). One cannot rescue somebody else's past; "objects anchor time" (187), and any attempt to intrude into the organic territory of the other is misleading, a phony act, since no memories can be associated with the stolen place.

Spatializing becomes an important artistic strategy that emphasizes the social aspects of the post-Civil War reality. In case of Christopher, an aristocrat, who should be a legal inheritor and legitimate owner of Blake Hall, the narrator equally alludes to spatial elements of his new dwelling, once a cottage inhabited by Fletcher. Though the simple cottage house shows signs of poverty, the atmosphere inside is lively and warm: "Here a cheerful blaze made merry about an ancient crane, on which a coffee-boiler swung slowly back and forth with a bubbling noise. In the red firelight a plain pine table was spread with a scant supper and cornbread and bacon and a cracked Wedgewood pitcher filled with buttermilk"(58).

Place gains meaning if it relates to a particular time, or experience of time of its inhabitants; the loss of the hereditary plantation together with its crucial center, the aristocratic mansion, shatters the essence of the Blakes' lives. On the mythic level, it makes the myth of the South, especially in its Arcadian version, devoid of its basic elements. It is the plantation that guarantees stability, order, harmony, sense of hierarchy, and patriarchal heritage. Place gives identity; Marcelle Thiébaux commenting on the three forces that shape the lives of the Blakes – history, environment, heredity – emphasizes that "[e]nvironment is more than setting. Not only does the earth provide a livelihood, but it affords an identity for all who live close to it" (58).

Alluding to Thomas Page's protagonists, Lucinda MacKethan, speaks about the organic attributes of a gentleman, "his land and his honor. Both are sacred, and both are the exclusive possessions of a particular kind of human being … 'the Virginia gentleman'" (49). That sort of gentleman is deeply anchored in history; Ritchie Devon Watson, emphasizing his mythic dimension, classifies him as the Cavalier and makes him reside mostly in Virginia: "Like most mythical figures, however, his origin is rooted in history. There existed in Virginia during the seventeenth and eighteenth centuries a class of wealthy planters who provided the broad outlines for the Cavalier myth. Many of these planters were in fact gentlemen of distinction, and they aspired to follow a distinctive code of conduct" (3).[1]

---

[1] However, it is sometimes emphasized that the concept of a gentleman lost some of its uniqueness in the 19th century. Apart from that outstanding positioning of a gentleman in the culture and history of the South, it must be admitted that, according to some historians, it lost some of its shine. As Bertram Wyatt-Brown emphasizes, "with the territorial expansions of the nineteenth century, the perceptions of gentility underwent corresponding changes. … [I]t was quickly apparent that the sobriquet 'Virginia gentleman,' for instance, had become so commonplace as early as the second war with Britain in 1812 that it had lost much of its exclusivity" (41).

But though the so-called dream of Arcady[2] is destroyed, and the hopes of white Southerners for the old good days shattered, men, though living in new times, often, in a sense, remain the same: "[N]either time nor condition can change blood. The Blake, poor and reduced to menial labor, still remained the Blake – the fine, splendid, aristocratic Blake. The Fletcher turned wealthy, still remained the Fletcher, coarse, brutal, vulgar" ("The Novel," 315). Living in the mansion is not enough to make "himself 'master' of 'Blake Hall.'" (Rouse, 58) Like Hamlet's stepfather, he is an usurper, not respected by anybody. Even the Blakes' former slaves are devoted to Christopher, ready to work for him any time he wants.

In that inverted Dixie world, the character that stands for the South and its myth is elderly Mrs. Blake. Christopher's mother lost her eyesight during the Civil War. However, she is made to believe, that Confederacy triumphed in the war, and that the South, now a nation, is a great place with its appropriate social order. Though a reviewer of *The Deliverance* finds the character of Mrs. Blake "absolutely unconvincing" (Anonymous, 119), one can also appreciate the role and function of Mrs. Blake, as a significant protagonist, the one that defends the *antebellum* South, being an expression of stability in the times of painful social transformations and shattered social order. With her memory of the past that is, as if, frozen, and with her conviction of living in the independent South, she imagines the world around her as undoubtedly noble, gallant, romantic, and happy, as the one in which family customs are observed. "After dinner you may take Mr. Carraway with you into the library and discuss your affairs over a bottle of burgundy, as was your grandfather's custom before you; meanwhile, he and I will resume our very pleasant talk which you interrupted. He remembers seeing me in the old days when we were all in the United States, my dear." (Glasgow, 72–73) Mrs. Blake belongs to the past though she also belongs to the present. But, as an elderly woman, she cherishes the past: "Well, well, I've had my day, sir, and it was the merry one. . . . The present is a very little part of life, sir; it's the past in which we store our treasures" (70). The past is to her reality idealized and unspoilt, and, paradoxically, due to the fact that she is blind, the present seems to her equally outstanding; her only tragedy is that she cannot see that victorious splendid South, which exists only in the blind woman's mind. The world of those who see is painfully devoid of that mythic quality; no stability, no social order, no slaves, no military victory.

The world that is inverted, "out of joint," is the world of clashing enemies; some personal sense of justice, as in case of Bill Fletcher, who bought Blake Hall

---

2   Lucinda Hardwick MacKethan states that the dream functions "almost always as a frame for artistic and in most cases ideological purposes" (8).

and can do with it whatever he wants, is set against deep injustice, as in case of Christopher Blake, who instead of inheriting the Hall, lost it to his treacherous ex-overseer. Christopher madly hates Bill Fletcher, and the feeling is reciprocal. Christopher, similarly to mad Hamlet[3], hates the usurper in "his" house, and, like Hamlet, he is obsessed by revenge. As Frederic P. W. McDowell writes, Christopher, "concentrates upon his diabolical schemes for humbling Fletcher; . . . and slowly matures his malignant plot" (77).

Mad with hatred towards Bill Fletcher, Christopher almost takes leave of his senses. Blinded by emotions, he turns from a noble person and a loving son and a brother to a man obsessed with revenge. That transformation is noticed by Mr. Carraway: "[Christopher's] voice, for all the laughter, sounded brutal, and Carraway, gazing at him in wonder, saw his face grow suddenly lustful like that of an evil deity. The beauty was still there, blackened and distorted, a beauty that he felt to be more sinister than ugliness" (84). Christopher practices his hatred and works out his sinful plan for revenge:

> It was his nightly habit, lying upon his narrow bed in the little loft, to yield some moments before sleeping to his idle dreams of vengeance – to plan exquisite punishments and impossible retaliations. In imagination he had so often seen Fletcher drop dead before him, had so often struck the man down with his own hand, that there were hours when he almost believed the deed to have been done – when something like madness gripped him, and his hallucinations took the shape and color of life itself. (156)

That hatred he so strongly feels towards Bill Fletcher is extended over anything connected with the ex-overseer. When Christopher notices that old Fletcher's grandson, Will, is totally vulnerable, he takes control over him, wins his friendship, and makes him finally break with his grandfather. When Will in an argument kills old Fletcher, it seems that the revenge is exacted. Even Christopher's growing affection and love for Maria is threatened by that consuming sinister feeling towards Fletcher. The hero wanders between hate and love, finding wisdom in an old family proverb: "A Blake can hate twice as long as most men can love, and love twice as long as most men can live." The power of love and Maria herself are the factors turning Christopher from sinner to saint. She not only changes Christopher but transforms the unpleasant interior of Blake Hall into a cheerful, livable place, nicely decorated, with "leather volumes on philosophy'" and "classic poets'" in the library. She, herself, "was abounding with energy, throbbing with life" (403,

---

3 In the novel, there are more Shakespearean echoes; the family feud resembles the Romeo and Juliet motif, though in *The Deliverance* it does not take such a tragic turn.

404). Love converts Christopher into a sensitive and responsible gentleman, "one of the 'real Blakes,'" (292) as Maria once called him.

Christopher, not an ideal gentleman with his poor education[4] and aggressive character, admitting his guilt to the murder that he did not commit, saves Maria's brother from being punished for the deed, this way behaving in a most honorable way, as a true gentleman should. Maria, though of a lower class than Christopher, possesses all features of a Southern lady; Godbold emphasizes that Maria "is educated, well-traveled, cultured, beautiful, and the epitome of what an aristocratic lady was supposed to be" (111). Thus now, Christopher, a gentleman by blood, and Maria, a Southern lady by education, beauty, and features of character, become appropriate and suitable inhabitants of the Blake Hall. The reversion of the property to its legitimate inheritor could not occur under better circumstances.

True that Glasgow "analysed the way aristocratic Virginians responded to the destruction of their *antebellum* social and economic order," (Watson, Jr., 213–214), but the writer gave the reader more than only that. Irrespective of showing the picture of the post-Civil War South, which to many white Southerners was, in a sense, a miserable imitation of their pre-war world, Glasgow expresses, with a dose of irony, the longing for the old good times, for the revival of the myth; the novel, after all, has a happy ending, the place of aristocratic Christopher is his plantation. As in some other Southern works of fiction created between 1895 and 1905, just to mention Thomas Page's *Red Rock*, also here in *The Deliverance*, one witnesses a return to the pastoral tradition, with its crucial plantation motif, this time as an expression of the longing for the lost world in the times when the machine enters the Southern garden.

Works Cited

Anonymous review of *The Deliverance*. *The Dial* 36. 16 Feb. 16 1904. 119.

Burke, Edmund. *The Works of the Right Hon. Edmund Burke*. London: Holdsworth and Ball, MDCCCXXXIV. Vol. 1.

Foner, Eric. *A Short History of Reconstruction 1863–1877*. New York: Harper and Row, Publishers, 1990.

Glasgow, Ellen. *The Deliverance: A Romance of the Virginia Tobacco Fields*. New York: Doubleday Page and Co., 1904.

---

4   Wyatt-Brown, however, states that "[L]earning, especially the venerable kind, marked the possessor as a gentleman. Yet in the South at least, too much of it allegedly spoiled the result. There was a strongly anti-intellectual streak in Southern society" (46).

Godbold Jr., E. Stanly. "A Battleground Revisited: Reconstruction in Southern Fiction, 1895–1905." *The South Atlantic Quarterly* 73.1 (1974): 99–116.

MacKethan, Lucinda Hardwick. *The Dream of Arcady: Place and Time in Southern Literature*. Baton Rouge and London: Louisiana State University Press, 1980.

"(The) Novel of the Month: Miss Glasgow's 'The Deliverance.'" *Current Literature* 36 (March 1904): 315–316.

Poe, Edgar Allan. "The Philosophy of Furniture." *The Complete Tales and Poems of Edgar Allan Poe*. No Ed. London: Penguin Books, 1982.

Rouse, Blair. *Ellen Glasgow*. New York: Twayne, 1962.

Thiébaux, Marcelle. *Ellen Glasgow*. New York: Frederick Ungar, 1982.

Tuan, Yi-Fu. *Time and Space: A Perspective of Experience*. Minneapolis and London: University of Minnesota Press, 2001.

Watson, Jr., Richie Devon. *The Cavalier in Virginia Fiction*. Baton Rouge and London: Louisiana State University Press, 1985.

Woodward, C. Vann. *Origin of the New South 1877–1913*. Baton Rouge: Louisiana State University Press, 1987.

Wyatt-Brown, Bertram. *Honor and Violence in the Old South*. New York and Oxford: Oxford University Press, 1986.

Agnieszka Podruczna

But Who Does Live? Postcolonial Identities, Authenticity, and Artificial Intelligence in Darryl A. Smith's "The Pretended"

Abstract: The following paper aims to analyze the ways in which Darryl A. Smith's "The Pretended" explores the power relations at the intersection between race, desire for authenticity, and the formation of subject's identity, positing that the literal constructedness of the Othered subject serves as a way to deconstruct the notion of the colonial Other.

Keywords: postcolonial studies, science fiction, African-American diaspora, authenticity, embodiment

Paradoxically, even though science fiction has been often regarded as the genre of the future and the unknown, it is, in fact, deeply rooted in the historical context from which it originates. The genre, therefore, founded – in its modern incarnation – upon the colonial, expansionist ideals of the 19th century, has always maintained a somewhat ambiguous and at times even deeply uncomfortable relationship with the subject of race. This practice of either obscuring or ignoring the issues of race, noted by several prominent contemporary critics of science fiction, finds an in-depth explanation in an essay on race and ethnicity in science fiction by Elizabeth Anne Leonard, who writes:

> By far the majority of sf deals with racial tension by ignoring it. In many books the characters' race is either not mentioned and probably assumed to be white or, if mentioned, is irrelevant to the events of the story and functions only as an additional descriptor, such as hair colour or height. Other sf assumes a world in which there has been substantial racial mingling and the characters all have ancestry of multiple races. These kinds of writing can be seen as an attempt to deal with racial issues by imagining a world where they are non-issues, where colour-blindness is the norm. This may be a conscious model for a future society, or a gesture to "political correctness" by an author whose interests in the story lie elsewhere, but either motive avoids wrestling with the difficult questions of how a non-racist society comes into being and how members of minority cultures or ethnic groups preserve their culture. (254)

The fact, then, that in the mainstream science fiction the portrayal of racial issues has been actively marginalised, and those issues themselves presented as unimportant or even nonexistent for a long time, despite the wealth of science fiction works which appropriated the colonial narrative of conquest and which elevated the narrative of the encounter with the Other to the most prominent, widespread narrative in the genre, owes to the origins of science fiction, deeply rooted in the ideals of the imperialist, colonialist project of expansion, conquest, and subjugation. Therefore, it should come as no surprise that, as John Rieder remarks, science fiction "appeared predominantly in those countries that were involved in colonial and imperialist projects" (375), and that it was actively shaped by the dominant ideologies of the times – ideologies to which a lot of mainstream science fiction subscribes until this day. It seems impossible, then, to regard science fiction as nothing more than a purely escapist phenomenon, a future-oriented genre which does not reproduce the existing power dynamics in any shape or form, as it would disregard the explicit link between the way the genre addresses issues such as gender, race, sexuality, or class, and the imperial legacy of the genre, which has shaped and continues to shape those approaches to a considerable extent in the mainstream science fiction cultural production.

It would be possible to state, then, that the sub-genre of postcolonial speculative fiction (and postcolonial science fiction in particular) has emerged as an essentially counter-discursive reaction to the colonialist roots of the genre and the continued erasure as well as racial bias inherently connected with mainstream science fiction writing. Effectively, then, it constitutes an attempt at the postcolonial act of writing back to the centre, a counter-discursive response to the imperialist notions of the Self and the Other which redefines the relationship between the centre and the periphery, thus situating itself within the broader framework of postcolonial practice. According to Helen Tiffin, "[p]ost-colonial counter-discursive strategies involve a mapping of the dominant discourse, a reading and exposing of its underlying assumptions, and the dis/mantling of these assumptions from the cross-cultural standpoint of the imperially subjectified 'local'" (98). In turn, postcolonial science fiction allows to dismantle the hegemonic forms of expression and expose their mechanisms, it hybrydises and fractures the narratives produced by the discourse, and it complicates the colonial power relations at the same time as it allows to recover and reclaim the silenced stories and voices, giving the voice back to the colonial Other. What is more, according to Michelle Reid, "[science fiction's] fantastic nature does not distance it from historical colonial projects, but gives a closer insight into the strategies used to create the ideological fantasy of colonialism" (258). And indeed, even though there is no general consensus as to how to define science fiction in precise terms, all the influential definitions (such as those proposed by Suvin, Scholes, or Broderick) emphasise the connection between science fiction and the realities from which it originates. Moreover, Suvin considers the principle of cognitive estrangement (Roberts, 8) to be the essential characteristic of the genre, as he remarks that without the interplay of estrangement (the *novum*, the alien, the unknown) and cognition (the familiar, the known, the historical) there can be, in fact, no science fiction (Roberts, 8). This rooting in the historical context, in turn, allows the authors to explore the power dynamics inherent in the narrative of the colonial encounter and formulate a more complex response to the hegemonic dynamics of difference, paving the way for revisionist, counter-discursive practices which question and interrogate the binary nature of the colonial discourse, facilitating the postcolonial act of writing back to the centre and the creation of polyphonic, ruptured narratives which reflect the non-homogenous, multiple nature of the colonial experience.

In keeping with the postcolonial practice of writing back, Darryl A. Smith, in his short story "The Pretended," published in an anthology of speculative fiction from the African diaspora entitled *Dark Matter* (2000) and edited by Sheree R. Thomas, interrogates the questions of power relations at the intersection between race, desire for authenticity, and the formation of subject's identity. The story, which takes place in a near future, following the total genocide of the African-American diaspora and the subsequent creation of racialised androids whose appearance and behaviour has been closely modelled on the now-extinct African-American minority, concerns the questions of ontology, authenticity, and identity, negotiated by Mnemosyne, the young protagonist of the story, not only at the intersection between the Self and the Other, but also between the human and the machine. Her liminality, embodied by her nature as an android – which, in turn, serves as a metaphor for the colonial Other – echoes the words of Donna Haraway, who, in her "Cyborg Manifesto," says:

> It is not clear who makes and who is made in the relation between human and machine. It is not clear what is mind and what is body in machines that resolve into coding practices. ... There is no fundamental, ontological separation in our formal knowledge of machine and organism, of technical and organic. The replicant Rachel in Ridley Scott's film *Blade Runner* stands as the image of cyborg culture's fear, love, and confusion. (313)

Haraway points to the inherent ambiguity of the figure of the android, located in between two worlds, existing at the fringes between the human and the machine, exposing the fragile equilibrium on which the humanity of the subject or lack thereof can be decided and, ultimately, testifying to the arbitrariness of that distinction. Therefore, the doubly Othered Mnemosyne becomes the transgressive locus of colonial ambiguity, exposing – in her own, literal constructedness – the constructedness of the colonial Other, thus facilitating the further deconstruction of the colonial myth.

In "The Pretended," the question of authenticity and the question of identity become inseparably connected as the protagonist attempts to contextualise her own existence within the broader cultural and historical framework. Mnemosyne, named for the personification of memory in Greek mythology, indeed comes to embody the collective memory of the ancestral past of the androids, whose minds have been modelled after actual, living members of the African-American diaspora before their genocide, and which manifests in inexplicable flashes of memories that she experiences throughout the story. Thus, what the authorities perceive as a malfunction, is in fact a manifestation of her role as a carrier of the ancestral memories – a role which to a large extent unconsciously informs her perception of her own identity. Since Mnemosyne understands that there exists an implicit continuity between the African-American diaspora and the androids, she is, therefore, incapable of reconciling the apparent difference between the "authenticity" of the African-American community and the artificial "imitation" personified by the androids. As a result, what becomes apparent is the fact that the protagonist perceives her existence as an android as being completely at odds with her self-established identity, which contributes to the feeling of alienation and anxiety that she experiences throughout the narrative. The link between the two manifests itself physically – at least to Mnemosyne herself – as Diva Eve, the consciousness of an African-American girl from before the purge, uploaded into Mnemosyne's mind at her creation. Diva Eve becomes thus the symbol of both transgression and connection between the authentic and the pretend, providing Mnemosyne with a broader framework which facilitates the development of her subjectivity regardless of the colonial narrative imposed upon her existence. In this way, the central conflict in the story becomes the struggle for self-identification and against the imposition of an outside, constructed identity forced on the androids by the hegemonic system to which they have no real access. Therefore, Mnemosyne's search for her own identity epitomises the processes of identity negotiation in colonial and postcolonial realities.

Moreover, Smith, in his examination of the postcolonial condition, echoes Said's understanding of the colonial Other as an artificial construct, a myth perpetuated by the hegemonic discourse on the basis of arbitrary assumptions (Said, 4), and exposes the covert mechanisms of the colonial system, as the Other in the story becomes constructed in more than one way, both metaphorically and literally – the androids, created in order to imitate the annihilated African-American diaspora, become the loci of marginalisation, forced into the frames delineated by the colonial discourse, previously occupied by their human "prototypes." What emerges, therefore, is the artificial, constructed colonial subject, once again relegated to the margin of the system, deemed inferior and dehumanised. This dehumanisation manifests itself in the story both in the general descriptions of the androids, such as the opening paragraph, in which they are referred to as "[t]he naked, shuffling brown slush of bodies" (Smith, 356), which suggests no individuality, humanity or agency on their part, and in the use of pronouns, since the androids are referred to by the authorities as "it" rather than "he" or "she." The artificiality of the imposed identity is further emphasised as the text explicitly states that the androids have been created on the basis of the image of the African-American community filtered through the lens of the hegemonic discourse. Therefore, they use the dialect stereotypically associated with the African-American community, and they look and act the way the white authorities *think* they should look and act, further complicating the issue of the ambiguity of the distinction between authenticity and imitation. Diva Eve comments upon that practice at one point in the story, saying, "Jes take thinkin outa real black people brains, put it into computers, rase the memory a bit, make our talk the way they think it should sound, and piss the whole kit'n'kaboodle into robots" (Smith, 362).

In addition, Mnemosyne's struggle facilitates a discussion of what it means to be Other and, at the same time, what it means to be human, since the two, Smith argues, are inseparable – something the hegemonic system cannot comprehend. His exploration of the connection between Otherness and humanity in the case of the androids runs parallel to his discussion of the link between Otherness and humanity in general, creating a narrative fraught with colonial tensions. The story, therefore, examines the precarious situation of the androids, who have been created in order to only pretend that they are black – so that the white society could return to pretending that black people are not people at all – but find themselves incapable of separating the quality of being black and the quality of being human. "You pretend you're black *and* people at the same time," remarks Diva Eve. "They tried to make it so you can't do that. But they couldn't. You always doin both. Cause they the same thing. Can't no robot pretend two things is different when they aint" (Smith, 362). This attempt at controlled, systemic and total dehumanisation of the black androids constitutes a perpetuation of the colonial notion that the Other can never be considered fully human, but its ultimate failure testifies to the arbitrariness and constructedness of the colonial discourse as a whole. This failure to uphold the colonial myth, in turn, becomes the catalyst behind the decision to exterminate all androids – the fact that they cannot stop pretending to be human, making it impossible for the white society to forget about the atrocities of the system they have created, forces the oppressors to face the one truth they do not want to admit, namely, that the African-Americans, who they were trying to recreate, were people as well.

What emerges as a result is a vicious cycle of creation, subjugation, transgression and destruction based upon the fact that, for the colonialist, the existence of the colonial Other is a necessary condition in the process of legitimising their position as the locus of central hegemonic power. This, in turn, echoes the remarks of Albert Memmi, who, in his discussion of the Nero complex (a situation in which the more the colonialist oppresses the colonised, the more aware he becomes of his own perverted status as a usurper, up to the point where his only wish is for the colonised to disappear and therefore release the colonialist from the position of the oppressor) and its effects on the coloniser (52–53), comments that "the colonialist realizes that without the colonized, the colony would no longer have any meaning" (66). In the story, the desire for the colonial paradigm to have any meaning is so strong on the part of the coloniser that not only do they usurp the power over all aspects of the lives of the androids, including their bodily autonomy, but they create the colonial Other in the most literal sense of the word. In this way, the story exposes the inconvenient truth about the colonialist – namely, that the colonialist cannot survive without the colonial Other if he wishes to remain at the centre of the hegemonic power structure, a fact which informs the initial decision concerning the creation of the androids. The colonialist's position, therefore, seems to verge on a fragile equilibrium which could be easily disturbed, but at the same time must be maintained at all cost, and in "The Pretended," Smith comments on both the fragility of the position of the coloniser within the system, and on the constructedness of the system as a whole – a system which does not tolerate void and can operate only on the basis of arbitrarily assigned binary oppositions.

However, ultimately, Mnemosyne transcends the restrictive binaries of the hegemonic discourse and becomes the locus of colonial ambiguity, dangerous in her liminality, transgressing the boundary between being and pretending. Her connection to Diva Eve and, by extension, to the collective memory of the exterminated African-American diaspora demonstrates that it is impossible to completely extinguish the lost stories and voices, as the collective memory bleeds through, disregarding the differences in biological make-up, and rebelling against the loss of access to the prohibited knowledge – a process referred to in the story as "forghettoization." The process, whose name combines both the notions of forgetting and of ghettoization (which denotes not only a physical restriction to a place, but also the lack of access to the hegemonic discourse), points to the importance of knowledge and memory in the formation of subject's identity, and the impossibility of establishing one's subjectivity without historical continuity and the awareness of belonging to a cultural community. Mnemosyne's imperviousness to those attempts at extinguishing memories signifies, therefore, that she rejects the colonial binaries imposed upon the androids and strives to establish her own identity, thus bridging the gap between the past and the present, the human and the machine, and, effectively, between the Self and the Other, existing in the hybrid, liminal space in between. Her awareness of the doubly-liminal status of her existence, in turn, points to the fact that, at the same time as she resists the colonial imposition of identity, Mnemosyne also resists the postcolonial desire for authenticity, since, as Helen Tiffin observes

> [p]rocesses of artistic and literary decolonisation have involved a radical dis/mantling of European codes and a post-colonial subversion and appropriation of the dominant European discourses. This has frequently been accompanied by the demand for an entirely new or wholly recovered 'reality', free of all colonial taint. (95)

Later on, however, she goes on to state that, in fact, "such pre-colonial cultural purity can never be fully recovered" (Tiffin, 95), and Mnemosyne's awareness of the ambiguity inherent in her condition signifies an attempt to do away with such essentialism. Ultimately, Mnemosyne becomes a source of anxiety for the hegemonic power structure, as she rejects the boundaries delineated by the system and exposes its constructedness, mirrored in her status as an android. Thus, her transgressive act of rebellion against the system becomes a "malfunction" to be eradicated, but her act of defiance at the very end of the story constitutes a final act of rejection of the colonial *status quo*, facilitating the reclamation of her identity and subjectivity.

Works Cited

Haraway, Donna. "A Cyborg Manifesto: Science, Technology and Socialist-Feminism in the Late Twentieth Century." *The Cybercultures Reader*. Ed. David Bell and Barbara M. Kennedy. London: Routledge, 2000. 291–324.

Leonard, Elizabeth Anne. "Race and Ethnicity in Science Fiction." *The Cambridge Companion to Science Fiction*. Ed. Edward James and Farah Mendlesohn. New York: Cambridge University Press, 2003. 253–63.

Memmi, Albert. *The Colonizer and the Colonized*. Boston: Beacon Press, 1993.

Reid, Michelle. "Postcolonialism." *The Routledge Companion to Science Fiction*. Ed. Mark Bould, Andrew M. Butler, Adam Roberts, and Sherryl Vint. London: Routledge, 2009. 256–66.

Rieder, John. "Science Fiction, Colonialism, and the Plot of Invasion." *Extrapolation* 46: 3, (2005): 373–94.

Roberts, Adam. "Defining Science Fiction." *Science Fiction: The New Critical Idiom*. London: Routledge, 2000. 1–46.

Said, Edward W. *Orientalism*. New York: Vintage Books, 1979.

Smith, Darryl A. "The Pretended." *Dark Matter: A Century of Speculative Fiction from the African Diaspora*. Ed. Sheree R. Thomas. New York: Warner Books, 2000. 356–71.

Tiffin, Helen. "Post-Colonial Literatures and Counter-Discourse." *The Postcolonial Studies Reader*. Ed. Bill Ashcroft, Gareth Griffiths, and Helen Tiffin. London: Routledge, 2002. 95–98.

Jacek Wiśniewski

Editorial Revision and Recovery: Authenticity and Imitation in John Clare's Early Poetry

Abstract: Most writers enjoy a fair degree of authorial control of their own work. They often supervise and edit the final versions of their texts; but not so John Clare, the Northamptonshire peasant poet whose poems were left in the hands of his London publishers. Vital decisions on selection, omissions, additions and alterations were not the poet's, therefore questions about authenticity, editorial revision and recovery of original texts are in this case crucial.

Keywords: authenticity, authorial control, censorship, literary fashion

Anyone embarking on an extensive critical study of John Clare's poetry today, more than two hundred years after he wrote his first poems, is at the very outset faced with a number of questions or conundrums – relating to authenticity and imitation – which one does not encounter when examining the work of other Romantic poets: Wordsworth and Coleridge, Byron and Shelley, even Keats. They were all in full authorial control of their own work, and often supervised the final editorial versions of their poems. A characteristic note may be found in Edward Dowden's Introduction to *Poems by William Wordsworth,* showing the way in which the poet, by claiming the exclusive possession of his poetry, is becoming responsible for the work of his own self-creation:

> Wordsworth began the revision of his poems at the earliest possible moment, in 1800; in each new edition – in 1803, 1805, 1815, 1820, 1827, 1832 – omissions, additions, and alterations were made. For the first stereotyped edition, that of 1836–1837, a very searching revisal was carried out; in 1840 the work was begun anew; further changes were made in the text of 1845, and many earlier readings were then restored. Even the edition completed in 1850, the year of Wordsworth's death, shows that to the last he had his eye upon perfection. (Dowden, lxxxiv–lxxxv)

The work of editing and revising Clare's poetry was taken out of the poet's hands – vital decisions on selection, omission, additions and alterations were not his: Taylor and Hessey, his London publishers, wanted to create a certain image of "poor Clare" as he was often referred to, the authentic 'Northamptonshire peasant poet', the true voice of the people of England, or 'the English Robert Burns'. But treating this amazingly prolific poet as 'a child of nature' will not bear closer scrutiny, in view of his excellent knowledge of Shakespeare, Milton, and all the major poets of the 18th century, including Thomas Gray, James Thomson and William Cowper. On the one hand, his editors realized that they were dealing with a genuine and authentic poetic talent – Taylor stresses in the Introduction to the first, 1820 edition of *Poems Descriptive of Rural Life and Scenery* that "it is now thirteen years since CLARE composed his first poem: in all that time he has gone on secretly cultivating his taste and talent for poetry, without one word of encouragement, or the most distant prospect of reward" (Clare 1820, xxi), so it is evident the experienced editor knows that he is dealing with an experienced and self-conscious artist – but on the other hand both editors felt an obligation to their genteel readers to present their Genius in a purified, smoothed, amended form. One gets the impression that Taylor is trying to send a veiled message to the readers of the Introduction, without hurting "poor Clare" too much:

> no Poet of our country has shewn greater ability, under circumstances so hostile to its development. And all this is found here without any of those distressing and revolting alloys, which too often debase the native worth of genius, and make him who was gifted with powers to command admiration, live to be the object of contempt or pity. (Clare 1820, xxvi)

Money or profit were never the principal objects of poetry publication in the first half of the 19th century, even in the case of the poorest of the Romantics, John Keats. Clare saw the publication of only about ten per cent of his work in his lifetime (in four collections between 1820 and 1835), and the choice of what to print and in what form to print it was not his, but his patrons' and the London publishers'. John Taylor (the same man who also printed Coleridge, Keats, Hunt and several other Romantics, and also the editor of the *London Magazine*) received from Clare eight manuscript books with well over three hundred poems in them, some of them very long. For instance "The Parish", a satirical poem written in the early 1820s, consists of 2200 lines in rhyming couples (occupying 80 pages of print in the second volume of *The Early Poems* in the monumental Oxford University Press edition, consisting of 9 fat volumes, on four and a half thousand pages). What was originally published in the first two volumes printed by Taylor and his business partner Hessey, in 1820 and 1821, was just a tiny part of the poet's early work, and not necessarily the best of it, not even the most characteristic for Clare's art, so that the authenticity of his poetic voice was very difficult to gauge. Some lovely poems were brutally cut short, or omitted for curious and diverse reasons which I will try to explain below, and were only printed for the first time 170 years after they were written. Other lively poems of love and betrayal, like "Dolly's Mistake", a boisterous tale of country matters and manners, made their appearance in the first printing of *Poems Descriptive*, to be removed, without Clare's approval, in the second, presumably under pressure from Clare's patrons who cared about modesty.

> Till dark night he kept me wi fussing & lying
>   How he'd see me safe home to my cot
> Poor maidens so easy & free in complying
>   I the show mans good caution forgot
> All bye ways he led me twas vain to dispute it
>   The moon blushed for shame nasty rake
> Behind a cloud sneaking – but darkness well suited
>   His baseness to cause the mistake (Clare 1989, v. 1, 534)

Clare's publishers were both well-educated gentlemen of the London elite, looking for the authentic voice of the people, the 'real language of men' which Wordsworth and Coleridge could only imitate in their poems. In passing let us recall that as a young man newly arrived in London in 1800, John Taylor assisted the printing firm of Vernor and Hood in publishing the poetry of Robert Bloomfield, thus becoming aware of the tremendous promise of 'native genius' of uneducated lower-class poets. The demotic and highly original language of dialect-poetry came naturally to Clare, who was raised on popular ballads, songs of tragic love, tales of horror and wonder, longer tales and ditties in verse, usually about murder, suicide, robbery or rape. It is worth recalling that John Clare's mother was "illiterate to the last degree" (Bate, 12), a simple country woman who believed that reading was a form of black magic, but Clare's semi-literate father knew over a hundred ballads by heart, and recited them often for the enjoyment of his family and friends. It is no wonder that narrative poems in dialect, often dealing with country matters in a down-to-earth way predominated in Clare's early work, but are unrepresented in 19th century collections. Instead, it seems, the genteel readers were more interested in Clare's poems of nature description which were imitations of 18th-century picturesque poets such as James Thomson or William Cowper. They are often derivative, they sound like awkward imitations, and are not Clare's best.

    Taylor and Hessey found in Clare the authenticity they were looking for, but they thought the genteel reading audience expected the voice of the people to be corrected, edited and polished. Eric Robinson and David Powell, Clare's 20th-century editors, say in the Introduction to *The Early Poems of John Clare, 1804–1822*: "If a poem was too unorthodox in its sentiments, its language, or its punctuation and grammar, its chances of survival into print were very limited" (Clare 1989, xi). The London publishers never offered poor Clare any written contract for these early volumes, and paid him according to their own sense of fairness, even though his first two collections, *Poems Descriptive of Rural Life and Scenery* (1820) and *The Village Minstrel and Other Poems* (1821), sold many more copies than either Keats's *Endymion* (1818) or Wordsworth's *The Excursion* (1814) – Clare's first collection went through four editions between 1820 and 1821 and overall sold over 3000 copies (Bate, 149), while 500 copies of Wordsworth's *The Excursion* sufficed for the sale of six years, between 1814 and 1820 (Dowden, xxxi). Wordsworth, his biographers remind us, came from an old and respectable Yorkshire family; at 17 he was entered as a student at St. John College, Cambridge; at 25 he had been made possessor of the sum of 900 pounds by a young friend, Raisley Calvert who died of tuberculosis; in 1813 he obtained the post of distributor of stamps in the county of Westmoreland: Dowden assures us that "the salary was 400 pounds a year and the duties not oppressive; his means, though not large, were yet sufficient" (Dowden, xxxii). Clare, on the other hand, felt that he failed to achieve the same financial success which had made Robert Bloomfield, the author of *The Farmer's Boy,* a man of considerable independence. John Clare, a landless peasant, often referred to by reviewers and patrons as "poor Clare", and his family of seven, had to rely on his irregular earnings as seasonal agricultural labourer and thresher, hedger or quarryman, road-builder or gardener, and on the generosity of aristocratic patrons and admirers of his poetry. The texts which were in the end chosen for publication had been heavily edited and censored, often cut short, altered and amended. Lovely and quaint dialect words were excised and replaced by more elegant and polite, more acceptable or more easily recognizable terms. All questionable texts, politically subversive or ethically risky, were dropped. After 1837, when Clare was incarcerated in a lunatic asylum at the age of forty-four, only a handful of his poems appeared in almanacs and literary magazines, though he continued writing fine poetry in the asylum (the volumes of *Clare's Later Poetry* in the Oxford Texts series contain almost one thousand poems on 1100 pages – these later poems were often composed by the elderly poet in his mind, recited to one of the house stewards who admired Clare's poetry and wrote it down). Eric Robinson says in the Introduction to *The Later Poems of John Clare, 1837–1864, volume I*:

> During the period from 1837 until a year or two before his death in 1864 Clare wrote an immense number of poems... As John Clare was probably the most prolific of all English poets, he was also one of the untidiest: the sheer bulk of the material, the intricacies of the handwriting, the state of the manuscripts which are often mere scraps of paper pasted into a larger book, the apparent disorder of Clare's creative processes which produced notes, poems, letters, and anagrams all mixed together in a furious welter. (Clare 1989, x–xi)

After his death in Northampton Asylum in 1864 he and his poetry fell into an almost complete obscurity, though strangely enough some of his most famous poems did appear in anthologies of Victorian poetry, which makes some sense in terms of chronology, because alone among the English Romantics of the second generation he lived a long life and died at the age of seventy one. The first critic to argue for a more prominent place for Clare and his poetry was Julian Symons, author of the first modern edition of a representative selection of Clare's poems, even in some cases going back to manuscripts rather than published versions. Symons's work was continued in the first half of the 20th century by Edmund Blunden, Geoffrey Grigson, Anne and John Tibble. Nonetheless, it took well over a century since John Clare's death for all his voluminous output to become available to readers and students of English literature, in the original authorial versions.

In John Clare's case the study of his manuscripts and the full recovery of authentic versions of everything he ever wrote is made available to the student of his poetry in two different ways which I believe must complement one another. The first avenue is the study of the Oxford English Texts edition of his collected poetry in nine volumes (published between 1984 and 2003), the life work and achievement of Eric Robinson and several collaborators: David Powell, Margaret Grainger and P.M.S. Dawson. These editors firmly believe in printing John Clare's poems in the authentic shape and form in which they were written, closest to original manuscripts, with Clare's characteristic and fanciful spelling, with regional words and expressions, almost without punctuation, and often with disregard for the rules of grammar (the full editorial apparatus, questioned and criticized by some 21st century scholars, is to be found in the Introduction to the Oxford English Texts series). The Robinson team rejected 19th-century editorial practice of 'correcting' or 'amending' the peasant poet's language and omitting the more controversial texts. Taylor and Hessey removed most regional, dialectical words, local names of birds and flowers, names of animals and descriptions of village games, onomatopoeic words and calls, names of agricultural tools and rural activities. In the first collection they printed a number of early poems, some of them written when Clare was a teenager, imitations of 18th century classics, such as James Thomson's *The Seasons*. They felt the reader should be warned about the difficulty of regional vocabulary and Clare's unconventional use of grammar, and they supplied the first printing of Clare's poems with a short glossary, containing only about one hundred words. It is my contention that an attentive reader, even a non-native reader of English poetry, is perfectly capable of understanding Clare without much effort; reading Clare is certainly much easier than reading Robert Burns.

The second avenue in the study of authentic texts by Clare, both verse and prose, is the hands-on work with the poet's manuscripts. This is made possible because of the good work of several libraries in England which hold the manuscripts of the poetry and prose by John Clare. The largest of these collections is the one in Peterborough, the town closest to Clare's village of Helpston, with the second important collection in Northborough. The Vivacity Library, Peterborough, next door to the imposing and ultra-modern John Clare Theatre, has an excellent Archives Service, with Richard Hunt its punctilious director. The Library has a huge collection of Clare's manuscripts, and the vast majority of everything else he ever wrote on microfilm. (Here, in passing, let me acknowledge the financial help of my University's grant-in-aid which made my research there possible). Working with original manuscripts which are 200 years old, and in some cases older, is a thrilling experience, and a quaint one (the researcher is politely asked to place the volume he is studying on a white cushion, to put on white cotton gloves and to use a special cardboard page-turner, to refrain from the use of fountain pens and biros – it is pencils only; there is no possibility of copying or photographing the manuscripts). Remembering that Clare right at the very beginning of his writing career had no money for ink and paper, and had to make do with pencils or home-made ink and his mother's shopping wrappers, which often disappeared in the kitchen stove as firelighters, one is moved to see the fat, well bound volume. It is obviously a poet's own collection of texts copied carefully in a neat hand, evidently a volume meant for the eyes of a potential editor, with short notes on the margin: "old", or "very old", or "recent", or "3 or 4 year ago", and occasionally supplied with a particular date. The paper is hand-made, larger than A-4, and folded to produce four pages (the tops of pages are slightly uneven, cut with a sharp knife). The paper is of good quality, but with no crest or markings in it. Clare's handwriting is very neat, the poems obviously copied from earlier manuscripts. He must have been writing with a fine pen and black ink, quite unfaded, so one can presume that this collection (MA A3) is a fair copy of early poems.

In some cases there are numerous corrections and erased words, so many that the author feels obliged to cross out whole stanzas and rewrite them, and to indicate the final version with clear marginal pointers, often in the shape of a funny little hand. To be on the safe side, he adds on the margin: "The author erases these verses" (MA A3, 69), before supplying the amended lines. There seems to be a kind of dialogue going on between the poet and the potential publisher on the margins of the book: next to a stanza of a little poem entitled "What is Life", there is a note "unintelligible, E.D." in a different hand and a blacker ink – this must be a comment by Edward Drury, a local publisher and the man who 'discovered' Clare and later recommended him to his younger cousin and publisher in London, John Taylor. In other places

Clare turns directly to the publisher with explanations or appeals: on page 32 of the manuscript, next to the second section of a long poem entitled "Helpstone", he says:

> The word "twitatwit" (if a word it may be calld) you will undoubtedly smile at but I wish you to print it as it is for it is the Language of Nature & that can never be disgusting.

In another place, after a long poem entitled "The Traveller: A Parody" (41–48 in MA A3-2), the poet addresses his editor with an explanation:

> Sir you may think I finish the story in an abrupt manner but in doing this I have no worse a poet than Homer for my pattern his pieces I am told are left (as it were) unfinish'd.

The subtitle of the next poem, "The Resignation" (49–51 in MA A3-2) provides the following gloss:

> (supposed to be written by the unfortunate Chatterton just before he took the deadly Draught that put a Period to his Existence)

Next to a poem entitled "Address to a Lark Singing in Winter" he explains his use of the phrase "egs on" (eggs on, line 34):

> "egs on" in the "address to the Lark" whether provincial or what I cannot tell but it is common with the vulgar (I am of that class) & heartily desire no word of mine to be alterd.

"*And heartily desire no word of mine to be alterd*"; this could be taken as the poet's appeal, directed to his editors, to respect his right to use his own authentic, regional version of the English language, to break away from what Tom Paulin called in his essay "John Clare in Babylon" "the long ice age of standard British English [which] clamped down on the living language and began to break its local and vernacular energies" (Paulin, 47). Repeatedly, the poet tried to defend the authentic character of his lines, asking his stanzas to be copied "verbatim et literatim", explaining the meaning of his "provincial expressions", but to little avail: wishing to see his poems in print, he simply had to accept the need for cuts and changes. He even accepted the need to be introduced to the readers as a kind of noble savage, a "peasant poet":

> I am not against having my humble Occupation, mean parentage, & scanty Education – or anything of the like hinted at in your Preface – just what you think suitable so you may do. (MA A3, 133)

A good example of how little editorial revision is really needed is a short poem written before 1820, "To the Fox Fern": it appears in the Peterborough MS D2 on page 6, written on a loose sheet of paper and pasted in the manuscript book, but it is deleted by the poet, and probably unfinished. It is perhaps just a bit untypical for Clare, since it is unrhymed (Clare seldom abandoned the rhymed couplet, the rhymed quatrain, the ballad stanza, or different forms of the sonnet). Jonathan Bate is certainly right in praising the little poem for the absence of grandiloquence and the matter-of-fact tone of voice; he says this brief lyric "has a quiet perfection in its precision and lack of pretension" (Bate, 153).

> Haunter of woods lone wilds & solitudes
> Were none but feet of birds & things as wild
> Doth print a foot track near where summers light
> Buried in boughs forgets its glare & round thy crimped leaves
> Feints in a quiet dimness fit for musings
> & mellancholy moods with ere & there
> A golden thread of sunshine stealing through
> The evening shadowy leaves that seem to creep
> Like leisure in the shade (Clare 1989, 469)

Bate gives us a slightly different version of the poem, with a gentle touch here and there, correcting Clare's spelling, adding a bit of punctuation, aiding the modern reader with the pronunciation:

> Haunter of woods, lone wilds and solitudes
> Where none but feet of birds and things as wild
> Doth print a foot track near, where summer's light
> Buried in boughs forgets its glare and round thy crimpèd leaves
> Feints in a quiet dimness fit for musings
> And melancholy moods, with here and there
> A golden thread of sunshine stealing through
> The evening shadowy leaves that seem to creep
> Like leisure in the shade. (Bate, 153)

A poem like this one may be seen as representing what is best in the tradition of English pastoral poetry: the speaker presents himself as a lover of simple encounters with nature, whose attentiveness to natural phenomena turns a seemingly trivial moment into something magical, but there is no moralizing, and no attempt at providing the poem with a reflective coda. If you see the point of keeping still in this enchanted wood, if you are not a careless passer-by, then this early lyric is for you the authentic voice of Clare. The language is matter-of-fact, avoiding the grandiloquence of imitation or the Latinate abstractions which Clare picked up as a teenage poet because of his early readings in Thomson, Cowper and others. A poem like this one must be confronted with Clare's attempt at imitation, for instance in a sonnet "To the Glow-worm", which famously opens with the following address, a good example of the case when imitation is the enemy of authenticity.

> Tastefull Illuminations of the night
> Bright scatter'd twinkling stars o' spangl'd earth . . . (Clare 1820, 193).

Going back to the "Fox Fern": I remember reading poems by Edward Thomas, written about a hundred years after Clare, for instance his "October", when I could not avoid associating the tone, mood, and use of specific names of plants and insects, birds and animals, with Clare's poetry.

> The green elm with the one great bough of gold
> Lets leaves into the grass slip, one by one. –
> The short hill grass, the mushrooms small milk-white,
> Harebell and scabious and tormentil,
> That blackberry and gorse, in dew and sun,
> Bow down to; and the wind travels too light
> To shake the fallen birch leaves from the fern;
> The gossamers wander at their own will,
> At heavier steps than birds' the squirrels scold. (Thomas, 88)

The reader of Edward Thomas's poetry is likely to exclaim, this is pure Clare, but then he must correct himself: Thomas wrote "October" in 1915, and Clare's "To the Fox Fern" appeared in print for the first time in 1989.

Now I'd like to demonstrate how the editorial revision of a poem, ostensibly motivated by reasons of correctness and clarity, melody and rhythm of individual lines, may conceal the intention to censor, to dull the edge of social satire. Taylor needed a rustic poet who could write beautifully about the countryside and nature; he did not need a poet of social protest and political statement, certainly not in 1820. "The Robin" starts with a brief description of harsh winter season, and the plight of the hungry birds (I am quoting from Clare's manuscript, the version printed by Taylor in 1820 is a bit different):

> Now the snow hides the ground little birds leave the wood
> And flie to the cottage to beg for their food
> While the domestic robin more tame than the rest
> (With its wings drooping down and rough feathers undrest)
> Comes close to our windows as much as to say
> 'I would venture in if I could find a way
> 'I'm starved and I want to get out of the cold
> 'O! make me a passage and think me not bold' (MA A3, 74)

Taylor's changes are slight, but significant. He capitalizes all the names of the birds appearing in the poem, the Robin, the Wren, and the Sparrows, bringing the text closer to the tradition of beast fable or parable. He corrects obvious irregularities of rhythm which appear e.g. in line 3:

> While the Robin, domestic, more tame than the rest (Clare 1820, 42)

(Robinson prints this line exactly as Clare wrote it, "while the domestic robin"; it seems this time the original editor, and not the 20th-century one, was – for once – the better judge).

Both editors, Taylor *and* Robinson, correct Clare's whimsical spelling of the word "peasant" (Clare always spelt it "pheasant"; we may suppose the editors did this for the sake of clarity, to avoid misunderstanding: after all, a "pheasant" might very well make an appearance in a poem about birds. In all other cases (and in other poems) Clare's odd spelling (e.g. childern = children) is corrected by Taylor but left unchanged by Robinson who declares in the Introduction to Volume 1 of *The Early Poems of John Clare,* 1989, that problems created by "misspellings, mistakes in grammar, and mispunctuation" are insignificant and disappear with just "a little practice in reading Clare" (Clare 1989, v. 1, xxiii).

The remaining thirty lines or so of the poem is a heartfelt animated response by the poet: he invites the little bird in, promises to do him no harm, but warns him against a cruel neighbour, a rich farmer who likes hunting and killing birds:

> – But O! little robin be careful to shun
> That house where the peasant makes use of a gun
> For if thou but taste of the seed he has strew'd,
> Thy life as a ransom must pay for thy food (Clare 1820, 43)

Editorial revision is quite insignificant here (with the exception of the word "pheasant"). The most intrusive adjustment of the text appears in the conclusion of the poem: in the closing passage we can clearly see the direction and reasoning behind Taylor's revisions. Clare compares the cruel rich hunters to "wolves of the appenine clan", they may outwardly look like men, but in nature they are like wolves. It is clear by now that the robin and other little birds in the poem represent the unfortunate simple folk, the landless peasants and seasonal rural labourers like Clare himself, who suffered so much poverty and destitution in the era of enclosures (Clare's own village of Helpstone was officially enclosed in 1807), while the land-grabbing yeomanry are the members of the Apennine clan. Clare's original reads:

> Like them his whole study is bent on his prey
> Like them he devours what e'er comes in his way
> Then be careful and shun what is meant to betray
> And flie from these men-masked wolves far away (MA A3, 74, ll. 25–28)

Taylor cuts this rather breathless jeremiad to just two lines, partly perhaps because Clare has a clear problem here with balancing his lines, and partly because there seem to be too many rhymes all on the same note: *prey – way – betray – away.* More importantly, Taylor knows that Clare is obviously speaking here about the cruel exploitation of the poor by the richer farmers who are presented as "men-masked wolves" bent on devouring "what e'er comes in his way" (l. 26). Taylor's version, the one which was printed in 1820, is shorter, smoother, and much less radical in its message:

> Like them his whole study is bent on his prey:
> Then be careful, and shun what is meant to betray (Clare 1820, 43)

So, Taylor corrects Clare where he sees a blemish (Clare usually agreed with his editor, respected his judgment, but often pleaded for particular words or lines to be left alone). More importantly, Taylor takes out the radical sting out of this poem. Early in 1820 (Clare's first volume was published on January 15th), less than six months after the infamous Peterloo Massacre, anyone who was a publisher, even a publisher of Romantic poetry, had to be extremely careful not to be accused of sedition. The aftermath of the Massacre was the Government's crack-down on reform, with the passing of the Six Acts (obviously by coincidence) just two weeks before the publication of *Poems Descriptive*. Act number 5, known as the Criminal Libel Act, made existing laws much tougher. Authors and publishers accused of sedition could be sentenced to long years in prison or transportation.

Another prickly problem was patronage. There were members of aristocracy, both in London and in Northamptonshire, who were prepared to offer Clare a decent home, or financial support, or an annuity for himself and his growing family, without any strings attached, and without any attempts to tell the poet what he must write and how. Lord Milton of Milton Hall was quite enthusiastic about the "natural genius" unexpectedly appearing in the manor of which he was lord. He bought ten copies of *Poems Descriptive,* invited Clare to meet him and his family – including his father, old Lord Fitzwilliam, second earl in the English peerage – gave his neighbour the poet a ten-pound note, and even offered to contribute one hundred pounds towards the purchase of an annuity for Clare. His wife promised to send Clare's parents "a good supply of blankets and every thing that can comfort old people" (Bate, 159). The visit ended in the servants' hall where Clare was fed and plied with ale. Clare's biographer, Jonathan Bate is full of praise for the Fitzwilliam family who provided the poet with financial assistance till the end of his long life (including the money needed for the poet's long stay in the lunatic asylums after 1837).

Clare was also invited to visit the Marquess of Exeter at Burghley House, a grand country residence near Stamford. He arrived one day late, because it snowed heavily on the Sunday he was expected, and he only possessed one pair of shoes. The Marquess received him kindly, however, and insisted on examining his manuscripts. He warned him about the duplicity of booksellers and publishers. He was sorry he had no regular job to offer the poet, but he promised to give him fifteen guineas a year for life, so that Clare could have two days every week, the Marquess said, to pursue his studies and his poetry.

Unfortunately for Clare, the friendship and support of another gentleman, first Baron Radstock, a retired admiral and a friend of Nelson, was not given with a free hand. Radstock was very active in the campaign for the promotion of Clare's poetry, sending the first volume of his poems to Sir Walter Scott, and trying to persuade Lord Milton that a rent-free cottage, a cow and a couple of pigs would be a better way to help the poet than gifts of money (here Radstock was perhaps right because Clare, like many other poets, did have a drinking problem). But as Clare's biographer says, "Radstock's support came with a price" (Bate, 164): he was a deeply religious man, an Evangelical Anglican who was very active in the Society for the Propagation of the Gospel. He cared about respectability and always insisted on removing all the "dirty verse" from Clare's volumes (this is why Taylor agreed to remove two lovely tales, "Dolly's Mistake" and "My Mary" from *Poems Descriptive*). Radstock was also eager to expunge all "radical and ungrateful" sentiments about enclosures, poverty, social reform and "accursed wealth" and greed, which, in an autobiographical poem entitled "Helpstone" are rightly blamed by Clare for the sad plight of poor people in the country. Clearly, patronage is a significant factor when we speak about the authenticity of Clare's texts, because patronage forced the poet to capitulate and remove all the offending lines and passages, occasionally also whole poems, radically changing the impression his poems make when original, manuscript versions of his texts are studied.

The questions of authenticity, editorial revision and possible recovery of original authorial versions of Clare's poetry are complicated. On the one hand, he was quite willing and happy to defer to Taylor and Hessey's superior education, literary taste and judgment, or to withdraw passages which might, in the period after Peterloo, be treated as 'radical slang'. On the other, he had the mature poet's self-confidence and certainty he was simply right in his choices. Robinson's contribution, his insistence on the need for a full recovery of Clare's authentic voice, is extremely valuable for anyone embarking on an extensive study of John Clare's poetry: we hear authentic Clare, speaking in his own voice, 'the real language of men'.

Works Cited

Bate, Jonathan. *John Clare: A Biography,* New York: Farrar, Straus and Giroux, 2003.

Clare, John. Manuscripts MA A3 (1 and 2), and MA D2. Vivacity Library in Peterborough.

—. *Poems Descriptive of Rural Life and Scenery,* London: Taylor and Hessey, 1820.

—. *The Complete Poems of John Clare in 9 Volumes,* edited by Eric Robinson and David Powell, Oxford: Clarendon Press, 1989.

Dowden, Edward. *Introduction* to *Poems by William Wordsworth*, Boston, New York, Chicago, London: Ginn and Company, 1897.

Paulin, Tom. *Minotaur: Poetry and the Nation State.* London: Faber and Faber, 1992.

Thomas, Edward. *Collected Poems.* London: Faber and Faber, 2004.

Eliza Borkowska

The Birth of the Poet:
The Role of S. T. Coleridge in
the Making of "William Wordsworth"

Abstract: The paper argues that most themes and attitudes perceived as the hallmarks of "authentically Wordsworthian" poetry were in fact an imitation, as they appeared in the poet's work under the influence of Coleridge – while, ironically, Wordsworth's less imitative and more independent works are considered non-canonical, unrepresentative and *un-Wordsworthian*.

Keywords: Wordsworth, Coleridge, pantheism, memory, imagination, imitation

The quintessence of William Wordsworth are a few familiar titles: *Lyrical Ballads*, including "We are Seven" or "Lines Written a Few Miles above Tintern Abbey" (composed in 1798), early books of *The Prelude* (written in 1798–99), "Preface" to *Lyrical Ballads* (1800, 1802), "It is a Beauteous Evening" (1802), "Ode: Intimations of Immortality" (1802–4), "Daffodils" (1804). These works seem to constitute the material from which most curricula build the notion of "authentic William Wordsworth," which, once fixed and defined, is then clashed with later poetry written by William Wordsworth. The poet lived till he was eighty (1770–1850) and was active practically till the end of that long lifespan. But "authentic Wordsworth" seems to have had a very short life: born in 1798 (the year of the publication of the first edition of *Lyrical Ballads*) – died in 1804, perhaps in 1805 (which is when the Thirteen-Book *Prelude* was completed). At any rate, he was dead by 1807[1] – the year of the publication of *Poems in Two Volumes*, including "It is a beauteous Evening," "Daffodils," and the "Ode."

The familiar keywords and key-phrases associated with the notion "William Wordsworth" are, among other things, childhood (featuring in all of the above-

---

1 Cf., e.g., the characteristic claim from the introductory note on "William Wordsworth" in *The Norton Anthology of English Literature*: "Most of Wordsworth's greatest poetry had been written by 1807" (Abrams et al., ii: 128). The same is said in the introductory note in *The Critical Tradition*: "Most of Wordsworth's best poetry was written in a single decade, 1797–1807" (Richter, 283). After explaining that within this decade Wordsworth published *Lyrical Ballads* and *Poems in Two Volumes* as well as completed his *Prelude*, Richter adds: "By his forties, when he published *The Excursion* (1814) he was in decline" (283).

listed poems but "Daffodils"), imagination (understood as a power that "half-creates" the object of perception), "emotion recollected in tranquillity" (part of the definition of poetry given in the "Preface" and illustrated in a number of these pieces, most explicitly in "Daffodils"), the backward glance, the return to one's private past, the "spots of time." One more key phrase is "Wisdom and spirit of the universe" and, related to it, Wordsworth's pantheism, his nature worship – which tends to be emphasised to such a degree that a book based on the above-mentioned canonical texts of "William Wordsworth," like Haines' *Redemption in Poetry and Philosophy*, treats him, unreservedly, as a post-Christian poet. What I would like to argue in this paper is that those hallmarks of Wordsworth's poetry, the "characteristically Wordsworthian" attitudes, did not really emerge until the poet met S. T. Coleridge. This is to say: "authentic Wordsworth" was not "born" but "made."[2]

It would be pointless to start arguing this point by referring to very early Wordsworth, to his first poetic attempts, like, e.g., "Lines written as a School Exercise at Hawkshead" (Wordsworth's earliest extant poem, composed in 1784–85): this imitation of Pope, relying heavily on the eighteenth-century poetic diction, was a school exercise and, as such, it was not meant to express the author – what it captured instead were the poetic fashions of the times of young Wordsworth that "William Wordsworth" will later combat in his "Preface." Conversely, the material that does merit attention in this survey of pre-Coleridgean Wordsworth are two works completed nearly a decade later: "An Evening Walk" and "Descriptive Sketches," both given to the press in 1793, when "W. Wordsworth, B.A. of St. John's, Cambridge"[3] was in his early twenties – just a couple of years before he first met S. T. Coleridge.

Each of these poems documents a familiarly Wordsworthian development: the concentration on the theme of nature (the topic that interested *him* rather than his teachers). Nevertheless, apart from the choice of the theme, neither of the poems seems to have the expected "Wordsworthian" features. The first of them, a descriptive piece in rhymed heroics, "an exercise in the sentimental, bucolic manner of James Thomson" (Buchan, 347), does not record the subject's recollec-

---

2   For a discussion of the opposite point, *viz.* to what extent Coleridge was made by Wordsworth, see, e.g., Sanders (367–69). For a reflection on how Coleridge was unmade by Wordsworth see Buchan.

3   The formula repeated in the subtitles of "An Evening Walk" and "Descriptive Sketches" as they were printed in 1793 for J. Johnson; citations from both poems, including line numbers, follow Hutchinson's "Appendix: Poems of 1793, Reprinted from the Quarto of 1793," pp. 591–617.

tions but his observations. The topic of memory (and childhood) appears only at the beginning (ll. 16–48) – as a wistful sigh after "departed pleasures;" otherwise the speaker has no past of his own. Practically the entire poem is written in the *Present* Tense and the "I" is largely limited to the "eye" – which registers the "objective reality" and knows how to tell a fact from a fancy;[4] there is no talk in this poem about imagination. "Descriptive Sketches" – with the subtitle: "In Verse [again, the regular Drydenian-Popian heroic couplet]. Taken during a Pedestrian Tour in the Italian, Grison, Swiss, and Savoyard Alps" – is, on the other hand, founded on recollections: of the walking tour with Robert Jones in the long vacation of 1790 (also described in Book VI of *The Prelude*). There are, however, no "characteristically Wordsworthian" insights into the functions of memory in this poem. Personal recollections – not of childhood but of the natural phenomena the author had observed, the scenes he had seen two years before he completed this work – just suggest the subject matter, providing the raw material for the poetry. Nothing is said here about the continuity of man's psychological life, no claims are made concerning the way one's present builds upon one's past (in fact, though based on private memories, most of the poem is written, once more, in the generalizing Present Tense, unlike Book VI of *The Prelude*). Neither is there any reference to pantheism in "Descriptive Sketches:" the "secret Power" which is said to "reign" in the Alps (424–25) seems to be associated with the fanciful "native Genii" mentioned in line 419. The most articulated religious sentiments of the composition are stilted couplets addressed to "great God" in the work's conclusion and a heartfelt turn to the *Catholic* pilgrims of Einsiedlen (654–79); indeed, the poem firmly supports the verdict Wordsworth's nephew, Christopher, pronounced in *Memoirs*: "at this period of his life [the early 1790s], his religious opinions were not very clearly defined" (II: 90).

There is one more early poem by Wordsworth that must be noted in this survey, namely "Guilt and Sorrow; or, Incidents upon Salisbury Plain," begun in 1791–92, completed in 1793–94. Its fragment was published among *Lyrical Ballads* of 1798, the entire composition appeared in print as late as 1842, eight years after the death of Coleridge; in this sense, the poem can hardly be claimed to represent "pre-Coleridgean" Wordsworth. It does deserve attention, however, because it drew young Coleridge's attention, which he would emphasise after the years in *Biographia Literaria* among his reminiscences of the beginnings of his acquaintance with Wordsworth: "I was in my twenty-fourth year, when I had the happiness of knowing Mr. Wordsworth personally, and while memory lasts, I

---

4   E.g., the "strange apparitions" of 175 ff.

shall hardly forget the sudden effect produced on my mind, by his recitation of a manuscript poem, which still remains unpublished" (44). What made "so unusual an impression" (45) first on Coleridge's "feelings" – "and subsequently," he adds, "on [his] judgement" – was "the union of deep feeling and profound thought; the fine balance of truth in observing, with the imaginative faculty in modifying, the objects observed" (45). Significantly, this is where the conception of imagination as a "modifying" power appears for the first time: in Coleridge's "judgement" of Wordsworth's early work,[5] not in Wordsworth's own reflection. The latter has no insight into the subject to offer – yet; he does not (yet) conduct any "intimate analysis" of the faculty of imagination, its "functions," "effects," or "marks." In point of fact, practically the only place where pre-Coleridgean Wordsworth employs the word that will become one of the keywords of "William Wordsworth" is a footnote attached to the description of a stormy sunset in "Descriptive Sketches" (332 ff.), where, dissociating the Alps from the notion of "Picturesque" ("the Alps are insulted in applying to them that term"), Wordsworth insists:

> Whoever, in attempting to describe their sublime features, should confine himself to the cold rules of painting would give his reader but a very imperfect idea of those emotions which they have the irresistible power of communicating to the most impassive imaginations. (Hutchinson, 608)

This is to say, in the early 1790s, imagination in William Wordsworth is passive. It does not co-create the object of perception but is controlled by it[6] – a conception that will be challenged by "authentic Wordsworth."

The birth and growth of the latter depended entirely upon his acquaintance and collaboration with S. T. Coleridge. Wordsworth met Coleridge briefly in 1795 (which is when the recitation of the manuscript of "Salisbury Plain" took place). In 1796 Wordsworth had the chance to "read and admire"[7] Coleridge's *Poems on*

---

5 Coleridge elaborates upon this point in the famous passage that follows the reminiscence: "This excellence, which in all Mr. Wordsworth's writings is more or less predominant, and which constitutes the character of his mind, I no sooner felt, than I sought to understand. Repeated meditations led me first to suspect – (and a more intimate analysis of the human faculties, their appropriate marks, functions, and effects matured my conjecture into full conviction,) – that Fancy and Imagination were two distinct and widely different faculties" (45).
6 "That controuling influence, which distinguishes the Alps from all other scenery," is what occupies Wordsworth in the remainder of his footnote (Hutchinson, 608).
7 The phrase is Jonathan Wordsworth's (henceforth, in notes and references, abbreviated as WJ). In this account I follow the timing given in WJ's "Table of Dates" (1995, xi–xii) and in Hutchinson's "Chronological Table" (xxvii).

Various Subjects, which were published in April 1796. In June of the following year Coleridge visited Wordsworth at Racedown, then, on 4 July 1797, Wordsworth visited Coleridge at Nether Stowey and, three days later, he leased a house in Alfoxden to live three miles from Coleridge's cottage. Within several months, by February 1798, William Wordsworth wrote his first "Wordsworthian" poem, "The Pedlar." The poet never published this piece, though, in a sense, it was published twice, in 1814 and in 1850 (I will deal with this contradiction towards the end of this paper).

The composition of "The Pedlar," in other words, marks the birth of "authentic Wordsworth," and the most remarkable feature of the event is that the man (or the concept?) was born in the *third* person: not as "I" but as "*he*." "Him had I seen," reads the poem's opening line, the inversion giving the right impression of who is this poem's protagonist: a pedlar of the "I's" acquaintance ("I knew him – he was born of lowly race/ On Cumbrian hills;" 19 [8–9]).[8] It is in this poem that Wordsworth, for the first time in his work, looks back to the past to account for the present: most "characteristically," he pays and calls attention to childhood, treating it as a seminal period when the future adult is formed:

> I loved to hear him talk of former days
> And tell how when a child, . . .
> He many an evening to his distant home
> In solitude returning saw the hills
> Grow larger in the darkness, all alone
> Beheld the stars come out above his head. . . .
> So the foundations of his mind were laid.
> In such communion, not from terror free,
> While yet a child, and long before his time,
> He had perceived the presence and the power
> Of greatness, and deep feelings had impressed
> Great objects on his mind. (19–20 [13–31])

Man's strengths are acquired when he is a child: this is when "the foundations of his mind [are] laid." The same idea will be most memorably expressed four years later (1802) in the famous adage "The Child is father of the Man" – one of the most cited lines from "authentic Wordsworth" (Wordsworth himself liked to cite it: he recycled the formula in the motto of his "Ode").[9] Critics reflecting on these

---

8   Citations from "The Pedlar," followed by page [and line] numbers, are from WJ's edition of 1985.
9   Originally, the line comes from "My heart leaps up" of March 1802. It did not appear in the first edition of the "Ode" (cf. Wordsworth 1807, ii: 145–46), but was first cited in the motto in the edition of 1815.

and other statements documenting Wordsworth's interest in the continuity of psychological life – e.g., the poet's insistence on "forms which once seen/ Could never be forgotten" ("Pedlar," 22 [75–76]), or "the curious links/ With which the perishable hours of life/ Are bound together" ("Pedlar," 22 [78–80]) – point to David Hartley's *Observations on Man, his Frame, his Duty, and his Expectations* (1749) as the source of these ideas, specifically to the Hartleyan "beneficial 'chains' of association at work within the mind" (WJ, 604). What needs to be underlined in this chronological account of the birth and growth of "William Wordsworth," however, is that no such "Hartleyan implications" appear in the poet's work before he settled in Alfoxden. The "link" between Wordsworth and Hartley is Coleridge – who, after his conversion to Priestley's Unitarianism at Cambridge (in the early 1790s), "had his portrait painted holding a copy of the *Observations*" ("David Hartley"), and who gave his first son, born in 1796 (the year when Wordsworth "read and admired" *Poems on Various Subjects*), the name of David Hartley. The little David Hartley Coleridge was more than one year old when first references to the associationism of David Hartley appeared in the verse of "William Wordsworth."

The father's father (*viz.* the child) was not the only "characteristically Wordsworthian" theme that was born with "The Pedlar." The other hallmark of "William Wordsworth" that was absent from the earlier work by William Wordsworth and appeared for the first time in the poet's opus in "The Pedlar" was "Wordsworth's pantheism" – again, attributed within this formative composition not to the "I," but to "him," the protagonist:

> He was only then
> Contented when with bliss ineffable
> He felt the sentiment of being spread
> O'er all that moves, and all that seemeth still.
> ... Wonder not
> If such his transports were; for in all things
> He saw one life, and felt that it was joy.
> One song they sang, and it was audible –
> Most audible then when the fleshly ear,
> O'ercome by grosser prelude of that strain,
> Forgot its functions, and slept undisturbed. (26–27 [206–22])

As this and the previously cited passage suggest, there was yet another element that entered Wordsworth's poetry along with his removal to Alfoxden, *viz.* his "characteristic" attitude to imagination. "Great objects" are preceded by "deep feelings;" the songs that pantheist nature sings are most audible when the fleshly ear sleeps – melodies that are heard are sweet, but those unheard are sweeter. From now on, imagination in "William Wordsworth" is "creative" ("Pedlar," 21 [53]). It is the "*active* power" ("Pedlar," 20 [40]; original emphasis) that gives quality to the world of both the child and the child's child (*viz.* the father).

While Alfoxden, three miles from Coleridge's cottage, is where the important keywords of Wordsworth's poetry were formed, the next vital "spot" on the map of the poet's growth were the banks of the Wye, "a few miles above Tintern Abbey," where Wordsworth wrote his "Lines;"[10] the poem was composed in the summer of 1798 and can be treated as a stepping stone between "The Pedlar," which belongs to the previous winter, and *The Prelude*, whose composition would begin among the frosts of Goslar in the winter of 1798. It is in "Lines" that the poet assumes for the first time what will from now on become the "distinctly Wordsworthian" stance: that of looking backwards, revisiting the past, over-viewing the path that has been trodden – not by a character (the Pedlar) but by the "I." Arguably, this element is not yet wholly articulated in "Lines," which mostly talk of the subject's *physical* return to the place he had been to five years back ("Five years have passed; five summers, with the length/ Of five long winters! And again I hear/ These waters;" 201 [1–3]).[11] A few months will pass before this evolves to what is so "quintessentially Wordsworthian:" the "I's" *mental* return – not a bodily excursion but a journey taking place within the traveller's memory, not a visit to a "spot" but to a "spot of time." Nonetheless, even though "Lines" do not fully capture it (yet), they do advance the philosophy that lies behind all Wordsworth's revisitings. In this poem of mid 1798, much like in *The Prelude* (and unlike in "Descriptive Sketches") the "I" recollects not just for the sake of remembering, but in order to reflect on the distance that has been travelled since: the chain linking the present with the past is a measurement of the growth of the mind. In "Lines" it is relatively short; it spans the period of five years, reaching back to 1793 (the year of the publication of "An Evening Walk" and "Descriptive Sketches"). In *The Prelude* the beneficial links of association will be bound together to form a much longer chain that stretches back to the limits of individual memory – the regions of "first childhood" (*1805*, iii: 474):[12] this is when "the foundations of [man's] mind [are] laid," claimed Wordsworth in his formative poem about the Pedlar; this is "the base/ On which [man's] greatness stands," he will assert, remodelling his "original" metaphor, in the poem about himself (*Prelude 1805*, xi: 330–31).

---

10 The full title of the poem in the 1798 edition of *Lyrical Ballads* is "Lines written a few miles above Tintern Abbey, On revising the banks of the Wye during a tour, July 13, 1798."

11 Citations from "Lines," followed by page [and line] numbers, are from the original 1798 edition.

12 Citations from *The Prelude* follow WJ's edition of 1995; bracketed references provide information about the version, book and line numbers.

It is also in "Tintern Abbey," the stepping-stone between "The Pedlar" and *The Prelude*, that Wordsworth for the first time appropriates – ascribes to himself – the attitudes that in his formative poem were attributed to the character. Specifically, the "I" in "Lines" takes over "The Pedlar's" approach to imagination: great objects result from deep feelings; this "mighty world" must be, first, "half-created" before it is "perceived" by the "ear" or the "eye."[13] And the same happens with the Pedlar's religion: in "the Poem upon the Wye" it is appropriated by the "I." The "presence that disturbs" in "Lines"[14] is no longer that "secret power" of the "native Genii" that accompanied the "I" during his climb with Robert Jones in "Descriptive Sketches." Here, this power is "[a] motion and a spirit, that impels/ All thinking things, all objects of all thought,/ And rolls through all things" (207 [100–2]). Wordsworth expressly defines himself in "Tintern Abbey" as a "worshipper of Nature" (210 [152]) – to the satisfaction of those critics who wish to discuss "authentic Wordsworth" as a post-Christian poet, and, be it added, much to the vexation of William Wordsworth himself (I will handle this last point by and by).

The final step on the path of the growth of the poet was "the Poem on [his] own Life" – which is how Wordsworth himself referred to *The Prelude*[15] (the more familiar title under which the work eventually became known to his readers was given posthumously by the poet's wife). In point of fact, this "autobiography" of "William Wordsworth," whose composition occupied William Wordsworth from late 1798 till 1805, should be treated as a ground upon which, after the intermediary "Lines," the author trained himself in the arts of appropriation.

Predictably, the Thirteen-Book *Prelude*'s "I" (in its two manifestations, that of the narrator and the narratee) is pantheist – like the Pedlar, and like the "I" in "Lines." In Book II, for instance, in a passage written for the Two-Part version of 1799 and preserved in *The Prelude* of 1805, while tracing "[t]he progress of our being" (*1805*, ii: 239), the "I" blesses the "infant babe," whose soul, he maintains, "[c]laims manifest kindred with an earthly soul" (*1805*, ii: 242). Later in the same Book, the "I" asserts of his earlier self: "in all things/ I saw one life, and felt that it was joy" (*1805*, ii: 429–30). This latter claim sounds familiar. In a sense, I have already cited it in this paper – much as I have quoted the whole passage within which these words are placed in the Thirteen-Book *Prelude* (*1805*, ii: 418–34).

---

13 The passage from which these citations are taken reads: "Therefore am I still/ A lover of the meadows and the woods,/ And mountains; and of all that we behold/ From this green earth; of all the mighty world/ Of eye and ear, both what they half-create/ And what perceive" (207–8 [102–7]).
14 See p. 207 [esp. ll. 93–99].
15 In a letter to George Beaumont of 1 May 1805 (Grosart, ii: 165).

A comparison of this passage (beginning: "I was only then/ Contented…") with the second long excerpt from "The Pedlar" cited above (beginning: "He was only then/ Contented…") makes it clear that *The Prelude* is indeed a development from "Lines," the next step, in which the author does not merely appropriate his protagonist's attitudes, including the Pedlar's belief in "one life," but he, literally, devours the character. By an adjustment in the pronouns (from the third person to the first), he decomposes the character to form the "I;" he un-writes the formative "Pedlar" in order to compose "the Poem on [his] own Life."

In this passage and elsewhere in *The Prelude* of 1805 the "I" similarly endorses "The Pedlar's" – and Coleridge's – judgement on imagination, the faculty that modifies – co-creates – the objects of perception: whose melodies are sweeter than those of the fleshly ear, which adds joy to what is communicated by the fleshly eye. Coleridge would give this idea a most succinct expression in line 47 of "Dejection: An Ode:" "We receive but what we give." Wordsworth repeats the exact formula, without even remodelling the expression, in *The Prelude's* Book XI,[16] composed in 1804 (WJ, 647), two years after the publication of Coleridge's "Dejection:" "thou must give,/ Else never canst receive" (*1805*, xi: 332–33). Intriguingly, the assertion appears in the same passage as the remodelled claim about childhood cited above;[17] in other words, this "quintessentially Wordsworthian" passage from his "autobiographic" poem is a cluster of quotes from the formative work written shortly after Wordsworth moved to live near Coleridge, and from Coleridge's "Ode." No wonder then that when, after his return from Malta, Coleridge heard Wordsworth recite *The Prelude*, he did approve of the poem (even though, by that time, he himself was no longer a pantheist). Indeed, he could not but appreciate this work founded on his own early fascination with associationism, depicting Wordsworth's past through the prism supplied by Coleridge himself, and echoing the theory of imagination that would later (after *Biographia Literaria*) become his own principal contribution to Romantic thought. Coleridge expressed his appreciation in "To William Wordsworth," a poem he composed on 7 Jan. 1807, "on the Night, on which [Wordsworth] finished the recitation" (Coleridge 1996, 309).

Sadly, that memorable occasion of Wordsworth's recitation of "the Poem on [his] own Life" to Coleridge, and Coleridge's composition of his tribute "To William Wordsworth," coincide with the death of "authentic Wordsworth." As noted at the beginning of this paper, the process of decline and decay was completed by

---

16 Given to the topic of "Imagination, How Impaired and Restored."
17 The entire passage reads: "I am lost, but see/ In simple childhood something of the base/ On which thy [man's] greatness stands – but this I feel,/ That from thyself it is that thou must give,/ Else never canst receive" (*1805*, xi: 329–33).

1807.[18] It might have begun as early as 1804, the year when Wordsworth conceived of his second (and last) major poetic work, *The Excursion* (WJ, xv).

Symbolically, the conception and then the composition of *The Excursion* meant the final decomposition of "The Pedlar." Most agonizingly, it sealed the fate of its protagonist: what once looked like Wordsworth's *alter ego* was dismembered and the leftovers – the bits and portions of the Pedlar that were not incorporated in *The Prelude* as part of the author's self-portrait – were now utilized to form the leading persona of *The Excursion*, the Wanderer. Then again, unlike "the Poem on [his] own Life" (which, though completed in 1805, near the death of "authentic Wordsworth," would not be published until the death of William Wordsworth in 1850), *The Excursion* appeared in print shortly after it was composed, in 1814, and the publication, among other reactions, provoked criticism, inducing some of the early readers to suspect the author of pantheism. What merits special attention in this place is the argument William Wordsworth used to defended himself. He admitted:

> There is indeed a passage towards the end of the 4[th.] Book where the Wanderer intrudes the simile of the Boy and the Shell, and what follows, that has something, ordinarily but absurdly called *Spinosistic*. (Hill, 172–73; original emphasis)

"But," he added in the next sentence, "the intelligent reader will easily see the *dramatic* propriety of the Passage" (again, the emphasis is original). This is to say, the Wanderer, made from the dismembered Pedlar, was a fantasy: it turned out after the years that the protagonist of the formative poem was not the author's *alter ego* but – simply – a character.

In another place of his defence (or else, his attack on unintelligent readers), Wordsworth argues that what might have (mis)led his audiences to (mis)take him, the author, for "a worshipper of Nature" was the "passionate expression uttered incautiously in the Poem upon the Wye" (Hill, 172). Indeed, as has been stressed before, "Lines" were a nuisance; still, what once appeared in print, as "the Poem upon the Wye" did in 1798 and the following editions of the *Ballads*, could hardly

---

18 "The causes of the decline have been much debated," states the note on "William Wordsworth" which I cited in footnote 1, "an important one seems to be inherent in the very nature of his most characteristic writing. Wordsworth is above all the poet of the remembrance of things past, or as he himself put it, of 'emotion recollected in tranquillity.' . . . But the memory of one's early emotional experience is not an inexhaustible resource for poetry" (Abrams et al., ii: 128). Other reasons behind the decline of Wordsworth – and the decay of his creative alliance with Coleridge – are themes addressed in the concluding chapters of the book I am currently writing, *The Presence of the Absence*.

be denied. Needless to say, Wordsworth never admitted that the thirteen Books of the long "autobiographical" poem whose composition had occupied him from 1798 to 1805 were likewise "*Spinosistic*" – and that they attributed the pantheist outlook not to a "*dramatic*" character but to the "I." Luckily, *The Prelude* of 1805 had not been published: and what did not appear in print did not need to be acknowledged – and could be rubbed out.

How many times William Wordsworth returned to "the Poem on [his] own Life" after the publication of *The Excursion* is not known (WJ, xlii), what is clear, however, is that there were at least three wholesale revisions: the first in 1819, then in 1832, and the last one in 1838–39. Within that lingering process of re-writing/ un-writing what had been written two/three/four decades before, Wordsworth re-modelled – adapted, rubbed out, or, according to his critics, ruined – a number of the most "characteristically Wordsworthian" claims of *The Prelude* of 1805. Many of these revisions involved the "Spinosistic" outlook of his autobiography. The assertion about the "infant Babe's" soul claiming "manifest kindred with an earthly soul," for instance, was cut out (cf. *1850*, ii: 232–37). Also the passage originally written for "The Pedlar" and then appropriated by the "I" – "Wonder not/ If such his[/my] transports were, for in all things/ He[/I] saw one life, and felt that it was joy" ("Pedlar," 27 [226–28]/ *1805*, ii: 428–30) – was modified:

> . . . Wonder not
> If high the transport, great the joy I felt,
> Communing in this sort through earth and heaven
> With every form of creature, as it looked
> Towards the Uncreated with a countenance
> Of adoration, with an eye of love. (*1850*, ii: 409–14)

Commenting upon this passage, Jonathan Wordsworth remarks: "Wordsworth in *1850* 409–14 not only replaces the great pantheist assertion of *1805* 429–30, but puts a careful theological distance between God, who is uncreated, and his adoring Creation," after which the critic adds:

> He wrote the original lines of joy and sharing at the end of the eighteenth century, aged 27; he revised them, with Queen Victoria on the throne, aged almost 70. (WJ, 567)

What underlies these critical remarks is a conviction that aging Wordsworth was falsifying the "authentic Wordsworth" by introducing (here and elsewhere) compromising concessions to Victorianism. It needs to be borne in mind, however, that the poet started replacing pantheist passages with what the editor of *The Prelude: The Four Texts* calls "concessions to Anglicanism" as early as 1819 (cf. WJ, xliii–iv) – the year in which Queen Victoria was *born* (and was still an "infant Babe" rather than a Queen "on the throne"). Perhaps then aging Wordsworth was not really falsifying the "original lines" but, just the reverse: purifying them of the concessions to pantheism that he had made several decades before? They were first incorporated into his autobiography along with the dismembered "Pedlar" and, aging Wordsworth might have come to realize, the protagonist of his formative poem was not a third-person version of himself but, through and through (including the features once appropriated by the "I"), a fiction – just a character.

Apart from the insertion of "concessions to Anglicanism" (or, perhaps, the removal of concessions to pantheism), the revisions of *The Prelude* involved a modification of the boldest assertions concerning childhood. These embraced, among other things, the entire "infant Babe" passage (cf. *1805*, ii: 237–80 vs. *1850*, ii: 232–65). According to Jonathan Wordsworth, the lines added in 1832 and the drastic cuts of 1832 and 1838–39 diminish the child (xliv), "weakening the great imaginative claims made by the poetry of *1799* and *1805*" (565). Here and elsewhere aging Wordsworth also modified many of his earlier claims concerning imagination, including changes introduced to Book XI. Summing up the effect of these revisions, Jonathan Wordsworth points out that "the poet's words [in the version of 1805] had had the force of a creed, proclaiming a faith in the mind's strength and self-sufficiency that was central to *The Prelude*" (xlvii). On the other hand, the addition of what the critic calls "ten gratuitous lines" (*1805*, xii: 326–35), demolishes the faith and the creed –

> telling of an old man who has quite forgotten the power of his original experience, the force of his original claims for inspiration and imaginative strength. (WJ, xlvii)

All these changes were made at the times when Wordsworth was no longer in touch with Coleridge; the last wholesale revision of 1838–39, to which belong the above-mentioned "ten gratuitous lines," took place after Coleridge's death. It is quite likely that these modifications were adjustments introduced to his autobiography by authentic Wordsworth, a maturing man re-viewing the "chain" of his "Life" to bind it more firmly with his past life, re-examining the individual links in an attempt to determine on his own – without the support of anybody's "judgement" – what "strength" he actually believed in, what was his "original" experience, what "creed" and what "faith" he had followed, who he was and who he had been. Still, criticism sees these revisions as inferior to the "originals." And anthologies and histories of literature treat the poetry of aging Wordsworth as non-canonical, unable to give the accurate impression of the phenomenon called "William Wordsworth."

Works Cited

Abrams, M. H. et al., eds. *The Norton Anthology of English Literature*. 2 vols. New York; London: W. W. Norton & Company, 1993.

Buchan, A. M. "The Influence of Wordsworth on Coleridge (1795–1800)." *University of Toronto Quarterly* 32.1 (1963): 364–66.

Coleridge, S. T. *Biographia Literaria*. London; Toronto: J. M. Dent & Sons Ltd, 1930.

—. *Selected Poems*. Ed. Richard Holmes. London: Penguin Books, 1996.

"David Hartley." *Stanford Encyclopedia of Philosophy*. 2013. 2 Dec. 2015. <http://plato.stanford.edu/entries/hartley/>.

Grosart, Alexander B., ed. *The Prose Works of William Wordsworth. For the first time collected, with additions from unpublished manuscripts*. 3 vols. London: Edward Moxon, Son, and Co., 1876.

Haines, Simon. *Redemption in Poetry and Philosophy: Wordsworth, Kant, and the Making of the Post-Christian Imagination*. Waco, Texas: Baylor University Press, 2013.

Hill, Alan G., ed. *Letters of William Wordsworth. A New Selection*. Oxford; New York: Oxford University Press, 1984.

Hutchinson, Thomas, ed. *The Poems of William Wordsworth*. London: Humphrey Milford, 1916.

Richter, David H., ed. *The Critical Tradition: Classic Texts and Contemporary Trends*. New York: St. Martin's Press, 1989.

Sanders, Andrew. *The Short Oxford History of English Literature*. Oxford: Oxford University Press, 2004.

Wordsworth, Christopher. *Memoirs of William Wordsworth*. 2 vol. Ed. Henry Reed. Boston: Ticknor, Reed, and Fields, 1851.

Wordsworth, Jonathan, ed. *William Wordsworth: The Prelude: The Four Texts (1798, 1799, 1805, 1850)*. London: Penguin Books, 1995.

Wordsworth, William. *Poems in Two Volumes*. London: Longman, Hurst, Rees, and Orme, 1807.

—. "The Pedlar." *"The Pedlar," "Tintern Abbey," The Two-Part Prelude*. Ed. Jonathan Wordsworth. Cambridge: Cambridge University Press, 1985. 19–32.

[Wordsworth, William, and S. T. Coleridge]. *Lyrical Ballads, With a Few Other Poems*. London: J & A. Arch, 1798.

Natalia Kamovnikova

Identity Blurred: The Use of Interlinear Trots for Translations of Poetry in the Soviet Union

Abstract: The article focuses on the verse translation from interlinear trots, which was a popular practice in the Soviet Union. Verse translation by means of a mediating prosaic text enabled the publishers and translators to introduce the readers to a variety of national literatures; the other side of this ability, however, was the regular blurring of the form, content and message of translated originals.

Keywords: translation, poetry, interlinear trot, identity, the Soviet Union

The popular practice of translating from interlinear trots made an important contribution into the shaping of the concepts of adequacy and creativity in Russian translation studies and translation practice. Interlinear trots – prosaic word for word translations of original verse – were used to create translated poetry by poet-translators, who were unfamiliar with the originals and their languages. And since translation was one of the most actively encouraged forms of literary activity in the Soviet Union, interlinear trots very soon found their application in the Soviet translation practice. In describing the role of interlinear trots in the Soviet literature, I shall here refer to the existing published materials on the subject, as well as the information provided to me in course of personal interviews by three Russian literary translators: Evgeniy Witkowsky from Moscow and Mikhail Yasnov and Viktor Andreyev from St. Petersburg. Witkowsky, Yasnov, and Andreyev were actively involved in poetic translation in the Soviet times; they now remain leading Russian literary translators, editors, and anthologists (Andreyev 2003, 2004; Apollinaire; Márquez; Rodenbach; Witkowsky 2006, 2007, 2012; Yasnov).

The use of interlinear trots for recreating foreign originals in the Russian language was a well-known practice, which Russia was introduced to long before the revolution of 1917. In the beginning of the 19th century, Russian literature was an alloy of original and translated literatures. Translations offered new genres and language forms to Russian writers and poets. At the same time, translations took the form of cultural appropriations, thus acquiring a new role in the receiving Russian literary context (Cooper, 75).

Therefore the Soviet period was not the only one in the Russian history, when cultural resistance to translation combined with a high demand for translations from other languages. For example, in 1916 the Russian poet and translator

Valeriy Brjusov edited an anthology of Armenian poetry, which was mostly translated from interlinear trots by poets Alexander Blok, Fyodor Sologub, Vyacheslav Ivanov, and Konstantin Balmont (Brjusov).

The revolution of 1917 set new requirements and standards for literature, which was supposed to provide the basis for education of the new generations of the new monarchy-free state (Gorky, 85–86). The orientation of Soviet literature towards education and the high demand for new literary texts for educational purposes created a foundation for the use of interlinear trots. Translation was a secure source of high-quality literary texts required for educational purposes, especially in those languages of the Soviet Union that had either undergone script reforms or were starting to introduce scripts for the first time. The use of interlinear trots also targeted education of literary translators: young translators were supposed to start their career translating from interlinear trots, thus gradually learning the language and eventually becoming able to translate from originals (Rossels, 45–6).

The multinational nature of the Soviet Union dictated the necessity of making the translation process in the country more intense, as the national literatures of the USSR were required to be translated into Russian. In fact, authors of the Soviet Union themselves struggled for the right to be translated into the dominating language of the country. Apart from that, the propagated friendship of nations and their joint efforts in constructing the new Soviet reality also called for active translation of literatures of the countries of the communist bloc. Interlinear trots were thus deemed useful to make it possible to introduce the readers to the variety of national literatures. It was the political necessity of rendering works of national literatures in the Russian language that made interlinear trots of both poetry and prose come into being (Rossels, 52–63). Interlinear trots of prose were used purely for translations from the languages of the Soviet Union into Russian; they were gradually replaced by direct translations from originals by the middle of the 20 century. But the translations of poetry via interlinear trots remained a regular practice until the fall of the Soviet Union: translations of poetry were often done via interlinear trots, at times even from the most popular and widely spoken European languages.

The use of interlinear trots was employed both by beginners in the field and experienced translators. Marina Tsvetayeva, who knew French, German, English, and Spanish, also translated from Czech, Serbian, Croatian, Bulgarian, Georgian, Polish, and Yiddish (Tsvetayeva). Samuel Marshak, the celebrated translator of Shakespeare, Keats, Burns, and Blake, is also known for his translations of the poems of Mao Tse-tung (Tse-tung) from interlinear trots. Another example is the great Russian poet Anna Akhmatova who was actively involved in poetic translation mainly using interlinear translations from Serbian, Czech, Bulgarian, Romanian, Korean, Chinese and Bengali (Akhmatova 1990b). Akhmatova found the use of interlinear translations quite natural and justified it by claiming: "We all translate from an interlinear: the translator who knows the language of the original sooner or later gets to see an interlinear translation in front of him" (Naiman 122). Joseph Brodsky actively translated from many languages, including Konstantinos Kavafis from Greek, Konstantyn Ildefons Gałczyński and Czesław Miłosz from Polish; he also translated from Czech, Dutch, Lithuanian, Estonian, and German (Brodsky).

Interlinear trots varied in the degree of detail they provided; they could be very detailed or very sketchy, depending on who prepared the interlinear trot and who was supposed to translate from it. In his interview given to the author of this article, Evgeniy Witkowsky remarked that there even existed a term *Stalin's interlinear trot (stalinskiy podstrochnik)*, when a variety of interlinear trots of one poem was provided, including the complete transliteration of the original made in the Cyrillic alphabet. In some cases, interlinear trots included information on phraseology, implications and allusions, or described in closer detail the prosodic features, stylistic devices or imagery, which is why a good interlinear translation was highly valued by poet-translators.

Due to the existence of interlinear trots poetic translation gradually turned into a steady source of income for many Soviet poets. Some of them, like Akhmatova, Tsvetayeva, and later Brodsky, translated to provide for their living and to remain involved in a literary activity which could result in publications. Unable to publish their original poetry, poets voluntarily dedicated themselves to translating poetry written by others, thus keeping their status of published poets. Other poets saw translation of poetry as easy earning – and, indeed, translation of poetry paid very well. Influential poets, who had worked their way out to recognition and approval of officials of different ranks, exercised greater influence in the selection of poetry for translation and were usually able to find someone to create interlinear trots for them. For several decades, as Witkowsky noted in his interview, there even existed an unofficial profession called *interlinear trotter (podstrochnikist)*, which eventually became extinct by the beginning of the 1980s. But even when interlinear trotters ceased to exist, interlinear trots continued to be widely used. Produced by other translators, editors, or even anthologists, interlinear trots were then employed by influential Soviet poets, who sometimes did not even know any foreign languages.

A literary translator in the Soviet Union was permitted to remain monolingual, however contradictory to the professional requirements this may sound. In this regard, the following statement made by Uvarov in 1981 is very demonstrative of the general tendency: "[T]he main quality of the translator is not the knowledge of two or more languages (the translator may not know languages and yet remain a translator), but the knowledge of his/her role. Rather than the one who knows languages, the translator is the one who behaves like a translator" (13). The quoted passage clearly indicates the tendency of text domestication, which was predominant in Soviet literary translation. The awareness of one's mission is defined here as more important than the knowledge of the source language, and hence the poetics of the original.

Translation from Soviet literatures was always at hand, it was a job, a source of income, and a chance of getting the translation published. This created favorable conditions for young translators who readily translated Soviet poetry from interlinear trots. Personal preferences of translators were not taken into consideration: beginners in the field of literary translation had little opportunity to write proposals, and therefore took every opportunity available. This, however, sometimes gave unexpectedly good results: young poets, open to new experiences and eager to get published, started close cooperation with authors of original texts. Most of the living authors had a decent command of the Russian language, and their personal wish to get their works translated into the politically dominating language of the country made them very cooperative with the translators. One of the examples is the close cooperation of translator Mikhail Yasnov with the famous Moldavian poet Paul Mihnea, who actually invited his translator to stay in his home in Chisinau for three weeks. Mihnea spoke decent Russian himself, and Yasnov was working with the interlinear trots consulting the author on the prosody and images at the same time.

In the 1980s, another translator, Viktor Andreyev, translated the poetry of Khaim Beider (1920–2003) who was one of the leading Soviet specialists in the Yiddish culture. Beider wrote poetry in Yiddish, too. Beider spoke perfect Russian but did not want to do his own poetic translations, which is why Beider hired Andreyev and provided him with interlinear trots, as well as detailed explanations of his poetry. Beider also read his poems aloud to Andreyev, so that the translator could get the feel of the metre and the sound structure.

As one can see, translation from interlinear trots, indeed, facilitated close cooperation of the peoples of the Soviet Union and strengthened friendly ties, as had initially been intended. It is also quite clear that interlinear trots were by nature target language oriented and the application of interlinear trots to translation was a domesticating practice. In some instances, Russian translations turned into free experimenting with the subject of the original. The widely supported opinion that the translation should become a reality of the target language culture endowed translators with greater authority. Translators were also encouraged by the general educational tendency of Soviet literature and the requirements of Socialist realism ("Ustav Soiuza Pisatelei", 712–3). This resulted in translations turning into literary variations. The general tendency was well described by the famous Russian poet Bella Akhmadulina (1937–2010), who translated from interlinear trots: "I never tried to conform to the formal features of the poem: meter, rhyming scheme – since the truth is that prosody differs with every language. Full of love and understanding towards the poems I was entrusted with, I wished only one thing – for them to become contemporary Russian poetry close to the contemporary Russian reader" (457).

This statement does not result purely from the sense of seeming impunity that the translator gets when working with interlinear trots; the experience described here is predetermined by the very essence of an interlinear trot, its mediating function, and the inability of the translator to make detached judgments regarding the text structure and its contents and, consequently, to decide independently upon the attachment of priorities and the translation strategy. This is vividly seen in the translations via interlinear trots done by the most celebrated and universally respected translators of the time. Let us, for example, take a look at the translation from Bulgarian made by Anna Akhmatova. Despite the close proximity of the Russian and Bulgarian languages, the poem of Elisaveta Bagryana *The Call* done via an interlinear trot underwent substantial semantic and structural transformation.

Bulgarian original (Багряна 1973)

Аз съм тук зад три врати заключена
и прозореца ми е с решетка,
а душата вълна, вълна птица в клетка,
е на слънце и простор научена.

Пролетни са ветровете полъхнали,
чувам гласове призивно ясни.
Моя плам непламнал ще угасне
в здрача на покоето заглъхнали.

Рзатроши ключалките ръждясали!
Дай ми път през тъмни коридори!
Не веднъж в огрените простори
моите крила са ме понасяли.

Tr. by Akhmatova (Багряна 1979, 27)

Здесь я замкнута, крепки засовы,
И в окне решетки черной прутья,
Ни запеть не в силах, ни вздохнуть я,
Ни в родной простор умчаться снова.

Как томятся в тесной клетке птицы,
Зов весенний слышу сердцем ясно,
Но огонь мой гаснет здесь напрасно
В душном сумраке глухой темницы

Так разбей замки – пора настала
Прочь уйти по темным коридорам.
Много раз по солнечным просторам
Я веселой птицей улетала.

И ще бликнат звукове ликуващи	Унесет меня поток певучий,
от сърцето трепетно тогава…	Что из сердца трепетного льется,
– Но зад тези три врати, сподавен,	Если до тебя он донесется…
моя пламнал зов дали дочуваш ти?[1]	– Слышишь из темницы зов мой жгучий?[2]

As we can see here, in her translation, Akhmatova introduced imagery different from that of the original. In the original, the focus is made on the image of the bird and the longing for freedom, in the Russian translation – on the bird suffering in captivity. Whereas in the first stanza the first and the second lines are mere statements and the other two are devoted to the memories of free life, in Akhmatova's translation the first two lines include extra characteristics of the cage, and the other two give a detailed description of the feelings of the captive. The omission of the mention of the tree doors here also destroys the closed-in structure of the poem, which in the original begins and ends with the mention of the tree doors. The second stanza of the translation introduces the word *call*, which is also the title of the poem. The word *call* in the translation is used in the sense *the spring call* which preempts the ending and, in fact, creates confusion: *the call* in the original is the call of the captive, the word itself is mentioned only once in the last line of the poem. In the translation there are, in fact, two calls that create an antithesis: there is a call of the spring and a call of the captive, that is, a call of freedom and the call of captivity.

---

1 Literal translation:
I am here locked behind three doors, / And my window is barred, / But my soul is a free, free bird in a cage / And it has been raised in the sun and the open space.
Spring winds have blown, / I hear voices invitingly clear, / My flame will go out unflamed, / Faded in the dusk of the quiet.
Destroy the rusty locks! / Give me the way through the dark corridors! / It was not once that to the lit up spaces / My wings took me.
And the joyous sounds will stream / Then from the thrilled heart. / – But from behind these three doors, smothered, / Will you hear my fervent call?

2 Literal translation:
I am locked here, heavy are the locks / And in the black window there are bars, / I have no power to sing, nor to sigh,/ Nor to fly away to the dear open space.
How the birds pine in the narrow cage,/ The spring call I hear clearly with my heart, / But my fire goes out here in vain / In the choky dusk of the blind cell.
So break the locks – it is time / To go away down the dark corridors. / Many times across sunlit spaces / I flew away a merry bird.
I shall be taken away by that canorous flow, / Which flows from a thrilled heart, / If it reaches you… / – Do you hear from the prison my burning call?

The third stanza of the translation sounds strikingly familiar to the Russian ear due to Akhmatova's accidental introduction of her own original imagery into translation. The phrase *the merry bird* is nowhere to be found in the original; however it is known to have been used by Akhmatova in one of her most famous and oft-quoted early works:

> And I buried my *merry*[3] bird
> Beyond the round well, near the ancient alder tree.
> (Akhmatova 1990a: 381)[4]

The adjective *merry (веселый)* is one of the favorite adjectives used by Akhmatova in sad and tragic contexts comparable to the context of Bagryana's poem (see, for instance, Akhmatova 1995, 15, 63, 71, 72, 88, 121, 202, 204, 212, 281, 353, 460, 524, 554, 560). This preference is obvious enough to have been well sensed by Akhmatova's translators who tend to observe a consistent usage of the adjective in their translations, like Judith Hemschemeyer in the translation quoted above and the following translations:

> I am cold… Winged or wingless,
> The *merry* god will not come to call. (Akhmatova 1990a, 217)[5]

> What fun to fan the *merry* wasps away
> From your green eyes. (Akhmatova 1990a, 323)[6]

> Forgive me, my *merry* boy,
> For bringing you death. (Akhmatova 1990a, 325)[7]

The use of interlinear trots, as we can see, led to active modifications of images and style of translated literary texts. The acceptance of translations from interlinear trots, however, was far from being universal. In 1963, a distinguished Russian scholar, translator, and literary critic Efim Etkind wrote that interlinear trots impeded both the transfer of creative expressivity of originals and the employment of creative abilities of translators (180–1). The result, in Etkind's view, was poor and unable to prove

---

3 Emphasis added.
4 И я закопала *веселую* птицу
  За круглым колодцем у старой ольхи. (Akhmatova 1995, 110)
5 Мне холодно… Крылатый иль бескрылый,
  Веселый бог не посетит меня. (Akhmatova 1995, 15)
6 Любо мне от глаз твоих зеленых
  Ос *веселых* отгонять. (Akhmatova 1995, 70)
7 Прости меня, мальчик *веселый*,
  Что я принесла тебе смерть. (Akhmatova 1995, 711)

credible to the reader. "Can one fall in love via an intermediate, get inspired with the help of an interlinear trot? It is counter-natural and unfeasible," argued Etkind (180).

Pointing out the usefulness of interlinear trots in establishment of cross-cultural contacts, the prominent Russian linguist and translation specialist Andrey Fedorov called the translation from interlinear trots "hybrid creativity", recognizing it as "individual creative work based on the impulse coming from the foreign source" (41). Fedorov thought it necessary that such translations should be marked as "free" or as "variations" to make the level of proximity to the original clear to the reader of the translation (42).

Despite the protests of leading translation specialists, domesticating practices prevailed in translations of poetry throughout the 20th century. Acceptance of translations made via interlinear trots was determined by literary, social, and political factors. Soviet publishing houses controlled the conformity of translations to clarity and other Socialist Realism requirements; the general reader wished translations to be clear and explicit. Driven by the necessity to provide for their living and to get published, the translators had to follow the dictated rules. As a result, many translations done via interlinear trots have survived until nowadays; they continue being quoted and admired by readers despite being at times very loosely connected with the originals.

Works Cited

Akhmadulina, Bella. "Stikhotvoreniye, podlezhashchee perevodu…" ["A poem to be translated…"] *Perevod – sredstvo vzaimnogo sblizheniya narodov.* Ed. A.A. Klyshko. Moscow: Progress, 1987. 456–9.

Akhmatova, Anna. *The Complete Poems of Anna Akhmatova. Vol. 1.* Trans. Judith Hemschemeyer. Ed. by Roberta Reeder. Somerville: Zephyr Press, 1990 (a).

—. "V to vremya ya gostila na zemle…" *Stikhotvoreniya. Poemy.* ["I was a guest on earth in those days…" *Poems.*] St. Petersburg: Lenizdat, 1995. Akhmatova, Anna. *Sochineniya v 2 tomakh. T.2. Proza, perevody.* [*Works in 2 volumes. Vol. 2. Prose, translations.*] Moscow: Panorama, 1990 (b).

Andreyev, Viktor, ed. *Romany magov.* [*Novels of magicians*]. St. Petersburg: Azbuka- klassika, 2004.

—. *Poezia magov.* [*Poetry of magicians*]. St. Petersburg: Azbuka-klassika, 2003.

Apollinaire, Guillaume. *Sobraniye sochinenii v 3 tomakh.* [*Collection of works in 3 volumes.*] Ed. Mikhail Yasnov. Moscow: Knizhnyi Klub Knigovek, 2011.

Bagryana, Elisaveta. *Amazonka. Izbrana lirika v dva toma.* [*Amazon. Selected poetry in two volumes.*] Sofia: Bylgarski pisatel, 1973. 10 July 2015 <http://www.slovo.bg/showwork.php3?AuID=183&WorkID=5356&Level=1> .

—. *Stikhi. [Poems]* Moscow: Khudozhestvennaya literatura, 1979.

Brodsky, Joseph. *V ozhidanii varvarov. Mirovaja pojezija v perevodah.[Awaiting the barbarians. World poetry in translations.]* St. Petersburg: Zvezda, 2001.

Brjusov, Valerij, ed. *Poeziya Armenii s drevneishikh vremen do nashikh dney. [Poetry of Armenia from the ancient times till now.]* Moscow: Moskovskiy armjanskiy komitet, 1916.

Cooper, David. "Vasilii Zhukovskii as translator and the protean Russian nation." *Contexts, subtexts, pretexts: literary translation in Eastern Europe and Russia.* Ed. Brian J. Baer. Amsterdam, Philadelphia: John Benjamins, 2011. 55–77.

Etkind, Efim. *Poesia i perevod. [Poetry and translation.]* Moscow-Leningrad: Sovetskii pisatel', 1963.

Fedorov, Andrey. *Iskusstvo perevoda i zhizn' literatury. [Art of translation and life of literature.]* Leningrad: Sovetskii pisatel', 1983.

Gorky, Maxim."Vsemirnaya literatura." ["World literature."] *Perevod – sredstvo vzaimnogo sblizheniya narodov: Hudozhestvennaya publitsistika.* Ed. Anatoliy A. Klyshko. Moscow: Progress, 1987. 85–6.

Márquez, Gabriel García. *More ischezaiushchikh vremen. [A sea of disappearing times.]* Ed. Viktor Andreyev. St. Petersburg: Azbuka-klassika, 2007.

Naiman, Anatoliy. *Rasskazy o Anne Akhmatovoi. [Tales of Anna Akhmatova.]* Moscow: ACT: Zebra E, 2008.

Rodenbach, Georges. "Stikhi." ["Poems."] Trans. Mikhail Yasnov. *Inostrannaya literatura* 11 (2011): 221–7.

Rossels, Vladimir. *Skolko vesit slovo. [How much the word weighs.]* Moscow: Sovetskii pisatel', 1984.

Tse-tung, Mao. *Vosemnadtsat' stihotvoreniy. [Eighteen poems.]* Moscow: Pravda, 1957.

Tsvetaeva, Marina. *Stikhotvoreniya i pojemy: V 5 tomakh. T. 3: Stihotvoreniya. Perevody. 1922–1941. [Poems: In 5 volumes. Vol. 3: Poems. Translations. 1922–1941.]* New York: Russica Publishers, 1983.

"Ustav Soiuza Sovetskikh Pisatelei SSSR." ["Regulations of the Union of the Soviet Writers of the USSR."] *Pervyi Vsesojuznyi Syezd Sovetskikh Pisatelei 1934: Stenographicheskii otchet.* Moscow: Khudozhestvennaya literatura, 1934. 712–4.

Uvarov, Viktor. "Paradoxy rolevogo povedeniya uchastnikov situatsii perevoda." ["Paradoxes of role behavior of the participants of a translation situation."] *Tetradi perevodchika* 18 (1981):13–5.

Witkowsky, Evgeniy, ed. *Sem' vekov angliiskoi poezii. Anglia. Shotlandia. Irlandia. Wales. V trekh tomakh. [Seven centuries of English poetry. England. Scotland. Ireland. Wales. In three volumes.]* Moscow: Vodoley Publishers, 2007.

—. *Vek perevoda: Antologiya russkogo poeticheskogo perevoda XXI veka.* *[A century of translation: Anthology of the Russian poetic translation of the 21 century.]* Moscow: Vodoley Publishers, 2006.

—. *Vek perevoda: Antologiya russkogo poeticheskogo perevoda XXI veka. Vtoroye desyatiletiye.* *[A century of translation: Anthology of the Russian poetic translation of the 21 century. Second decade.]* Moscow: Vodoley Publishers, 2012.

Yasnov, Mihkail, ed. *Proklyatye poety.* *[Les poètes maudits.]* St. Petersburg: Nauka, 2005.

Hanna C. Rückl

Imitation and Creativity: Ernst Jandl's Writing in Translation and Completion

Abstract: Translation and creative writing share several similarities. This is demonstrated by comparing English translations of poems by Ernst Jandl with completions of unfinished Jandl texts. The work considered was written by translators and completers who are also poets. The translators' agency is highlighted by the creativity that is necessary in literary translation as well as the socially constructed authority that author-translators have. The translations are not imitative, but products of creativity.

Keywords: literary translation, creative writing, concrete poetry, author-translator, postmodernism

Ernst Jandl's experimental poetry has been deemed untranslatable. This paper argues in favor of translatability. Any poem can be translated if the translator rewrites the poem in another language while taking certain constraints, which vary from source text to source text, into consideration. Translation is a creative act. More specifically, this paper deals with the translation and the completion of experimental poetry in the realm of creative writing. There are several similarities that translations and completions share. Due to these shared similarities, terms such as "source text" and "target language," taken from translation studies, are also applied to completions throughout this paper.

Two volumes connected to Ernst Jandl are at the center of this study. The first includes translations of poems by Ernst Jandl which were done by American poets; the other book contains poems which were created by poets who took unfinished Ernst Jandl poems as their starting point. As a consequence, this paper deals exclusively with the work of translators and completers who are also poets, and who may thus be called author-translators. The creativity that is necessary in literary translation, as well as the socially constructed authority that author-translators have, highlight the translators' agency. Instead of characterizing translations as imitative they are recognized as products of creativity.

Austrian experimental poet Ernst Jandl (1925–2000) was one of the most important twentieth century writers in the German language. It has been observed that "[d]espite his radical avantgardism, he enjoys a mainstream popularity rivaled only by the most traditional of German-speaking poets" (Stuckatz, 31). Jandl also functioned as a translator, translating, among other works from English, lectures by Gertrude Stein (Ernst, 285).

Jandl, who wrote concrete poems, defined concrete poetry as "poetry that uses the elements of language. The concrete poem is an object, not a statement about an object. In concrete poetry, the word appears mostly in isolation, the single word encounters another single word" (Ernst, 66, translation mine). Jandl refers to an aestheticization of language when speaking of isolated words. An example of aestheticized everyday language is the use of lists in poems:

> Die Liste, deren praktischer Nutzen noch dazu ihr prominentestes Merkmal ist, gehört zu einer kleinen Gruppe von literarischen Formen, die direkt aus dem Alltag übernommen sind. … Dadurch, dass die KP [Konkrete Poesie] das Montierte oder Zitierte adoptiert, verschiebt sich der Fokus von der ursprünglichen, konventionellen Funktion der jeweiligen Form, einer referentiell und pragmatisch mit der „Wirklichkeit" in Kontakt tretenden, zu einem Blick von außen auf das Funktionieren selbst. (Cotten, 50)

Concrete poetry is poetry that tends to be non-mimetic. However, the extent of it being different from conventional mimetic poetry varies in degree (Cotten, 35–36). It is a kind of poetry that is an example of the sort of text which, to a great extent, makes readers part of the texts' production due to language being used in new ways and not as a mere transmitter of information. This feature of concrete poetry has its origin in the countering of the Third Reich's ideological appropriation and misuse of language (Ernst, 276–277). One vivid example of such a use of language is sound poetry. Sound poems need to be read out loud. Therefore, readers play an active role in creating poems by using their voice. Jandl wrote many such *Lautgedichte* that put the focus on sound.

Clearly, a concrete poem is postmodern in the sense that it tends to refer to itself, to the material it is made of, rather than anything outside of it. Naturally, this produces certain constraints when translating a concrete poem. These constraints are different from those that have to be dealt with when translating other kinds of literature.

Let us now turn to the material examined. In 1973, Ernst Jandl designated a number of fragmentary poems which he had begun to write but never finished as "gedichte zum fertigstellen," i.e. poems to be completed. He intended to give these incomplete poems to the public, urging readers of poetry, who wanted to do more than just receive poetry, to become writers. The reader-turned-completer should in consequence try to publish his/her poem in order to assess its quality. In the case of publication the poem should be acknowledged as having its origins in a Jandl fragment. Jandl is equally clear on the subject of copyright – it lies solely with the completer. The completer is the author and his/her name should come before Jandl's. If other poets want to use Jandl's idea of having other people use their unfinished material, they should acknowledge that they are doing this "nach dem muster der 'gedichte zum fertigstellen' von ernst jandl" (Jandl 2010, 124).

Contrary to Jandl's intention, the only people publicly known to have produced completions were professional poets, not dilettantes. This occurred in 2010 when the editors of the exhibition catalog of *Die Ernst Jandl Show*, Bernhard Fetz and Hannes Schweiger, asked a number of contemporary authors to create poetry from some of the fragmentary poems. *Die Ernst Jandl Show* is the title of an exhibition that took place at the *Wien Museum* in Vienna (2010/2011) and at the *Literaturhaus* in Berlin (2011). According to the catalog, the manuscripts in which Jandl describes his idea of letting other people finish writing poems begun by him, as well as the unfinished poems themselves, were taken from Jandl's literary estate. Jandl's outline of his idea, the fragments that were used by the poets, and the completed poems are a part of the book. It is therefore possible to compare the poem pending completion with the completed poem. It is worth noting that one and the same unfinished poem was sometimes used by more than one poet.

The second group of poems that are the subject of this paper consists of Jandl poems and their English translations. These poems are part of the collection *reft and light* (2000), which is part of a translation series edited by Rosmarie Waldrop. The first section of said volume contains poems by Jandl in German as well as their English translations created by a number of American poets.

Comparing the two books, one can observe several correspondences between completing and translating, based on the poems in the exhibition catalog, which are the completed poems, and those in *reft and light*, which are the translations:

1. The contemporary poet who was asked by the editors to complete a poem and did so is equivalent to the American author-translator.
2. In both books Jandl is the creator of the source texts, i.e. the unfinished poems and the German poems.
3. A poem pending completion is equivalent to the source text of a translation.
4. Several people being completers of the same fragment is equivalent to several translators translating the same poem individually.
5. Both the catalog and the collection of poetry provide the reader with Jandl's poems and his unfinished poems, respectively, not just the poems produced by poets other than Jandl. Due to this, the reader has easy access to the source as well as the product. This shows that there are similarities between the two books in terms of the presentation of these poems.
6. The process of completing is equivalent to translating. Both are creative processes.

This last point makes it necessary to go into detail concerning the creative turn in translation studies, which Perteghella & Loffredo describe as having occurred due to "the significance increasingly bestowed upon the creativity inherent in rewritings, such as literary translation, and upon the mental processes occurring during these rewritings" (2). They also remark on the emphasis that is put on the translator's agency in the framework of translating being a creative activity.

In light of this, creative writing and translating are to be seen as similar activities placed at different points on a continuum, a view likewise described by Lin (97). Creative writing and translating do not stand in opposition to each other, as if the one were the creation of original art and the other the copying of an original. Rather, translations are texts in their own right.

The collection *reft and light* is part of a book series containing "current German writing in English translation" (Jandl 2000, no p.). In view of this reference to translation, let us take a look at the editor's note, which is noteworthy for its remark on translatability:

> Most of Ernst Jandl's poems are so engrained in the German language that they are impossible to translate. But their procedures can be imitated. Here is an experiment: several American poets respond to each poem so that the original is encircled by multiple English analogues. The responses (which range from close imitations to freewheeling versions that continue Jandl's thinking into other semantic areas) form the first part of this book. The version that seems closest to Jandl's text is usually the first to follow the German. ... (Waldrop, no p.)

I disagree with the verdict that Jandl's poems are "impossible to translate." I contend that any time one is able to identify a system in a text, one can try to recreate the same system in another language. Regarding experimental poetry such as Ernst Jandl's, one must remember that the focus tends to be on the language material. Instead of calling it an imitation of procedure, I call it translation. I agree with Xavier Lin, who writes:

> the complexity and difficulty resulting from the incommensurability between any two languages or two cultures also render poetry translation more than just an activity of choice-making. The gaps emerging from this incommensurability will have to be bridged by what the translator draws out of his/her own creativity. ... poetry translation should not be reduced to or thought of as an activity of mere replacement, but it becomes one of recreation. (97)

The translators of *reft and light* use their creativity and interpretation in order to produce translations rather than imitate anything. The term 'recreation' is preferable to 'imitation' as the former gives more agency to the translator. The translators' agency is further acknowledged due to their visibility, as their names appear below each of their poems and are listed on the back of the book.

The editor's note also points out that *reft and light* contains several translations of each poem and not just one. The poems are arranged in such a way that the source text precedes the translations. It is rather unconventional for a translated work to offer multiple translations. The inclusion of more than one translation exposes the possibility of numerous translations of a single source text and shows the creative potential the source poem has, making each translation no less authentic than the next. The authenticity of each poem is strengthened by the fact that the translators are *bona fide* poets. Each translation is different; all are connected to the same source, i.e. a Jandl poem.

We have seen that completion and translation are very similar. The significant difference lies in whether the source text is considered complete or incomplete. This difference, which in this case depends on Jandl, the author of the source texts, who categorized his texts thus, has little or no impact on the outcome of the creative processes of translating and completing. All completions and translations are analyzable poems.

We can find information on how Jandl defined a completed poem in his poetic manifesto *Die schöne Kunst des Schreibens*, where he describes what a poem is in the following way:

> Ein Gedicht ist ein Ganzes, das aus Teilen besteht, die jeder für sich ein Ganzes sind, das aus Teilen besteht, die jeder für sich ein Ganzes sind. Ich spreche natürlich von einem Gedicht, das aus Wörtern besteht, die ein Ganzes sind das aus Teilen besteht die ein Ganzes sind.[1] (Jandl 1995, 75)

And on the nature of finished poems Jandl states:

> Es ist ein Ganzes, sobald es für den Autor fertig ist, seine Arbeit daran abgeschlossen, was in dem Augenblick geschieht, wenn er erkennt, daß er daran keine verbessernden Änderungen mehr vornehmen kann, bzw. wenn er erkennt, daß er daran überhaupt keine Veränderungen vornehmen kann.[2] (Jandl 1995, 78)

According to Jandl, poems are complete entities and it is the writer who decides when a poem has been completed. In the description of his idea to give fragments to the public so that others could create poetry from them, Jandl states that none of the fragments were meant to become "poems pending completion" by design. He does not say why he was unable to finish them, only that the reasons were manifold.

---

1   A poem is an entity that is composed of parts, each of which is an entity consisting of parts. I am of course speaking of a poem which consists of words, which are entities that consist of parts which are entities [translation HR].

2   A poem is completed as soon as the author is done with it, which happens when the author cannot make any improvements or any changes at all [translation HR].

To illustrate my point of a translation being a poem in its own right, I have selected the list poem "reihe" by Ernst Jandl and two translations of it, one by Benjamin Friedlander and one by Julie Patton. (All in all, *reft and light* contains seven translations of this poem.)

> reihe
>
> eis
> zweig
> dreist
> vieh
> füllf
> ächz
> silben
> ... (Jandl 2000, 19)

The poem "reihe" consists of a list of ten words that are similar to the numbers one through ten, going from lowest to highest. All the words are German words. The words are similar to the German numerical terms insofar as they are composed of the same letters or sounds as the words for one, two, three, etc., but acts of addition, deletion, and substitution have transformed them. Spelling is also an issue. The word in the sixth line of the poem, "ächz" (for 'sechs'), exposes that German orthography is not consistently logical. From the perspective of sound and pronunciation there is no need for both the letter 'ä' and the letter 'e', since they sound the same. By using these two different ways of spelling the same sound, the poem exposes a certain inconsistency within German orthography. As we can see, the poem works on the level of letters and sounds. The words in the poem resemble the number terms in form and not in meaning. This poem clearly points to the material it is made of. It is a poem that makes apparent how crucial the reader's capacity to interpret is and how necessary the reader is for creating meaning and creating the text.

Turning to the translations, it is striking that three translations of "reihe" have the same title, which is "series." The words in these three poems are English words and resemble the English terms for the numbers one through ten. Benjamin Friedlander's poem does the same thing as Jandl's, which is making the reader aware of the fact that it is an object made of language.

> series
>
> wan
> too
> tree
> fur
> fife

sics
severance
… (Friedlander, 20)

In this poem we can identify exchanges of sounds in the word "tree" for 'three' and "fur" for 'four.' The word "too" in line two is a homophone of the number two. "[A]te" spelled in this way likewise is a homophone of the number eight, at least in American English. All words in this poem need to be seen as English except for the word "nein," which is German and is best pronounced as German. This use of German can be seen as a reference to the source language.

Whereas Friedlander's and others' translations recreate Jandl's poem with mostly English words resembling other English words, Julie Patton's translation uses English words to recreate the sound of German words. To achieve this effect one has to connect the sounds across word boundaries and speak with a French accent. The result is a poem that is composed of English words that need to be pronounced in a French way so that it will sound like German. This translation takes pointing to language as material a step further and does not only do that but also points to three different languages.

hind
size
wire
fear
fund
sexy
bent
… (Patton, 21)

Depending on how the poem works, certain things are required in the translation. Jandl's poems in *reft and light* are characterized by self-referentiality, an emphasis on the shape and the arrangement of words on the page, as well as the relationship of sound and sign. The constraints for the translator are on the level of form, sound, and orthography, less so on the level of meaning. An analysis of the translations shows that a number of brilliant poems can be created through translation. Also, translation can involve more than just one target language.

Part of the definition of translation is that the target language is different from the source language. Regarding completion, however, one would assume that the incomplete poems would be perfected in German, the source language. Interestingly, this is not always the case. *Die Ernst Jandl Show* includes work by two poets, Brigitta Falkner and Yoko Tawada, who completed fragments employing another language or code besides German.

The poem pending completion by Jandl titled "gruppen" (2010, 128) consists of a list of German words ending in -tik, such as "taktik," "nautik," "gotik," "erotik," etc. Each of these words is followed by -tak, making tik/ tak a recurring item throughout the list. Falkner and Tawada both created poems from this fragment. Brigitta Falkner's poem "poe / tik / tak" (128) takes the last three lines from Jandl's text, which can be found right next to Falkner's on the same page, and converts them into its title. The words in the poem are placed in a similar fashion to Jandl's text. Apart from words, the poem also includes pictograms of bombs as well as a series of black-and-white photos depicting the collapse of a tower being bombed. The pictograms, which are iconic signs, and the photos are signifiers of another code besides languages. This other code is exclusively visual.

Yoko Tawada's poem completions (129) stand out from the others since they use Japanese characters in addition to the Latin script. Explanations are given in German in order to make the ideograms' meanings known to anybody who does not know Japanese. These completions using a language other than German connects them closely to translation, as using a language different from the source language is a defining characteristic of translation. Language clearly cannot serve as a distinguishing factor between translation and completion. Rather, the use of a different target language constitutes a striking similarity between some completions and translation.

Turning to other completions, we find that the source text is – at least partially – part of the target text *verbatim*. This is the case to a larger or lesser extent in all completed poems. Taking the poems "mundfauler staub" (Rautenberg, 131) and "kleidungen" (Rautenberg, 132) by Arne Rautenberg as examples, the former is a poem incorporating very little of the source text, whereas the latter has the source text figure as a strong backbone. In all completed poems Jandl's writing is discernible but only due to it being available to the recipient on the same or facing page. If we did not know that a part of the poem was by Jandl, we would think it was all Rautenberg.

The poems pending completion, i.e. the source texts in *Die Ernst Jandl Show*, look like poems. The only reason we know that they are fragmentary is because Jandl designated them as such. This is an example of the author having power over his creation. The author did not, however, have any power over the decision of who the completers of his unfinished poetry would be (several years after his death). Contrary to his wish, the people whose completed poems are contained in the book *Die Ernst Jandl Show* are not, as noted before, mere readers of poetry, the kind of people Jandl originally had in mind; rather, they are established poets, people who have created poetry in the past. The fact that accomplished poets are the completers makes each of the poems authentic. Regarding authenticity, the same can be said about the 30 American author-translators of *reft and light*, among them such prominent poets as Anselm Hollo and Charles Bernstein, and their work.

In conclusion, I first of all contend that it is possible to translate Ernst Jandl's poems. Further, each translation is an independent work of art and in no way inferior to the source text. Each translation affords creativity on the part of the translator. Recognizing the creativity that is inherent to literary translation emphasizes the translators' agency. In the case of author-translators, which the translators of Jandl's poems are, their status as established poets adds to the poems' authenticity.

The completions of incomplete poems that Jandl had started are poems that share resemblances with the translations. Both translation and completion use source texts that pose various constraints to the poet. The translations of Jandl's poetry are tied to form and – to a lesser extent – meaning, as well as other defining characteristics, such as self-referentiality or sound. Most poems were completed solely in German, but not all. Using a language or code different from the source language is not a defining category for translation only; it can also be part of the creative writing activity of completion.

In terms of presentation, both books have a similar way of presenting the source texts and target texts. The reader has access to the source texts as well as the numerous target texts. One way in which a completed poem can be distinguished from a translation theoretically is its incomplete source text. This comparison involving the source texts by Ernst Jandl, their translations, and their completions demonstrate the close affinity between translation and creative writing. Thinking of translation as a creative process, we can add to the afore-mentioned writing continuum the specific creative writing form of "completing fragments."

Works Cited

Cotten, Ann. *Nach der Welt: Die Listen der konkreten Poesie und ihre Folgen*. Vienna: Klever, 2008.

Ernst, Ulrich. *Konkrete Poesie: Innovation und Tradition*. Wuppertaler Broschüren zur Allgemeinen Literaturwissenschaft. Nr. 5. Wuppertal: Bergische Universität – Gesamthochschule Wuppertal, 1991.

Falkner, Brigitta. "poe / tik / tak." *Die Ernst Jandl Show*. Ed. Bernhard Fetz and Hannes Schweiger. St. Pölten: Residenz, 2010. 128.

Fetz, Bernhard and Hannes Schweiger, eds. *Die Ernst Jandl Show*. St. Pölten: Residenz, 2010.

Friedlander, Benjamin. "series". *reft and light: Poems by Ernst Jandl with Multiple Versions by American Poets*. DICHTEN = 4. Ernst Jandl. Providence: Burning Deck, 2000. 20.

Jandl, Ernst. *Die schöne Kunst des Schreibens*. München: Luchterhand, 1995.

—. *reft and light: Poems by Ernst Jandl with Multiple Versions by American Poets*. DICHTEN = 4. Providence: Burning Deck, 2000.

—. "reihe". *reft and light: Poems by Ernst Jandl with Multiple Versions by American Poets*. DICHTEN = 4. Providence: Burning Deck, 2000. 19.

—. "gedichte zum fertigstellen." *Die Ernst Jandl Show*. Ed. Bernhard Fetz and Hannes Schweiger. St. Pölten: Residenz, 2010. 124–125.

—. "gruppen". *Die Ernst Jandl Show*. Ed. Bernhard Fetz and Hannes Schweiger. St. Pölten: Residenz, 2010. 128.

Lin, Xavier. "Creative translation, translating creatively: a case study on aesthetic coherence in Peter Stambler's Han Shan." *Translation and Creativity: Perspectives on Creative Writing and Translation Studies*. Ed. Manuela Perteghella and Eugenia Loffredo. London: Continuum, 2006. 97–108.

Patton, Julie. [hind]. *reft and light: Poems by Ernst Jandl with Multiple Versions by American Poets*. DICHTEN = 4. Ernst Jandl. Providence: Burning Deck, 2000. 21.

Perteghella, Manuela & Eugenia Loffredo. "Introduction". *Translation and Creativity: Perspectives on Creative Writing and Translation Studies*. London: Continuum, 2006. 1–16.

Rautenberg, Arne. "mundfauler staub." *Die Ernst Jandl Show*. Ed. Bernhard Fetz and Hannes Schweiger. St. Pölten: Residenz, 2010. 131.

—. "kleidungen." *Die Ernst Jandl Show*. Ed. Bernhard Fetz and Hannes Schweiger. St. Pölten: Residenz, 2010. 132.

Stuckatz, Katja. "Atemschrift: Ernst Jandl's Experimental Poetics of Affirmation." *Journal of Austrian Studies* 45. 1–2 (2012): 31–49.

Tawada, Yoko. "lärmmusikmaschine." *Die Ernst Jandl Show*. Ed. Bernhard Fetz and Hannes Schweiger. St. Pölten: Residenz, 2010. 129.

—. "taktiktak." *Die Ernst Jandl Show*. Ed. Bernhard Fetz and Hannes Schweiger. St. Pölten: Residenz, 2010. 129.

Waldrop, Rosmarie. "Editor's note." *reft and light: Poems by Ernst Jandl with Multiple Versions by American Poets*. DICHTEN = 4. Ernst Jandl. Providence: Burning Deck, 2000. No p.

Joanna Gładyga

The Birth of the Editor: On Authenticity in Raymond Carver's Writing and Editing

Abstract: Raymond Carver's literary career was significantly influenced by his editor, Gordon Lish. One can, in fact, state that it was Lish who created Carver's minimalistic style. Does such an extensive intrusion leave room for authenticity? And is it authenticity that makes an author unique? These questions continue to be relevant in the context of artistic and cultural practice.

Keywords: editor, authenticity, minimalism

Authenticity has long been seen as a crucial issue in all art forms. Plagiarism, feigning and forgery are not only illegal but perceived morally inadmissible. Thus, the need for genuineness grew to be the virtue of art genres, and literature is not an exception in this respect. It is then essential to raise the question of whether a writer is the authentic creator of their literary work. The process of creating a literary work does not consist solely in authors preparing their manuscripts. The subsequent work of editing is frequently of great consequence too. In this article I intend to analyze the course of Raymond Carver's career and, if possible, its authenticity. I wish to concentrate mostly on the writer's cooperation with his editor Gordon Lish, whose extended editorial changes into the manuscripts were at some occasions compared to ghostwriting rather than editing. I will also use the classic text by Roland Barthes "The Death of the Author" as an attempt at defining who or what the authentic creator of Carver's writing was.

Raymond Carver started his career writing poetry, yet it was short stories that brought him fame and recognition. Soon after publishing his first short stories collection, "Will You Please Be Quite, Please" in 1976, Carver was declared a great minimalist. Both literary critics and readers praised his style, whose main feature was economy on words. However, not many knew at that time that Carver's writing was strongly influenced by his editor, Gordon Lish. Only many years later it turned out that the amount of changes Lish introduced in Carver's stories was enormous (Max). What seemed to be specific for the writer's style was actually Lish's invention. He deleted not only words but full paragraphs, changing the endings or main character's behavior. Lish replaced the names of characters with simple, characterless pronouns like *he, she*.

Carver's relation with his editor was not strictly professional. The friendship between the two men developed simultaneously with their business cooperation. Yet, reading the letters written by Carver to Gordon Lish, one can notice how self-conscious and dependent on the editor the writer was. This might have been caused by the fact that from the beginning of his career in the early 1970s Carver was tortured by his addiction to alcohol. The problems in his personal life intermingled with difficulties to find a publisher for his writing. It was Gordon Lish who first showed the genuine interest in placing Carver's stories in *Esquire* magazine where the editor worked. Lish also enabled Carver to print his first book form collection (Sklenicka, 272) Lured by the opportunity to have his works published Carver accepted extensive changes imposed by Lish.

As Carver regained his sobriety and met Tess Gallagher, who later became his second wife, he wished to become more independent in his writing. It was not effortless, though, to persuade Lish into letting the writer make his own decisions about the final look of his stories. Just before publishing the collection "What We Talk About When We Talk About Love" Raymond Carver accepted Lish's first edition of the stories. Having received the second edition from Lish, Carver signed the contract for publishing the collection without reading its final version. Only later did he discover that the range of changes was incredibly wide. In his letter to the editor Carver literally begged Lish to keep at least some of the stories in their original versions. At the same time the writer made numerous apologies to his editor. „Please help me with this, Gordon. I feel as if this is the most important decision I've ever been faced with . . . I ask for your understanding. . . . I don't want to lose your love or regard over this, oh God no. It would be like having a part of myself die, a spiritual part," Carver wrote (Stull, and Carroll, 991–996).

Despite Carver's initial determination to prevent the publication of the collection in the form suggested by Lish, "What We Talk About When We Talk About Love" was finally released in the version which was "lishified", to use the words of Daniel Bourne (Bourne). The title story was the result of Lish cutting by 50% the 33-page manuscript called "Beginners". Some of the other stories included in the collection were: "Mr. Coffee and Mr. Fixit." which was the result of cutting the 15-page manuscript titled "Where Is Everyone?" by 78%; "I Could See the Smallest Thing" as a cut by 56% form of the 11-page manuscript "Want To See Something?" and "So Much Water So Close To Home" – the effect of cutting by 70% the 27-page manuscript of the same title (Stull, and Carroll, 999–1003). It was only after Carver's death when all the original manuscripts of his short stories were published thanks to immense engagement of Tess Gallagher.

One might wonder if the job performed by Gordon Lish consisted in editing or ghostwriting. In one of his emotional letters to the editor Carver wrote: "Please help me with this book as a good editor, the best… but not as my ghost" ("Letters to an Editor"). While preparing the texts for his next collection "Cathedral" Carver was determined again to regain the control over the final look of his writing. In the letter of August 11th 1982 Carver stated, "I can't undergo the kind of surgical amputation and transplant…" ("Letters…"). The comparison of what happened with Carver's earlier writing due to Lish's editorial work to amputation and transplant proves how painful the writer felt with what *his* stories became.

In the end "Cathedral", published in 1983, was written with very little help from Gordon Lish. Yet, it was highly praised and acclaimed by many Carver's best publication. The stories in the collection were fuller, more descriptive and more optimistic. However, what was perceived by critics as the writer's new, more expansive style was, in fact, his "old" style, only not revealed before, because of the editor's minimalistic preferences. Moreover, Carver included in the collection his early story "A Small, Good Thing" which cut by 70% and renamed "The Bath" by Lish was published many years earlier.

The extent of Lish interference into Carver's text can be seen below:

"A Small, Good Thing"
"How is he?" Howard said. "What's all this?" waving at the glucose and the tube.
"Dr. Francis orders," she said. "He needs nourishment. Dr. Francis said he needs to keep his strength. Why doesn't he wake up, Howard?" she said. "I don't understand, if he's all right."
Howard put his hand at the back of her head and ran his fingers through the hair.
"He's going to be all right, honey. He'll wake up in a little while. Dr. Francis knows what's what."
In a little while he said, "Maybe you should go home and get a little rest for yourself. I'll stay here. Just don't put up with this creep who keeps calling. Hang up right away."
"Who's calling?" she asked.
"I don't know who, just somebody with nothing better to do than call up people. You go ahead now."

"She shook her head. "No," she said, "I'm fine."
"Really," he said. "Go home for a while, if you want, and then come back and spell me in the morning. It'll be all right. What did Dr. Francis say? He said Scotty's going to be all right. We don't have to worry. He's just sleeping now, that's all." (Carver 807)

"The Bath"
"What's this?" the father said.
"Glucose," the mother said.
The husband put his hand to the back of the woman's head.
"He's going to wake up," the man said.
In a little while the man said, "Go and let me take over."
She shook her head. "No," she said.
"Really," he said. "Go home for a while. You don't have to worry. He's sleeping, is all." (Carver 253)

"A Small, Good Thing" tells a story of a boy called Scotty, who on a day of his birthday has an accident in consequence of which he cannot regain his consciousness. Scotty's birthday party must be cancelled and his devastated parents, Ann and Howard wait at the hospital bed. They only leave the hospital to have quick baths at home where they are tortured by harassing phone calls. A baker reminds them that a birthday cake ordered for Scotty was prepared but never picked up. Soon the boy dies from what the doctors call "hidden occlusion" which is "one-in-a-million circumstance" (Carver, 823). Since Ann and Howard receive another phone call from the baker they decide to visit him. Having heard what happened to the boy, the baker apologizes for his behavior and asks for forgiveness explaining that he is only an exhausted worker trying to earn the living. The final scene of the story resembles almost biblical reconciliation, as the couple treated with fresh bread "ate what they could. . . . talked on into the early morning . . . and did not think of leaving" (Carver, 830). Jerzy Jarniewicz even compared the baker to Jesus Christ sharing the bread and stated that the closure of the story is nearly "evangelic". According to Jarniewicz, ending the story with *the good* is natural, and this is what the whole piece of writing leads to (299).

Lish's version of the story, "The Bath", does not finish in the same way, though. Instead of the sacred harmony, the parents answer another phone call only to hear: "Scotty. It is about Scotty. It has to do with Scotty, yes." (Carver, 257). Even though the boy dies only in the manuscript version, it is "The Bath" which maintains more pessimistic atmosphere. What strikes in Lish's version is not simply economizing on words, but also the lack of emotions. Moreover, from the very beginning till the end it is the feeling of threat that dominates. As Miriam Marty Clark commented on the story, "the threat never gives way to a good talk, good things" (241). In Carver's story, though, the good thing is announced in the very title. The title invented by Lish, on the other hand, has a connotation with fear. The narrator of the text says, "Fear made him want a bath". Yet, these words cannot be found in the original text, as it was also Lish who introduced them into the story. Fear remains present till the very last words of the story.

The example of "A Small, Good Thing" and "The Bath" proves that Carver's style was significantly different from the one Lish created for him. After Carver's death Tess Gallagher engaged in attempts to show the readers how distinguished a writer he was, regardless of Lish's intervention. When asked about her attempts to publish Carver's manuscript versions, Gallagher once said: "I'm just looking forward to the time when some wonderful reader doesn't rush up to me and say, 'Did Gordon Lish write all of Raymond Carver's stories?'" (qtd. in Rich).

Who then is the authentic creator of "Carver's" short stories? In his essay "The Death of the Author" Roland Barthes used the words uttered by Balzac's Sarrasine about a castrato: "it was a woman, with her sudden fears, her irrational whims, her instinctive fears, her unprovoked bravado, her daring and her delicious delicacy of feeling" (qtd. in Barthes, 2). Barthes then speculates about the producer of this utterance. Is it the story hero? The man Balzac? The author Balzac? A universal voice of wisdom? Very similar questions could also be raised concerning the voice speaking in Carver's writing. Who is the voice in his writing? Is it the alcohol addict Carver? Is it the sober man Carver? Is it his editor? Is it his ghost or a ghostwriter? Is it his wife Tess Gallagher being his inspiration? Is it his life experience or inexperience? To use the answer suggested by Barthes: "it will always be impossible to know" as "all writing is itself this special voice, consisting of several indiscernible voices" (2).

In fact, in the web of voices tangled in Carver's writing, it is truly difficult to praise one as the solely causative. However, in this labyrinth of the ghostly voices, Lish's seems to be dominating. It is Lish who decides whether to let the characters speak or not, the latter one being more frequent choice. It is also Lish who deprives protagonists of their names and does not allow for any display of their emotions. It is finally Lish again who chooses how a piece of writing shall end.

In his work Barthes also states that "literature is the trap where all identity is lost, beginning with the very identity of the body that writes" (2). In Carver's writing the situation is more complicated as one might in fact state that there were two bodies that wrote. Thus, the necessity to "lose" the identity turns out to be even of a greater importance. The two identities, Carver's and Lish's, appear to be so closely integrated that "losing" them may be the only method to benefit from the reading itself.

Barthes argues that the absence of the Author is a historical fact, yet it also changes the text. We – the readers – used to perceive the author "conceived as the past of his book". If we accept the Author as true "he is supposed to feed the book, he pre-exists it, he thinks, suffers, lives for it, maintains the same relation of antecedence a father maintains with his child". However, this idea is no longer valid. Barthes argues that:

> time is no longer the same . . . , the modern writer is born simultaneously with his text; he is no way supplied with a being which precedes or transcends his writing, he is no way the subject of which his book is the predicate; there is no other time than the time of utterance. (4)

What Barthes claims seems particularly accurate as far as Carver's literary career is concerned. Time truly is no longer the same. The first short stories Carver wrote were, in fact, rewritten by Lish and published receiving acclaim. When, already sober, he later decided to terminate the cooperation with Gordon Lish, write in his own (no longer minimalistic) manner and even publish some of his original versions of "lishified" stories, the public got the situation wrong. Readers and critics had the feeling that Carver's sobriety not only made him rewrite some of his old minimalistic and gloomy stories to give them more positive tone. It was also believed that the abstinence resulted in Carver's writing the new stories in a "fuller" style. However, it is known now that if his sobriety had some influence, it was the courage to reveal his own *old* style, not the inspiration to create in a new manner. It is essential to keep in mind that Carver had already gained the status of a distinguished writer when he published "Cathedral". One may only wonder whether the collection would have received such positive acclaim without author's earlier success. But not only the very chronological order of writer's and text's birth (or rebirth) should be questioned here. As Barthes talks about "antecedence a father maintains with a child" it can also be considered who this early writing should be affiliated with. Is it Carver or Lish who holds the pride of paternity?

Referring to the question concerning Balzac's sentence, Barthes finally gives the answer: "no one utters it: its source, its voice is not to be located: and yet it is perfectly read; this is because the true locus of writing is reading" (5). Let us then look back again at Carver's history. If writing, in fact, is about reading, then no matter who the "authentic" creator of these short stories is, there are those who read them, there is , (to use Barthes' word) a destination. And masses of Carver's readers constitute this destination. Yet, it is vital to note that Carver's readers differ. For some the feeling of "real" Carver is to read his minimalistic stories. Carver is perfect; they would say, and the only real Carver is the economist of words. However, one could also hear the voices stating the opposite opinion, the opinion that Carver's genuine talent was only revealed along with publishing "Cathedral" – a collection of his *own* stories.

Finally, there are also those loving each piece of Carver's writing. As Jerzy Jarniewicz stated in his afterword to the Polish edition of "Cathedral", there is no doubt Lish was responsible for creating what is called "Carver's style". It shouldn't, though, affect the pleasure of reading (205).

There is always a ghost standing behind. The editor. The ghostwriter. Barthes's final argument is: "the birth of the reader must be ransomed by the death of the Author." Analyzing Carver's creation, however, one might state that *the death of the author is the birth of the editor*. What does the birth of the editor mean, though? Is the birth of the editor the death of the authenticity, or quite the contrary? It is important to remember that there are different types of editors and editing work. Gordon Lish's editing, as mentioned before, consisted mostly in cutting. Vladimir Nabokov, however, allowed his editors only to correct spelling or punctuation mistakes (Sklenicka, 283–284). Jerzy Pilch, on the other hand, openly admits that his editor Antoni Libera wrote a few chapters for the book "Spis Cudzołożnic" for which the writer seems truly grateful. Pilch also claimed that Libera's editorial work inspired him to write fiction himself (Wolny-Hamkało).

Robert Miola in his text about types of intertextuality, which he understands as "the widest possible range of textual interactions," talks about two ways of text revision (13). One type of revision may be simply what Miola calls "author's subsequent wishes." Both critics and readers usually seem to accept such "authorial revisions." However, as Miola states, it may also become problematic. After a few hundred years it is not possible for the public to know for sure if the changes were really motivated solely by author's free second thoughts or by some other external factors.

The second type of revising described by Miola is the revision "prompted by external circumstance" (14). He gives the example of Shakespeare, who replaced the name Oldcastle with Falstaff as a result of the Oldcastle's descendants' protests. Miola commented on this kind of editing with the following words: "Editors who define the text more as a product of cultural and social factors than as individual property necessarily place less emphasis on authorial intention as a criterion of textual authenticity" (14).

Raymond Carver's authorial intentions probably received little attention from his editor Gordon Lish. However, is this really relevant? Numerous factors and, as Barthes called it, "indiscernible voices" are involved both in the process of writing and reading. The case of Carver is obviously an extreme one, yet it proves the complexity involved in the relationship between edition and authorship, also in the context of ghostwriting. Since it seems unachievable to determine authenticity of a written work and its creators, including editors, it might be valuable to focus on Barthes' 'destination' – the reader. What is definitely authentic in writing is the reading.

Works Cited

Barthes, Roland. "The Death of the Author." Trans. Richard Howard. Web.
Bourne, Daniel. Interview with Tess Gallagher. *Artful Dodge*. N.d., 30 Sept. 2015. <http://artfuldodge.sites.wooster.edu/content/tess-gallagher-0>.
Carver, Raymond. *Collected Stories*. New York: Library of America, 2009.
Carroll, Maureen P., and William L. Stull. Chronology. *Collected Stories*. By Raymond Carver. New York: Library of America, 2009. 957–978.

—. "Note on the Texts." *Collected Stories*. By Raymond Carver. New York: Library of America, 2009. 979–1004.

Clark, Miriam Marty. "Raymond Carver's Monologic Imagination." *Modern Fiction Studies* 37 (1991): 240–247.

Jarniewicz, Jerzy. "Od Końca Do Końca." *Literatura Na Świecie* 12 (1999): 191–193.

—. "Donikąd." *Literatura Na Świecie* 3–4 (2006): 299–301.

—. [Afterword] Posłowie. *Katedra*. By Raymond Carver. Trans. Jerzy Jarniewicz. Warszawa: Czuły Barbarzyńca, 2010. 199–206.

"Letters to an Editor. Letters from Raymond Carver to Gordon Lish." *The New Yorker*. 24 Dec. 2007. 30 Sept. 2015. <http://www.newyorker.com/magazine/2007/12/24/letters-to-an-editor>.

Max, D.T.. "The Carver Chronicles." *The New York Times*. 09 Aug. 1998. 30 Sept. 2015. <http://www.nytimes.com/1998/08/09/magazine/the-carver-chronicles.html?pagewanted=all>.

Rich, Motoko. "The Real Carver: Expansive or Minimal?" *The New York Times*. 17 Oct. 2007. 30 Sept. 2015. <http://www.nytimes.com/2007/10/17/books/17carver.html?pagewanted=print&_r=0>.

Saltzman, Arthur M.. *Understanding Raymond Carver*. Columbia, S.C.: University of South Carolina Press, 1988.

Sklenicka, Carol. *Raymond Carver: a Writer's Life*. New York: Scribner, 2009.

Wolny-Hamkało, Agnieszka. "Redaktor też autor." *Polityka*. 6 Oct. 2007. 30 Sept. 2015. <http://archiwum.polityka.pl/art/redaktor-tez-autor,359453.html>.

Nafize Sibel Güzel
Abdullah Küçük

A Non-Existent Source, A Successful Translation: Nihal Yeğinobalı's *Genç Kızlar*

Abstract: This paper examines one of the pseudotranslations in Turkey: Nihal Yeğinobalı's *Genç Kızlar*. Yeğinobalı, at the age of 23, could not dare to acknowledge her authorship due to the existing attitudes towards obscenity and authorship in Turkey then, since the novel included a group of young girls' romantic affair with their teacher and translation was highly rewarding. However, when her motives behind her pseudotranslation changed, she revealed the fact having great impact on Turkish chick-lit.

Keywords: pseudo-translation, repertoire, shaping the canon, chick-lit, authenticity

One of the assumptions of pseudotranslation is, as Toury defines, "texts which have been presented as translations with no corresponding source texts in other languages ever having existed" (Toury, 1995, 40). The introduction into a culture of a new text which is non-existent in the source language/culture can be a deliberate act of intervention, either by power holders or free agents, in culture planning (Zohar, 2002; Gürçağlar, 2014). This deliberate act of intervention may arise from ideological reasons, aimed at resisting the extant social and cultural norms. Such a case is *Genç Kızlar* [*Young Girls*], the first novel of Yeğinobalı, a successful 23 year old female translator. Claiming this is a translation, she shows that she lacks the courage to acknowledge authorship, since the subject matter deals with a group of young girls from wealthy families, all boarding students at a theater academy, and their romantic affair with the new oratory teacher. The authentic text, claimed Yeğinobalı, is *The Curtain Sweeps Down* by Vincent Ewing, an American author. At a time when sexual relations was a taboo subject for writers, especially for a female author (1950s), Yeğinobalı's work is worthy of a cultural analysis. Without such a literary forgery, would the novel have had a chance of being published? On the other hand, due to the gradual spread of liberalism in the country, Yeğinobalı continues writing and publishing novels under her own name in the same subgenre, and confesses to this forgery years later. The subject matter of this text are Yeğinobalı's motives for her behavior as well as the changing climate in the reading public of Turkey, considering the ethical perceptions of obscenity in the years following the novel's publication.

Translation studies, as any discipline, has evolved greatly in the recent years. It has experienced several changes, particularly the shift from studies which focus on the linguistic level in which equivalence is important, to cultural focus. This shift constitutes the gist of the studies of the prominent Israeli culture researcher Itamar Even-Zohar (1990). Even-Zohar considers translated literature as a part of the socio-cultural systems, and recommends that translation strategies should be determined by the role of the translated text in the target system. Moreover, he instituted a polysystem theory, which views translation and literature in a wide cultural and social context; and in which literature is divided into center and periphery, moving within the system in a dynamic stratification principle. He sheds further light on the subject by stipulating the following condition: provided that translation occupies primary position in the polysystem, and the literary model of the source polysystem does not exist in the target one, adequacy to the norms of the source language and culture will be sought in translations. (Even-Zohar 1990). Based on this theory, Gideon Toury developed a method for applying the polysystem theory to translation (Toury 1995).

As the field has developed, the scope of translation studies has been broadened to include new aspects. One prominent researcher on translation in Turkey, Şehnaz Tahir-Gürçağlar, describes three main contributions of the cultural approach to translation studies:

1. Widening the scope of the definition of translation
2. Bringing a new approach to the concept of equivalence
3. Broadening the scope of translation studies research to include pseudotranslations, (Tahir-Gürçağlar 2005, 20) which is the subject matter of this study.

The concept of pseudotranslation was first taken up by the prominent Slovak translation scientist and text theoretician, Anton Popovic, in *Dictionary for the Analysis of Literary Translation* (1976). In this study, Popovic proposed the term "fictitious translation" for the concept of "original works" published as translations by their authors for the specific goal of "winning a wide public". He also defined the aim as manipulation of the readers' expectations through fictitious translation (Popoviç 1976). A later definition of fictitious translation suggested by Toury was "texts which are regarded as literary translations though no genuine source texts exist for them" (Toury 1980, 45). In the light of Toury's definition, it would be reasonable to claim that his notion of 'assumed translation' (1995, 32) enables pseudotranslations to be regarded or treated as such. In the second definition, Toury explained the concept as "texts which have been represented as translations with no corresponding source texts in other languages ever having existed" (Toury 1995, 40). Tahir Gürçağlar claims that Toury's definition emphasizes the agency and intentionality of the authors and publishers in pseudotranslations (Tahir-Gürçağlar 2014, 517). Gürçağlar adds in the same article that these texts have variety of forms and functions; and they contribute to understanding the concepts and norms of translation in a given culture (Tahir-Gürçağlar 2014, 517).

There may be a variety of motives behind the pseudotranslation. On the one hand, Toury suggests that the primary motives are to introduce innovations to a target culture; and to evade sanctions and censorship; and to give new direction to literary production (Toury 1995, 41–44). On the other hand, Lefevere states that motives may be simply financial or the desire to expose colleagues, critics or both (Lefevere 2000, 1123). Furthermore, pseudotranslations defined as "a deliberate act of intervention either by the power holders or free agents into an extant or crystallizing repertoire" by Even-Zohar can be used for culture-planning in the alleged target literatures (2002, 45). This form of writing is also associated with culture, politics and society (Tahir-Gürçağlar 2014, 519).

Considering the above mentioned motives and functions of pseudotranslation, it can be claimed that Turkey has been a key party in the dissemination of pseudotranslation. Turkish literature has been exposed to considerable degrees of prohibition, restrictions, loyalty, rivalry and ideological conflict. Hence, the literati have frequently resorted to pseudotranslations in order to publish work, and increase financial gain, foreseeing the prominence and power of translation in the developing literature, and understanding its potential to bypass censorship or legal sanctions. The dominant motive for pseudotranslations has been that the reading public has always been more tolerant of translations than indigenous works. It seems that many novels and other works read in Turkey are pseudotranslations, although this status has yet to be proven by academic studies. The two well-known Turkish writers of pseudotranslations, whose work has been revealed as such by academic studies, are Kemal Tahir, famous for his *Mike Hammer* translations and pseudotranslations; and Nihal Yeğinobalı, known for the novel *Genç Kızlar,* the focus of this paper.

Nihal Yeğinobalı is a Turkish female author and translator, born in Manisa, a province in the Aegean Region of Turkey, in 1927. Her father is the owner of farms, vineyards and orchards; and her mother, an Ottoman lady whose ambition of becoming a teacher is prevented by war and marriage. Nihal Yeğinobalı's great desire for an education most probably stems from her mother's deprivation. After completing primary school, her father's new job entails a move to Istanbul. With her elder sister, Nihal enrol in Arnavutkoy American College for Girls. This choice of school proves how westernised the parents are, in spite of their rural origins. However, the family undergoes a dramatic change on graduation from her secondary education and Yeğinobalı is forced to earn a living instead of starting a university due to her parents' divorce. As very few in Turkey are competent in English at the time, she starts a career as a translator for Türkiye Publishing House. She has already translated a popular novel *The Garden of Allah* in her lycée years. After five successful translations for the prominent publishing houses in Turkey, she feels confident enough to write her own novel, using a similar structure and theme to the translated novels, however, the editors with whom she was previously on friendly terms doubt her ability to produce her own novel. During a holiday in Manisa, when she was only 21, her editors asked her to do a new translation. Reluctant to return to Istanbul, she decided to kill two birds with one stone, extending her holiday and taking the opportunity to write her own novel, though introducing it as a translation from an American author.

Thus, in accordance with her decision to present the book as a translation, Yeğinobalı invented a biography for a fictitious American male author, Vincent Ewing, and chose a picture of a suitably aristocratic looking man from a French fashion magazine. She claimed to have found the English version of the novel among the magazines published as weekly serials with the name *The Curtain Sweeps Down* among her uncle's personal belongings at their family home in Manisa. The novel tells the story of young girls from wealthy families studying at an American Academy of Dramatic Arts. Three of the girls fall in love with their new oratory-teacher. Yeğinobalı, afterwards, confesses to using an exact description of her own school as the setting in her book. Her school was an American college for girls, founded by Cyrus Hamlin, an American missionary who devoted himself to education in 1863, and the school premises were identical to the ones in America. The school's status and aura are said to be the inspiration for Yeğinobalı's imaginary institution. The book provides the reader with detailed descriptions concerning the physical and psychological features attributed to American female students. The established perceptions about American girls' sexual and romantic relationships are at the core of the dramatic love story between the two protagonists: Miss Bee and Gabriel Samson. The novel receives wide acclamation, firstly from Yeğinobalı's publishing house colleagues, and then from readers, and is republished many times, even though it is regarded as highly erotic for its time. The news that Yeğinobalı is the translator of such an erotic book is greeted with much astonishment by her colleagues, and she fears the possible reactions to news of her authorship, and continues the myth of the fictitious author.

After writing and publishing *Genç Kızlar*, she marries Morton Schibel and starts studying literature at New York State University in the USA, but drops out after the birth of two children. She feels uncomfortable in her new environment, since she has no role other than that of a desperate house-wife. Having lived in America for 7 years, homesickness overcomes her love for her husband and she returns to Istanbul with her children. When she is back, she learns that her attempt at literary forgery has been exposed. However, Altın Kitaplar, which takes over from Türkiye Publishing House publishes *Genç Kızlar* with Vincent Ewing named as the author and Nihal Yeğinobalı as the translator for the second time in 1963 so as to benefit from the fame of Ewing. At this time a movie version of *Genç Kızlar* is made with the prominent Turkish actors, which, like the book, wins wide acclaim.

Nihal Yeğinobalı continues writing and translating. Moreover, she makes a new pseudotranslation, serialized as an original work under the title *Eflatun Kız* [*The Lilac Girl*] in *Vatan Newspaper* in 1959, then published in the book form, again as a translation from Vincent Ewing, in 1964. In 1987, *Eflatun Kız* was published with revisions as an original novel under the title *Mazi Kalbimde Yaradır* [The Past is a Wound in my Heart]. Now 88 years old, Yeğinobalı is no longer active as an author but, as one of the most successful literary translators, has introduced the novels and stories of numerous classical and modern authors into Turkish, in addition to contributing to Turkish literature with her indigenous works.

Numerous scholars studied Nihal Yeğinobalı and her place as a pseudotranslator and *Genç Kızlar* and analyzed it from different theoretical and methodological perspectives. These can be listed as follows:

1. A descriptive analysis by Işın Bengi-Öner in *Çeviri Bir Süreçtir... Ya çeviribilim?* [*Translation is a process..., what if it were a Discipline*] (1999). This is the first study of *Genç Kızlar*: Bengi-Öner proposes a descriptive analysis of the book within Toury's preliminary and operational norms, and supports her strong analysis with interviews with Yeğinobalı;
2. A presentation delivered by Sündüz Öztürk and Serap Gür Birdane at the VI. International Language, Literature and Stylistics Symposium held at Süleyman Demirel University in 2006. The presentation is based on textual analysis and discusses the conditions and the historical and sociological context at the time *Genç Kızlar* was written and published. The presentation discusses the semiotic relations between *Genç Kızlar* and its movie version, produced in 1962. They conclude that pseudotranslation is an effective device for avoiding social and political pressure; and for introducing innovations into the extant cultural and literary system.
3. A master thesis entitled as "A Gender-based Study of Nihal Yeğinobalı's Genç Kızlar" by Nil Alt at Boğaziçi University in 2008. This dissertation is the only one to analyse *Genç Kızlar* as a case study. The core of the study is to bring to

the foreground the relation between the case and the gender issues. Two main issues addressed by the study are:
a. Yeğinobalı's pseudo-identity as a male Anglo-Saxon to allow her novel to be published;
b. the novel's status as a deliberate challenge to the established notion of the role of women.

There are also academicians who cite Yeğinobalı and *Genç Kızlar* in their studies, such as Şehnaz Tahir-Gürçağlar (2001, 2005), Müge Işıklar Koçak (2007), Pınar Sabuncu Artar (2007).

The most recent study on *Genç Kızlar* is an article by Ahu Selin Erkul Yağcı which is yet to be published. In this paper, Erkul-Yağcı considers Yeğinobalı as a free agent, and an agent of change in the Turkish literary canon, and emphasizes her contributions to Turkish literature.

Our presentation accords with the opinion of Yağcı. The thematic and a cultural analysis of the text employed in our study justifies the view that Yeğinobalı's *Genç Kızlar* has encouraged other authors and publishers to produce novels within the same sub-genre, and there has been an increase in the publications of such literature since then. Hence, it is entirely justifiable to describe Yeğinobalı as an agent of change.

The sub-genre of *Genç Kızlar* falls within the category of chick-lit which, as Necdet Neydim (2005) defines it, is a type of literature dealing with the issues of young adult females, their maturation processes and love affairs, which are integral to the formation of their personalities and social identities. Moreover, the real protagonist of the chick-lit is expected to be a girl, not a boy (Neydim 2005, 16–36). The chick-lit characteristic of Yeğinobalı's text is made clear from the cover of its 1951 edition, on which four girls are portrayed in the attire and manners of contemporaneous Hollywood stars. As well as the author, Yeğinobalı, the illustrator of the book was also successful in understanding the mainstream American culture of the 50's. The cover preconditions the prospective readers regarding the content matter. Toury suggests that the pseudotranslations are not only presented as such, but they are written as if they were genuine translations from the very start of the writing process (Toury 2005, 7). Though pseudotranslations are original works, they differ from the indigenous works existing in the target repertoire (Tahir-Gürçağlar 2014, 516). The difference mentioned here starts from the very beginning of the book with the paratextual elements, i.e., both peritexts and epitexts, which surround the text (Genette 1997). Peritextual elements are also worth examining. The name of the fictitious author and the source title are indicative in this respect.

Figure 1- Vincent Ewing

Yeğinobalı selected one of the least risky names and surnames to introduce her author, to increase the credibility of the authenticity of the source text. On the one hand, Vincent and Ewing are widely used as names of locations and people in America. On the other, Vincent is the surname of a prominent French bacteriologist (Jean Hyacinthe Vincent), appealing to the dual French-American based structure of the Turkish literature at the time. The photo of the pseudo author, as *Figure 1* illustrates, comes from a French magazine, which is another irony that Yeğinobalı employed.

The character names in the text are not random, either. Prissy is an adjective used to refer to a woman who is excessively proper. It is also the blend of two words, prim and sissy; Yeğinobalı frequently makes Prissy tell her friends sexually-explicit stories. Prissy displays her body shamelessly in front of the other girls. Her rather westernised bodily gestures may seem pretentious, but the genre requires them. Furthermore, such manners have often been attributed to college girls at the time. Again, as her name suggests, Prissy can be very serious and demure in front of her teachers and the newly made friends, and is adept at hiding her shamelessness when required.

Beatrice Karova is the only daughter of a wealthy family, and generally referred to as Miss Bee in the novel. This abbreviation too, suggests many things. Miss Bee is to inherit all the money and family plantations. She is as productive and industrious as a bee. This makes her unique in the novel as she both works as a businesswoman, and continues her education at the academy. Many privileges are bestowed upon her; she lives in a mansion within the school premises with her nanny. In other words, she is the one who has realized the so-called American dream.

Despite her mature approach to business, she is rather inexperienced as regards emotional issues and sexual relationships. When she develops an intimate relationship with her teacher, Gabriel Samson. Keeping it within the norms of her education and family values, she is supposed to say "no" and avoid sexual intercourse, although she feels his overwhelming power over her body. However, she does not resist, but, instead aims at complete fulfillment in their relationship, overcoming the obstacles on the way.

Miss Bee forces Gabriel to divorce his wife. In spite of her great love for him, she makes sure that unless Gabriel is free, like her, complete happiness cannot be achieved. Miss Bee's opinion on divorce reflects the debate popular at the time Yeğinobalı wrote her novel. Catholic prohibitions on divorce at the time are compared to the more liberal ideas of Miss Bee. She explicitly states that if either side in a relationship or marriage is unhappy, the peer pressure or the religious obligations imposed upon couples to remain married are cruel and inhuman.

Through Miss Bee's character, Yeğinobalı sends clear messages to Turkish readers. It is possible to say that Miss Bee is created as a model for her implied readers. She manages to be herself, uses her free will, is radical in her decisions, and never accepts defeat. She comes to terms with real love, but this does not mean giving up all her social benefits. Instead, she demands changes from the society; she requires the society to allow individuals to end marriages when necessary. Yeğinobalı also emphasizes that unless a woman has financial independence, similar to Miss Bee, she will have no opportunity to change society.

Yeğinobalı's most courageous female character is Mariana. She is beautiful and charming, and behaves like a mentor in many cases. However, she refuses emotional intimacy, preferring sensual love in her relationships. When needed, she gives herself to a man, and argues that to keep the man, it is necessary to sacrifice your body. In her opinion, men can desire women, by which she mainly refers to the body of women, but women are supposed to keep their integrity. The integrity of women is disrupted when they yield to their passion. In this respect, the name Mariana is apt, reminding the readers of the mother Mary, who kept her virginity.

Hindley Bell is the only character that can be claimed to represent the stereotype of a Turkish girl. She is introduced as a character for whom it is impossible to externalize and face her feelings. Anonymous letters are sent to her, and she is victimised by the group as a result. Later on, the source of these letters is understood to be Prissy. Why Prissy chooses her for this treatment is obvious enough. Due to her unrequited love towards her teacher, and her learning of her best friend, Miss

Bee and her beloved teacher's feelings towards each other, she attempts a suicide, which is prevented by the protective figure of Mariana. Mariana, similarly to Miss Bee, is the mentor, the voice of the common sense in this regard as well. After these experiences, Hindley becomes introverted, and filled with self-hate and guilt for her unrequited love. Moreover, she blames herself alone and finds herself worthless, abnormal, like an abominable creature that should be annihilated. To build an independent self under such conditions is extremely difficult. Again similarly to a Turkish girl, she is never willing to hear obscene stories about other girls. She is "the other" and "outcast" in the Art Academy, someone belonging to a different, more conservative culture.

Yeğinobalı places her only male character in the midst of these four different female characters. Gabriel Samson is introduced as the new oratory teacher of Ludlow Art Academy in the novel. He is the youngest male teacher of the school, is admired by almost all the girls in the academy, but is loved by these three. Like an owl, he is often silent as if trying to hide something that has happened to him or that is still happening in him. The novel proceeds to revealing his marriage to Alison who initially enthralled him with her charm and femininity. However, after the marriage, he realizes his mistake, but he must endure the situation even when she is unfaithful to him, although they have a daughter. Despite all the difficulties, because they both are Catholics, divorce is forbidden. Samson does not allow himself to fall in love again and lives an unhappy life, until he meets Miss Bee whom he eventually marries.

Does Gabriel's devotion to his religion mean something for the Turkish reader? Certainly, yes, since in Islamic belief a man is expected to take on all the responsibilities for his wife after marriage. However, in spite of his wife's infidelity, Gabriel quietly accepts his fate. In this respect he is more than an average man, which is reflected in his name, Gabriel, meaning an archangel who typically serves as a messenger from God. This name symbolizes his good side, while his surname symbolizes his sinful nature. As it is also deliberately chosen for reference to Shamshoun, or Samson, one of the last of the judges of the ancient Israelites mentioned in the Book of Judges of the Old Testament. Samson is portrayed as a hero of great strength who breaks his oath due to a compulsion for relationships with young women. Similarly to the original Samson, Yeğinobalı's oratory teacher can no longer keep faith to his religion after meeting Miss Bee (*Bible Gateway*).

To conclude, considering the strategies employed in the text, it may be said that Yeğinobalı was successful. She had a clear notion of her implied readers, she was able to predict the features they would appreciate, which is shown by the continued popularity of her novel half a century later. She maintained a close adherence to a foreign culture, as it is proven in her choices of names, places, settings and the specifics of her characters. She maintained such coherence in creating this aura of a foreign culture that the origins of her work were not questioned until her confession years later.

In this attempt, she is, of course, motivated by the preferences of the Turkish readers of the time. Yeğinobalı most probably felt that her readers needed to learn to tolerate other ways of living. Chick- lit was the genre to serve her aim. The graph below shows the numbers of chick-lit novels produced in Turkey in each decade since 1950's. During the period in which *Genç Kızlar* was first published, there were only 16 books. After Yeğinobalı's book won wide acclaim, the number rose to 26. Beginning with the 2000's, the genre peaked, reaching 100 books during the 10-year period in which *Genç Kızlar* was published with Nihal Yeğinobalı named as the author for the first time. This increase proves Yeğinobalı's unintentional creation of a canon, although this has yet to be further analyzed and studied. The last few years show another decline in the popularity of chick-lit, most probably because of the variety of new genres introduced into Turkish literature, including the postmodern ones, science fiction, and gothic literature.

Graph 1 - *The data has been obtained and the lists have been recorded from the database of the Turkish National Library and the National Collective Catalogue (TO-KAT) and two other bibliographies.*

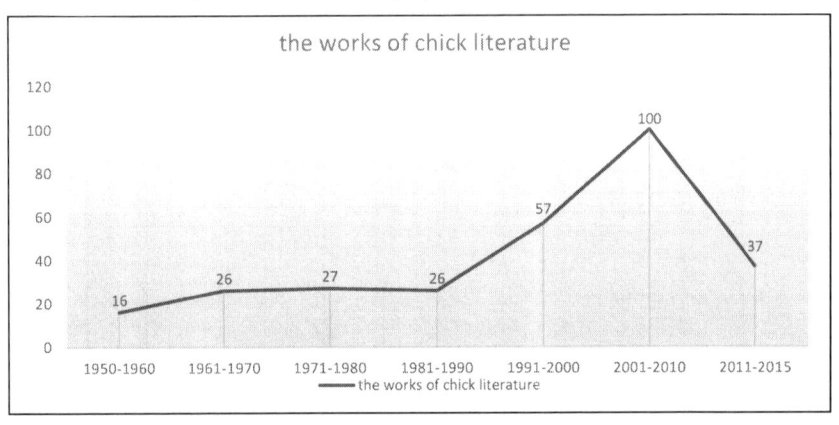

Period	the works of chick literature
1950-1960	16
1961-1970	26
1971-1980	27
1981-1990	26
1991-2000	57
2001-2010	100
2011-2015	37

Yeğinobalı at the time knew that if society only produced girls identical to Hindley Bell, there would be no improvement in the female understanding and appreciation of the opposite sex. Yeğinobalı was courageous enough to attempt to mold her society so as to create a different cultural outlook. At the time she was not courageous enough to put her name to her creation, the decision which she reversed later due to the changing social norms. Our calling her "a successful translator" in the title of this paper stems from the opinion that Yeğinobalı was an intermediary between two cultures. She knew the American culture of the 1950's, as reflected in the books she read, and she seemingly faultlessly disclosed her subconscious knowledge in the text she formed.

Works Cited

Alt, Nil. "A Gender-Based Study of Nihal Yeğinobalı's Pseudo-Translation Genç Kızlar." Diss. Boğaziçi University, 2008.

Bal, Baha. *Kadın Yazıları: Kadınların Edebiyat Ürünleri, Kadınlar Üzerine Yazılanlar ve Tezler Bibliyografyası: 1955–1990.* Istanbul: KEKBVM & TETTV, 2000.

Bengi-Öner, Işın. "Çeviribilim, Çeviri Kuramı ve Sözde Çeviriler". *Çeviri Bir Süreçtir...? Ya Çeviribilim.* Istanbul: Sel Yayıncılık, 1999. 25–35.

Bible Gateway. Biblegeteway.com. 11 March 2015.

Davaz, Aslı, Bekir Kemal Ataman, İmren Sipahi, Jale Baysal, and Zehra Toska. *Kadın Konulu Kitaplar Bibliyografyası 1729–2002.* Istanbul: İletişim Kadın Eserleri Kütüphanesi ve Bilgi Merkezi Vakfı Yayını, 2006.

Erkul Yağcı, Selin A. *Nihal Yeğinobalı.* Unpublished paper.

Even-Zohar, Itamar. "Polysystem Studies." *Poetics Today* 11:1 (1990). 1–268.

—. "Culture Planning and Cultural Resistance in the Making and Maintaining of Entities." *Sun Yat-Sen Journal of Humanities* 14 (2002): 45–52.

Ewing, Vincent. *Genç Kızlar.* Trans. Nihal Yeğinobalı. İstanbul: Altın Kitaplar, 1964.

Genette, Gerard. *Paratexts: Thresholds of Interpretation.* Trans. Jane E. Lewin. Cambridge: Cambridge University Press, 1997.

Işıklar-Koçak, Müge. "Problematizing translated popular texts of women's sexuality: A New perspective on the modernization project in Turkey from 1931 to 1959." Diss. Boğaziçi University, 2007.

Lefevere, Andre. "Pseudotranslations." *Encyclopedia of Literary Translation into English,* Vol. 2. Ed. Olive Classe. London: Fitzroy Dearborn, 2000. 1122–23.

Milli Kütüphane Katalog Tarama. Web. 15 Apr. 2015.

Neydim, Necdet. *Genç Kız Edebiyatı.* İstanbul: Bu Yayınevi, 2005.

Öztürk, Sündüz, and Serap Gün Birdane. "Sözde-çeviride söylem ve biçem [Discourse and style in pseudotranslation]." For VI. Uluslararası Dil, Yazın, Deyişbilim Sempozyumu, Süleyman Demirel University, Isparta. 1–2 June 2006.

Popoviç, Anton. *Dictionary for the Analysis of Literary Translation*. Edmonton: University of Alberta, 1976.

Sabuncu Artar, Pınar. "A Comparative Analysis of Mike Hammer in Turkish'Translation.'" Diss. Dokuz Eylül University, 2007.

Tahir-Gürçağlar, Şehnaz. "The Politics and Poetics of Translation in Turkey 1923-1960." Diss. Boğaziçi University, 2001.

—. *Kapılar Çeviri Tarihine Yaklaşımlar*. İstanbul: Scala Yayıncılık, 2005.

—. "Scouting the borders of translation: Pseudotranslation, concealed translations and authorship in twentieth-century Turkey." *Translation Studies* 3:2 (2010): 172-187. 11 March 2015.

—. "Pseudotranslation on the Margin of fact and Fiction". *A Companion to Translation Studies*. Ed. Sandra Bermann, Catherine Porter. Wiley-Blackwell Publishing, 2014. 516-527.

Toplu Katalog Tarama. Web. 15 Apr. 2015

Toury, Gideon. *In search of a Theory of Translation*. Tel Aviv: The Porter Institute for Poetics and Semiotics, Tel Aviv University, 1980.

—. *Descriptive Translation Studies and Beyond*. Amsterdam and Philadelphia: John Benjamin Publishing, 1995.

—. "Enhancing Cultural Changes by Means of Fictitious Translations." *In Translation and Cultural Change: Studies in History, Norms and ımage-Projection*. Ed. Eva Hung. Philadelphia: John Benjamins, 2005. 3-17.

Yulia Nanyak

Language Personality: Problems and Opportunities in Translation (Based on the Characters from the Tragedy *Faust* by Johann Wolfgang von Goethe and its Ukrainian and Anglophone Translations)

Abstract: This paper is aimed at giving a short summary of problems with cognitive and pragmatic aspects of language personality which translators may face. The paper is based on the model of language personality suggested by Yuriy Karaulov with the main characters of Goethe's *Faust* in Ukrainian and Anglophone translations serving as examples.

Keywords: language personality, individualization, translation, Goethe

This paper is aimed at giving a short summary of problems with cognitive and pragmatic aspects of language personality which translators may face. The paper is based on the model of language personality suggested by Yuriy Karaulov with the main characters of Goethe's *Faust* in Ukrainian (translated by Ivan Franko, Dmytro Zahul, Mykola Ulezko, Mykola Lukash) and Anglophone (by Anna Swanwick, Charles Brooks, George Priest, Anthony Kline) translations serving as examples.

The term language personality was first used by Viktor V. Vinogradov in a book on artistic prose published in 1980. Shortly after that this area of linguistics started to be actively developed in Soviet Translation Studies, because the category of language personality meets the needs of the anthropocentric stage of the development of linguistics that started to be actively elaborated at that time (Караулов 1987, 21–23).

According to Yuriy Karaulov language personality is understood as a personality that is expressed in language and reconstructed in its main features based on the linguistic data.

The most accurate and the closest to the specifics of this study is such a definition of language personality: the type of person representation, based on the analysis of the speaker's discourse in terms of using means of a language for reflection of his/her vision of reality and for achieving specific communicative goals.

While dealing with the structure of language personality almost all researchers refer to the language personality model suggested by Yuriy N. Karaulov. It is often used as a basis for analysis of various language personalities and is often modified. The model consists of three levels: verbal-semantic (verbal-grammatical) or lexicon, linguo-cognitive or thesaurus and motivational or pragmaticon. Each level is characterized by its set units that collectively cover all the units used in the speech study, originally redistributing them according to the specificity of these levels (Караулов 1997, 672).

The basis of the language personality model is Humboldt's metaphor – language surroundings, a set of communicatively significant characteristics that define a person as a representative of a particular civilization, ethnic or social group and as an individual. In this case to define also means to limit.

This understanding is applied to language personality of the literature character, which is a language personality modeled for the fiction world that only reflects the characteristics of the real world. Analysis of a language personality gives researchers the opportunity to consider both external and internal, dialogue and monologue utterance, and certain features of individual verbal behavior of the character.

The study of the belles-letters characters provides certain advantages. First of all, we have a full discourse of a personality, which is impossible in the analysis of real language personality. Secondly, not only the external speech, but also internal can be analyzed, following the work of consciousness and mental processes (Бондаренко, 181).

Speech individualization on the cognitive level implies putting different social and educational backgrounds into the character's speech. Individualization on this level is clearly seen in the tragedy *Faust* by Johann Wolfgang Goethe as Faust and Gretchen are opposed to each other because of different mental pictures of the world and social backgrounds. This is manifested through all possible means of individualization: the choice of lexis, grammar, intentions, motives, reaction etc.

The problems that arise before the translator on this level can be divided into:

1. Differences between source culture and target culture, including traditions, established social roles, perception of religious and mystic concepts;
2. Differences in the time of original writing and translations that includes difficulties with decoding political and social allusions.

To justify these statements, the character of The Witch, as it might be considered a very typical literary character, can be analyzed:

Ukrainians, Germans and Englishmen perceive evil forces in different ways. The roots of the German word "Hexe" can be found only in the West Germanic language area: Middle High German "hecse", "hesse", Old High German "hagzissa", "Hagazussa", medium Dutch "haghetisse", Old English "haegtesse" (Ghostly beings) – shortened in modern English to "hag" early 13c. (ugly old woman). The "*hægtesse*" was used to define a powerful supernatural woman.

Though both Ukrainian "відьма" and English "witch" derived from "veda" – sacral knowledge (Sanskrit), the fortune of these words in Ukrainian and English was quite different. In Ukraine "відьма" is the woman communicating with evil spirits, who does harm to the others (СУМ1, 666). It is derived from Old Slavic "вѣдъ" that is connected with "відати" – to know.

The witch in Ukraine is feared much less that the witch in Europe because the harm she does is supposed to be not very serious, though everywhere witchcraft was considered to be an activity punished by law. In the Ukrainian translations we even notice hierarchization of witches: in the translation by Ivan Franko is the word "чарівниця". Ukrainian researcher Ivan I. Ohiyenko stresses that one should differentiate between the notions of "відьма" and "чарівниця", as the second can do good things, whereas the first – only harm (Огієнко,16). At the time when *Faust* was written by Johann Wolfgang von Goethe the very perception of evil spirits was changing. It was the epoch of Enlightenment and one was trying to get rid of the frights and to explain everything by ones intellect. People were trying to make fun of the things they were afraid of, because what is funny cannot be scary.

DIE HEXE,	THE WITCH	ЧАРІВНИЦЯ
Du mußt verstehn!	This must thou ken:	Се знай: з одного
Aus Eins mach Zehn,	Of one make ten,	Зробити много,
Und Zwei laß gehn,	Pass two, and then	А два – овва!
Und Drei mach gleich,	Make square the three,	А три зрівняти,
So bist du reich.	So rich thou'lt be.	То будеш багатий.
Verlier die Vier!	Drop out the four!	Чотири пусти.
Aus Fünf und Sechs –	From five and six,	З п'яти і шести,
So sagt die Hex –	Thus essays the witch,	Сім, вісім вкрути.
Mach Sieben und Acht,	Make seven and eight.	А дев'ять – одниць,
So ists vollbracht:	So all is straight!	А десять – то нич,
Und Neun ist Eins,	And nine is one,	Оце рахуба чарівниць!
Und Zehn ist keins.	And ten is none,	(Франко)
Das ist das Hexen-Einmaleins!	This is the witch's one-time-one! (Swanwick)	
(Goethe)		

THE WITCH	ВІДЬМА	ВІДЬМА
Remember then!	На ум бери!	Премудрость! трав міть
Of One make Ten,	Бо десять – раз,	З ,дного десять зробить,
The Two let be,	А два зітри	Два – так пустить;
Make even Three,	То три якраз.	Три миттю взяв, -
There's wealth for thee.	І все гаразд!	Багатий став.
The Four pass o'er!	Чотири змий,	Похіри чотірі!
Of Five and Six,	А шість і п'ять	З п'яти з шести –
(The witch so speaks,)	В лічбі моїй	Рече відьма, – ти
Make Seven and Eight,	Порахувать	Сім, вісім зроби,
The thing is straight:	Як вісім – сім.	От і все тобі!
And Nine is One	І вже по всім.	Дев'ять – це раз,
And Ten is none--	Бо девять раз,	Десять – ні раз.
This is the witch's one-time-one! (Brooks)	Десять ні – раз. Так лічить відьма кождий раз. (Загул)	Це в відм чин множення й наказ! (Улезко)
THE WITCH	ВІДЬМА	The Witch
This you must ken!	Як досягти	You shall see, then!
From one make ten,	До десяти?	From one make ten!
And two let be,	Один – як дим,	Let two go again,
Make even three,	А два – сплива,	Make three even,
Then rich you'll be.	А три – зітри,	You're rich again.
Skip o'er the four!	Чотири ж – виріж,	Take away four!
From five and six,	А п'ять – украдь,	From five and six,
The Witch's tricks,	А шість – ізчисть,	So says the Witch,
Make seven and eight,	А сім – знесім,	Make seven and eight,
,Tis finished straight;	А вісім – повісім,	So it's full weight:
And nine is one,	А дев'ять що? – Невідь що.	And nine is one,
And ten is none,	А десять ку десять.	And ten is none.
That is the witch's one-time-one! (Priest)	Отак-то лічим ми – відьмИ. (Лукаш)	This is the Witch's one-times-one! (Kline)

In these lines some researchers see the mocking of the ten commandments. But another variant is more probable – the mocking of belief in cabbalistic numbers (as into '666' etc.) (Улезко, 314–315). Aleksander Ankist suggested that it was a challenge for the church of that time, which is seen a bit later when Mephistopheles uttered: «Durch Drei und Eins und Eins und Drei/Irrtum statt Wahrheit zuverbreiten.» It was against the dogma of the Trinity of God (Гете 1976, 462).

The history of the belief in the magic power of the numbers has started long ago. In the Bible, we can find reference to "The Tower of Babel"; it was a tower that represented the «stages» between earth and heaven. For the first time, numbers expressed the world order. The seven steps often appear in magical philosophy. In Ukraine we even had a god for counting – Chystoboh who was given seven numbers by the goddess Lada. Mykola Lukash expresses the idea that it was just a satire on those beliefs and even Johann Wolfgang von Goethe was laughing at the way some researches were trying to decode the inner sense of the Witch's counting.

This piece is written in two feet iamb. The thirteen lines are aaabbcddeejjj, but, despite the fact that the line "Verlier die Vier" is not rhymed to any other line, it has the inner rhyme (epiphora). In this very poem the main point is sound and image, words being nonsense. From the point of view of the author it sounds ridiculous, but from the point of view of the character it is a very important ritual.

The variants of the first phrase translation are interesting: "Du mußt verstehn!" In two English translations (by Anna Swanwick and George M. Priest) the word "ken" is used. It was a rather good choice, as it has the semes both of knowing and understanding (Longman, 771). In other English translations the word «must» is used as well. Generally it is absolutely adequate variant to render the phrase of the original. Charles T. Brooks translated it as: "Remember then!" But here the seme of understanding is lost; one can remember but not understand. This seme is very important in the understanding of this piece. The Witch is trying to convince everybody around that there is some inner sense, higher knowledge and that one has to understand it. In the original the Witch just wants to show that she is very smart and wise; the other cannot reach that level of knowledge. Ivan Franko included only the seme of knowledge into his translation: "Се знай". But it gives the association of teaching, maybe not even aiming at being understood. Dmytro Zahul and Mykola Ulezko have rendered it in a more precise way, translating not the lexis, but the meaning and associations: "На ум бери!" by Dmytro Zahul and "Премудрость!" by Mykola Ulezko. But in the translation by Mykola Ulezko the mocking of church rituals already starts here, as the word "Премудрость!" is very often repeated during divine service in the church. Mykola Lukash introduced a rhetorical question. In his translation the association appears that it is very hard to reach ten: "Як досягти /До десяти?" It stresses the willingness of the Witch to show that she is wise: she puts a question and then she answers it.

Proktophantasmist.
Ihr seid noch immer da! Nein, das ist unerhört.
Verschwindet doch! Wir haben ja aufgeklärt!
Das Teufelspack, es fragt nach keiner Regel.
Wir sind so klug, und dennoch spukt's in Tegel.
Wie lange hab' ich nicht am Wahn hinausgekehrt,
Und nie wird's rein; das ist doch unerhört! (Goethe 1969, 252)

Some translators provide a detailed analysis and historical background of this piece, without which a modern reader cannot understand what was really meant by Johann Wolfgang Goethe. The whole Walpurgis Night is just a senseless fairytale without these comments. Ukrainian translator Mykola Ulezko has decoded it as a two levels story: a fairytale and philosophical worldview. But actually it has three levels – it is also a very strong mocking of and satire on Goethe's contemporaries.

The very word "Proctophantasmist" was invented by Goethe. It is derived from two Greek words meaning "rump" and "fancy". A skit on Friedrich Nicolai, the Berlin publisher and rationalist, who though he had all his life denied the existence of spirits, began to see visions in 1791. He cured himself of these however by a timely application of leeches, hence the allusion of Mephistopheles later on.

The words «Das Teufelspack, es fragt nach keiner Regel./Wir sind so klug, und dennoch spukt's in Tegel» also have implications. In German there is an expression «es spukt in Tegel», meaning the devil playing the cast iron; it is used to say that there are some evil forces in the house. Tegel was the country estate near Berlin; it was said to be haunted, and Nicolai lectured to the Academy on these apparitions.

Almost all the translators have preserved this name, except for Anthony Kline, who decided to explain it "The Rationalist (Nicolai)" and Ivan Franko, who used "Дерев'яний ясновидець" to indicate that the clairvoyant was lifeless and inanimate (made of wood) without references to Nicolai.

The pragmatic aspect of the character's individual speech cannot be fully explored, as intonation plays a major role in identifying a speaker's attitude and motivation, and graphically it is not fully expressed.

Individualization of the character's speech on the pragmatic level implies the motives, tactics, behavioral rules, pragmatic meaning of the utterances, pragmatic presupposition and the attitude of the speaker to the addressee. All these before mentioned aspects can be analyzed only on the level of words as one can notice certain markers – words that define certain motives, intentions and attitude of the speaker.

Due to the above, there can't be any serious difference between the translation and the original on this level as it would change the whole work. That is why most differences occur at the micropragmatic level. These are: omission of expressions that carry blurred pragmatic information (i.e. "O!"), changing and omission of certain types of deixis, compensation or omission of performatives etc. Nevertheless, the attitude to the character can be modified because of cultural differences (as with the Witch) and it influences certain communicative situations.

In every challenge and problem there is an opportunity. The first full translation into English was done by A. Hayward and for a long time seemed to have been accepted as the standard, in default to anything more satisfactory: the English critics, generally sustaining the translator in his views concerning the secondary importance of the form of poetry, practically discouraged any further attempt (Goethe 1912, III).

Already in 1894 Anna Swanwick's translation was considered to be one of the five best English verse translations of the tragedy *Faust* by J. W. Goethe (McLintock). By 1967, there were over forty printings of it (Goethe 1967, xiii). In spite of the fact that Anna Swanwick rendered the original carefully, there are some features peculiar to her style: for example the translator uses the word "soul" twice as much as it is used in the original. She also would often change masculine rhymes into feminine. But despite these inaccuracies she was the best among English translators to grasp the image of Gretchen.

Ivan Franko translated using the language of his time, which is a bit old-fashioned for today. But by his translation Ivan Franko has brought to the Ukrainian readers the eternal questions of the sense of existence and human cognition which are central to this poem which was given the name of tragedy by the author – the tragedy of a human being on the verge of mundane knowledge, the tragedy of a fighter of the terrifying struggle of faith and knowledge (Цимбалюк, 127). The first part of *Faust* was translated by Ivan Franko in 1881, by Dmytro Zahul in 1919 and by Mykola Ulezko in 1926.

Ivan Franko started his translation activity with the creation by Johann Wolfgang Goethe, namely *Faust* (one of the songs of Margarethe). Ivan Franko resembles Goethe in the perception of the world. That is why this translation is a masterpiece by itself despite the fact that Ivan Franko in his foreword claimed:

> Перекладаючи *Фавста* на нашу мову, я старався передовсім про те, щоб зробити його приступним для нашої письменної — чи, сказати правду, малописьменної— громади. Я поклав головну вагу на зрозумілість і ясність бесіди. (Translating *Faust* into our language, I was trying mostly to make it accessible for our literate, – or telling the truth illiterate – community. I was mostly paying attention to understandability and-clearness of interlocution.).

That is why Ivan Franko's opportunity was to be the first and to give the possibility to people not knowing foreign languages to read *Faust* in Ukrainian.

Mykola Ulezko expressed his intention to translate the whole of *Faust* in the preface to the first part. Mykhailo Johansen highly estimated the mastery of translation, arguing that he has two main features: accuracy and nationality. «Точність перекладу дуже велика, і в місцях ліричних вона могла-б бути навіть менша – вони б від цього тільки виграли» (The accuracy of translation is very high, and in some lyrical pieces it could have been even lower – it would win this way) (Гете 1926, 5).

The translation of the first part of *Faust* by Mykola Ulezko is the result of ten years of work. This translation excels in closeness to the original (Цимбалюк, 128). It is very important for Ukrainian literature as it is followed by detailed comments and explanations of historical and cultural background of *Faust* creation.

Mykola Lukash managed to do the first full translation of the tragedy. He was blamed for overusage of archaisms and dialectisms. As Leonid Pervomaiskyi wrote: «Тінь травестійного Енея стояла за спиною перекладача» (The shadow of travestied Aeneas was behind his back) (Первомайський, 370). Of a similar opinion was Viktor Koptilov, indicating that such a number of pages cannot avoid certain mistakes and inaccuracies. But the main fault of the translator according to V. Koptilov is that he did not listen to the comments of the editors of the first edition (Коптілов, 107).

Mykola Lukash did not publically react to the review of Leonid Pervomaiskyi but internal review of Viktor Koptilov has forced him to join the debate. Mykola Lukash wrote three articles as an answer «Хто такі були двораки», «Про змішування західноєвропейських реалій з польськими та про тінь Франца-Йосифа», «Про зниження стилю та про скривдженого Мефістофеля» (Лукаш 1995, 503), where he grounded his translation solutions that caused the criticism. While studying these examples very carefully one can come to the conclusion that that very variant of translation that seems odd at first sight is the most precise of all.

Ukrainian and Anglophone translators of Johann Goethe's *Faust* apply domestication strategy more often to cognitive categories rather than the pragmatic ones. This can be explained by the fact that for an adequate understanding of the work at the cognitive level, characters can be slightly different from the original, especially in relation to national coloring, but intentions and aspirations of heroes must remain intact to preserve the essence. And while micro pragmatic categories may differ in the translations, full reproduction of macro and mega pragmatic categories is essential for the translation to be adequate.

Most problems with rendering the language personality occur at the cognitive level because of cultural differences and different social and political background. But these challenges provoke translators to seek for opportunities. If these opportunities are used and the translators create something new to a reasonable extent – the translation wins as it cannot be a carbon copy of the original and has to compete for its place in the target literature.

Works Cited

Goethe, Johann Wolfgang. *Faust*. Trans. B. Taylor, Cleveland, Ohio New York, N.Y., 1912.

—. *Faust: A Tragedy*: Parts I and II. Trans. B. Taylor. Introd. A. Scenna, 2nd printing, New York: Washington Square Press, 1967.

—.*Faust*. Gesamtausgabe. Leipzig: Insel-Verlag, 1969.

—.*Faust*. Trans. A. S. Kline. 17 Nov. 2014 <http://www.poetryintranslation.com/PITBR/German/Fausthome.htm>.

—.*Faust*. Trans.Anna Swanwick. London: G. Bell and Sons, Ltd., 1928.

—.*Faust*. Trans. Charles T. Brooks. 25 Dec. 2004. 1 Sept. 2015 <http://www.gutenberg.org/cache/epub/14460/pg14460-images.html>.

—. *Faust*. Trans. George Madison Priest. New York: Alfred A. Knopf, 1941.

Longman Dictionary of Contemporary English, Pearson Education Ltd. 2000.

McLintock, R. *The Five best English Translations of Faust*, Mackie & Co., Limited, Warrington. 1894.

Бондаренко, Яна "Комунікативно-когнітивна характеристика мовлення персонажа (на матеріалі мовлення М. Герцога з однойменного роману С.Беллоу)" *Вісник Житомирського держ. ун-тету ім. Івана Франка* 8. (2001): 180–184.

Гете, Иоганн Вольфганг "Фауст Трагедия."*Собрание сочинений. В 10-ти томах*. 2. пер. с нем. Б. Пастернака. Под общ. ред. А. Аникста и Н. Вильмонта. Коммент. А. Аникста. Москва: Худож. Лит. 1976.

Ґете, Йоган Вольфганг *Фавст*. Перекл. І. Франко. Іван Франко. Зібрання творів у п'ятдесяти томах13. Київ: Наук. думка, 1978. 174–424.

—.*Фауст. Траґедія*. І частина, з нім. мови вірш. переклад Д. Загула; з портретом Ґете та 12 ілюстраціями Ліцен-Маєра. Київ-Відень: Вернигора, 1919.

—.*Фауст. Траґедія*. І частина, перек. з нім. мови М. Т. Улезко. Держ. вид. України, 1926.

—.*Фауст*; *Лірика*. Пер. з нім. М. Лукаш. Київ: Веселка, 2001.

Караулов, Юрий *Русский язык и языковая личность*. Москва: Наука, 1987.

—.*Русский язык. Энциклопедия*. Большая Российская энциклопедия, 1997.

Коптілов, Віктор "Німецькі класики українською мовою" *Всесвіт* 6 (1970): 105–108.

Лукаш, М. "Хто такі були двораки; Про змішування західноєвропейських реалій з польськими та про тінь Франца-Йосифа; Про зниження стилю та про скривдженого Мефістофеля" [публікатор М. Стріха] *Записки НТШ: Праці філол. секції* Т. CCXXIX (1995): 505–517.

Огієнко, Іван *Українські чари*. 2-ге вид., стереотип., Упоряд. О. М. Таланчук. Київ:Либідь, 1994.

Первомайський, Леонід "*Фауст* Гете в перекладі М. Лукаша: Замітки на полях рукопису"*Твори : Творчий будень: Статті. Спогади. Замітки7*. Київ, 1970. 362–378.

СУМ Словник української мови в 11 томах, ред. кол. І. К. Білодід та ін. Київ: Наукова думка, 1971.

Цимбалюк, Д. "Ґете по-українському." *Жовтень 12* (1970): 126–129.

Шевченко, О. Н. *Языковая личность переводчика (На материале дискурса Б. В. Заходера)*: Дис. … канд. филол. наук : 10.02.19 Волгоград, 2005.

Debora Biancheri

Representations of Identity in Italian Translations of Seamus Heaney: Rewriting Poetry "True to Life"

Abstract: The article investigates issues of authenticity in the articulation of poetic recollections in translation. By way of an attentive critical engagement with Italian translations from the work of Nobel laureate Seamus Heaney, the study shows how boundaries of representation are often actively redefined by target texts and supporting paratext, thus implicitly contributing to a re-modelling of the readers' perception of the artistic "truth".

Keywords: Seamus Heaney, Irish poetry, the Troubles, memory, Italian publishing industry

This essay focuses on the phase of Seamus Heaney's career hailed as the culmination of his mythopoetic journey: the poems where his flight from commitment and clear commentary about the situation of his homeland, Northern Ireland, becomes the object of self-critical assessment. This is achieved by moving his attention from his native county Derry to the unearthing of a pre-historical epoch's sedimented evidence, as recorded by the bog in Jutland. Hence, the preserved corpses catalogued in P.V. Glob's book *The Bog People*, declared inspiration behind Heaney's lines, acquire the valence of symbolic mediums, which allow ancient rituals to become a site of re-signification of contemporary predicaments. *North* (1975), a collection that received massive critical attention, is the volume where Heaney's project "to define and interpret the present by bringing it into significant relationship with the past" (Heaney 2014, 60) found its most successful, albeit questioned, fulfilment. One of the central questions addressed, however, is whether translation can function as a threshold to effectively access *North*'s suspended historical time, and recreate the complexity of representation sought as a way forward in tackling the contentious subject of sectarian violence.

The first poem developing Heaney's poetic discourse of ground towards the use of Jutland as an objective correlative for Northern Ireland, which is precisely the controversial juxtaposition underpinning *North*, is nonetheless predating this collection. It is "The Tollund Man," included in *Wintering Out* (1972), a collection never translated into Italian. Nevertheless the poem is translated as part of a couple of anthologies. Originally published in 1995 and later reprinted in 2013, Erminia Passannanti's *Terra di Palude* is one of those volumes compensating for what would be an otherwise important lacuna in the Italian construction of

Heaney's poetic profile. Despite being released by an independent publisher and currently targeting primarily the online market, the book's strategic release after the Nobel Prize award and subsequently shortly after Heaney's sudden demise, makes this contribution by one of the first scholars and translators to ever engage with Heaney particularly relevant. The Italian title, though, "La mummia di Tollund," immediately reveals the difficulty of maintaining the poet's perspective – his use of memory not only as a tool of "recollection in tranquillity" to create bridges between past and present, but to actively defy the boundaries of temporality. The corpse of the Tollund Man, as explained by Heaney in an interview (Randall), struck him for the familiarity of his features, the thought that this man could be one of his forefathers or anybody else's. His title, thus, captures the humanity of this corpse by referring to him simply as the Tollund *man*. The Italian translator, instead, decides to emphasise the archaeological rather the human dimension of the relic. Yet, in so doing, she partly defies the tentative overlapping of Jutland's remoteness with the poet's homeground, as stressing temporal displacement is essential to trigger the geographical dislocation that underpins the source text. These movements are what in turn allow the reading of present adversities in the light of past brutalities: an angle that will find its climax in "The Grauballe Man," in *North*, where the shift from the singular of the "archaeological" discourse to a more plural engagement with ethical and social discourses is even more evident.

The close proximity of these two poems is somewhat emphasised by their concomitant inclusion in *Terra di Palude*, and yet the affinity between the two bodies is slightly undermined by the translation of the other title as "L'Uomo di Grauballe." While this solution seems to recuperate the poet's subtle superimposition of the bodies and his ancestors – that in the source text is also strengthened by a language reflecting the diction of Heaney's own group – the use of two different terms weakens the connection between the Tollund and the Grauballe men, whose relation is also partly revisited by having the poetic predecessor from *Wintering Out* appearing sequentially after the poem from *North*.

After all, Passannanti's anthology posits itself as an independent project, which does not intend to capture the macro-dimension of Heaney's *oeuvre*, as exposed by the curious combination of poems translated, deceivingly presented as an Italian version of the *Bog Poems* but excluding from the selection the iconic poem "The Bog Queen," for instance. Accordingly, conveying the conceit that, by virtue of linguistic affinity, the term "bog" fosters the assimilation of the distant soil in Jutland with Irish farmland, is not a priority for *Terra di Palude*, as the framing chosen for this anthology is rather a depiction of Heaney as a telluric poet more so than as a spokesperson for the Troubles. By having a closer look at Passannanti's translation of "The Tollund Man," it is possible to note that minor divergences are mostly consistent with this general outlook. The conflation of different spatial and temporal dimensions, for instance, consecrated by the last stanza of the source text, is hardly reproduced by the target text.

> Out here in Jutland
> In the old man-killing parishes
> I will feel lost,
> Unhappy and at home.
>
> Laggiù nello Jutland,
> nelle vecchie parrocchie assassine,
> mi sentirò perduto,
> infelice e a casa. (32)

In the English text, the imaginative poetic journey has brought the poet "there," or rather has brought "home" the Scandinavian bog and its archaeological memory, as the deictic adverb "here" indicates. In Italian, the first line evokes Jutland as "out there" and, by inserting a comma at the end of the line, increases the impression of something distant, unreachable and ultimately unconnected. In the second line "parishes" is translated in its religious sense of *parrocchia*, etymologically close, but with an explicit reference to churches in modern Italian, whereas Heaney's term is most likely employed with the broader meaning of "district," partly considering that no religious parish existed in the pre-historic time he is evoking. Furthermore, the compound "man-killing," that seems to strip the act of killing of every legal or even moral connotation, is translated by the adjective *assassino*, which derives from the verb *assassinare*, to murder, thus carrying implications of ethical judgement absent from "to kill" and not necessarily relevant to the climate of human sacrifices to the Earth Goddess referenced by Heaney. Finally, the English "feeling lost" is rendered by *sentirsi perduto*, which has a rather distinct connotation of desperation and ineluctability, close to an expression like "feeling doomed." The impression of somebody who has lost his bearings and found himself, from being a stranger in a strange land, to being suddenly at home, would have been perhaps better conveyed by *perdersi/essersi perso,* or simply by adding a "s" and using *sperduto*. This adjective would have captured both the sense of the speaking voice's geographical disorientation and the feeling of being confused and at a loss, equally valid for the interpretation of Heaney's ambiguous line.

In synthesis, this final stanza also misses an effect of superimposition between Jutland and Northern Ireland. However, this is not necessarily an unintentional mishap. It should be remembered the obvious: target readers are Italian and, in order to comprehend Heaney's epiphany linking homeland with Jutland, they should preliminary achieve an understanding of themselves as Northern Irish. Otherwise, the poem would promote a bizarre identification between modern Italy and ancient Jutland, but in this case the coordinates of interpretation would be completely disarranged. What the translation is arguably trying to achieve is first and foremost the recognition of Heaney's speaking voice as Other, and subsequently his possible identification with the Tollund Man. That is arguably why the Italian title presents readers with a mummy and Jutland remains "out there." They are looking at the process from the outside: they are not part of it, because the poem derives its significance from an awareness of the Northern Irish situation that is impossible to fully recover from the poem alone, unless somebody is highly familiar and possibly emotionally connected with the events indirectly being commented upon. By recalling the deaths of Catholic labourers and four nameless brothers, for instance, Heaney is creating a direct reference to actual atrocities committed in the North. Although the details of those events might not be recovered by the translator, the overall critical support given to her anthology is vast enough to include references to the Northern Irish conflict, so as to allow the attentive reader at least a basic understanding of the overall parallelism.

All things considered, Passannanti's "Tollund Man," although it might offer a different *angle* on the events, or emotions described and memories evoked, constitutes an important tile in the complex mosaic of the elements constituting Heaney's profile in Italy. Furthermore, her projection of Aarhus as a faraway, indeterminate place, achieved in the textual dimension of translation thanks to a clever use of adverbs of space, anticipates a strategy that Roberto Mussapi will employ in his translations from *North* for major Italian publisher Mondadori. In the poem "The Seed Cutters," for instance, the effect of a distant landscape is accomplished thanks to a minor re-visitation of the line "With all of us there, our anonymities." This time the adverb is already distal; yet the first half of the line before the caesura flows uninterrupted, so that the personal pronoun "us" and the adverb "there" almost combine to create one identity strongly defined by spatial coordinates. The Italian version, instead, isolates the adverb *lì*, there, so that there is no continuity with the pronoun *noi*, which remains locked out, looking towards the spatial dimension defined by "there" from a distance. The Italian text's perceived separateness between the personal pronoun and the adverb of space serves to underline the gap between the speaking voice of the poet, comprised within the collective nature of the pronoun "we," and the receiving ear of the reader, rather than encouraging a misleading identification with people and circumstances that are "other" to the Italian context. "The Seed Cutters" in particular embodies the attempt to give a symbolic voice to collective identities whose individual names are lost to history. Heaney's perspective might be temporally displaced, as the poem takes the form of childhood memories, like snapshots of a past that no longer exists. Yet the historical and geographical coordinates that define those anonymous identities are carefully reconstructed through Heaney's act of recollection: their worth defined by the poet becoming part of their lineage to describe them, to "get them true." This line also encompasses the poet's concern with authenticity and the role of art, also stirred by the mention of Breughel. The reference to a Flaming painter who famously portrayed a similar scene to the one described by the poet, although "hundreds of years away," significantly expands the scope of his depiction of reality precisely in its attempt to zoom in and "get them true." Nonetheless, while the boundaries of representation might be blurred across space and time, Heaney's preoccupation with authenticity is clearly on focus. The target text, instead, while highlighting the parallelism with art through the choice of the verb *ritrarre*, characteristically associated with painting, does not capture with the same colloquial incisiveness the reflection on the relation between artistic representation and truth at the core of "The Seed Cutters." An English gloss of the last Italian line, *se li saprò ritrarre esattamente*, would read something like "if I will be able to portray them exactly," which is somewhat different from "if I can get them true." Quite significantly when discussing a poetic composition, the subject "them" and the attribute "true" lose their strong positions at the end of the line. The Italian pronoun is expressed through the weaker accusative form *li* and the adjective "true" is replaced by the adverb "exactly," which also evokes an idea of precision that is not necessarily what the source text suggests as an essential trait of authenticity.

The source text is also advocating a stronger identification between speaker, readers and the subject matter in the part preceding the caesura: "you'll know them." Not only the personal pronoun "you" makes explicit the implied addressee, as entailed by English grammar, but the verb "know" has a deeper semantic scope than the Italian *riconoscere*. Thanks to the activity of the poet the readers will not only "recognize" the seed cutters, they will *know* them, in a more profound manner, inasmuch as their anonymity will become one with the poet and reader's identities, defying the constraints of spatial and temporal determination. The challenge for the translation of this poem lies precisely in reproducing his capacity to reach out for universal meaning while rooting the momentum of its significance in very precise historical, geographical and personal circumstances. All that while simultaneously interrogating the reliability and effectiveness of his poetic statements.

Another poem in which the theme of memory in relation to authenticity is crucially touched upon is the "The Grauballe Man," where the poet compares the past image of the body depicted in a photograph with the image "perfected in [his] memory" after his visit to the site where the mummy is conserved.

> ... but now he lies
> perfected in my memory
> down to the red horn
> of his nails,
>
> hung in the scales
> with beauty and atrocity:
> ... (36)

The source text presents an intricate intersection of details that assert and question the materiality of the body, and its metaphysical nature, at the same time. In Italian, this delicate balance between the overlapping of different temporal dimensions and epistemological approaches is partly altered by the possible use of *perfetto* as past particle of the verb "to perfect," normally rendered in Italian by *perfezionato*. The term *perfetto,* however, is much more commonly used as an adjective, equivalent to the English "perfect." In other words, due to its remarkably more common usage, the Italian translation of that crucial line is likely to be interpreted as "perfect in my memory."

> ... ma ora giace
> perfetto nella mia memoria,
> giù fino al conrno rosso
> delle unghie,
>
> in equilibrio
> atrocità e bellezza,
> ... (37)

Mussapi's translation, therefore, potentially misses the idea that memory is conceived of as a tool that shapes the actuality of the body in the poet's mind. Only through the act of recollection the Grauballe Man is endowed with its full significance of something "hung in the scales/with beauty and atrocity." In Mussapi's text the act of remembering seems to "reflect back" reality without questioning its static nature or reliability, and the translation of this following line is accordingly rendered as *in equilibrio/ atrocità e bellezza*. The Italian text seems to allude to a perfect, i.e. unchangeable balance, thus overshadowing the problematic relationship between ontological truth and representation – especially a poetic representation imbued with symbolic connotations.

Another poem from *North* which is clearly centred upon the organic relation between materiality, representation and memory is "Punishment," but here the equation is virtually overturned:

> . . . her shaved head
> like a stubble of black corn,
> her blindfold a soiled bandage,
> her noose a ring
>
> to store
> the memories of love.

> . . . la sua testa rasata
> come una stoppia di grano nero
> la benda agli occhi una fascia sporca,
> il cappio un anello
>
> a custodire
> i ricordi d'amore.

This time it is the "noose" that stores memories, rather than memory storing something. In this case, therefore, the subjective element is missing, as the noose as an object is only capable of passively retain the dead girl's memories. In Italian, however, the neutral expression "store the memories" becomes the more personal *custodire i ricordi*, where the verb in particular is generally used in connection to something precious, to be safeguarded. *Ricordo* as well is etymologically linked to *ricordare*, literally to remember, which again implies a human agency absent from a word like storing.

In the target text *custodire i ricordi* seems to imply a conscious act of preservation of fond memories, an interpretation supported also by choosing *d'amore* as opposed to *dell'amore*, which would be closer in meaning to memories of loving, intended more as an act than as an affection. This creates a sort of friction not only with the kind of love referred to in the poem – the adulterous love that caused the young girl's death – but, more importantly, with the overriding theme of memory as a site that incubates "the spilled blood," as the title poem "North" recites. This means that in the context of Northern Ireland the act of remembering often nourishes and promotes acts of violence and in Heaney's poetry, by reflection, the "cud of memory" is seldom allayed ("Funeral Rites"). Moreover, the complex articulation of the relation between art and authenticity is partly compromised in translation by downplaying the noose's passivity, as the idea of "safeguarding fond memories" introduces an element of subjectivity at a moment where Heaney is rather focusing on the objective. This creates a sense of absoluteness that is crucially extended to the body as an emblem of timeless violence.

In other words, the poet employs the materiality of the ground, the bodies, and the objects as symbols of a kind of memory that is unaffected by the morphing power of the human act of remembrance, to be set in opposition to poetry as an act of recollection.

In this context, the "shaved head" and the "tar-black face" come to stand as tokens of that ineluctability of violence that caused considerable outrage amongst critics, especially in Northern Ireland. The overall impression given by the Italian *North*, instead, is quite far removed from the problems of Ulster, partly because Mussapi deliberately loopholes this subject in the introduction his translation, or at least give it a very limited visibility. His disposition is to prioritize layers of meaning with more general significance, in order to make them more relevant to the target readers. By re-inscribing the complex configuration between art, authenticity and violence within new coordinates, though, partly obscures its visibility. His choice of *abile* as translation for "artful," for instance, does not posit the subtle but direct connection between the eye of the voyeur and that of the artist. Heaney's playfulness with words' etymology is admittedly harder to release within the perceived constraints of translation. While the "poet's version" is an enticing theoretical stance, eminently formalized by Venuti in recent years, back in the nineties Italian publishers' and readers' expectations were very much moulded around a notion of a "punctuality" of translations, based on a rather specific set of parameters. Those parameters of chimeric linguistic equivalence have been arguably the main reason for the target text's need to resolve textual ambiguities within Heaney's work, thus failing to achieve the source text's carefully balanced structure between static images and the poetic voice, where ambiguity stands out both as the precondition and the outcome of an artistic engagement that strives to be authentic.

In "Punishment," the poet is deliberately embracing the role of "artful voyeur," which reveals his will to simply record factuality without any intervention, as he is unable to find a tenable position. In this poem he is reclaiming the greatest authenticity of poetic art right in the moment when he claims its non-interventionist nature. In this light, "Punishment" functions as a manifesto of the "forked-tongued" diction of *North*, as perfectly articulated in the last two stanzas of the poem:

> I who have stood dumb
> When your betraying sisters,
> Cauled in tar,
> Wept by the railings,
>
> Who would connive
> in civilized outrage

> Yet understand the exact
> And tribal, intimate revenge.

Here the poet acknowledges his inaction, his refusal to take a stand, precisely because he can understand both "the civilized outrage" and "the intimate revenge." "Yet," one of the few conjunctions in English that can carry a coordinating and disjunctive meaning at the same time, becomes a way to capture this ambiguity through the use of language. It is a device used by Heaney throughout the collection and consecrated in the final poem, "Exposure:"

> Rain comes down through the alders,
> Its low conducive voices
> Mutter about letdowns and erosions
> And yet each drop recalls
>
> The diamond absolutes.
> La pioggia cade tra gli ontani,
> le sue basse voci conduttive
> mormorano di erosioni e delusioni
> ma non c'e' goccia che non risvegli
>
> adamantini assoluti.

In this case the reconciliatory act is metaphorically carried out by the rain, with its action of letdowns and erosion coexisting with the diamond absolutes of each drop. It is a powerful analogy, as in the act of allowing the legitimacy of fragile and unstable stances, it envisages the possibility of "absolutes," which are thereby attested and denied at the same time. A stalemate resolved by the following line through another linguistic device, the disjunctive "neither" supporting the final famous statement of this collection: "I am neither internee nor informer," where the poet exposes the lack of absolutes as an integral part of his own human and artistic condition.

In the crucial line from "Punishment," however, the conjunction "yet" becomes in Italian a merely coordinating *anche*, meaning also. Moreover, Mussapi, is also using this line to deliberately place emphasis on the narrating Self, by way of explicitation of a first person pronoun absent in the source text: *io comprendo*. While this preserves in the Italian text a preoccupation with individual responsibility, the poem's significance is partly removed from the seemingly endless violence and inbred hostilities of Ulster. Mussapi shifts the emphasis from Heaney's quest for an alternate imaginative plane where resolution is found through language determining its own reality, to an endeavour of reconciliation between individual ethic and the so-called *legge del branco*. This is not so much due to the minor linguistic variations analysed so far, that only corroborate a specific framing set up by a paratext that overlooks that the moral dilemma in *North*, and indeed the poignant stalemate uttered by "Punishment," have been openly traced back by Heaney to the situation in the North of Ireland:

> It's a poem about standing by as the IRA tar and feather these young women in Ulster. But it's also about standing by as the British torture people in barracks and interrogation centers in Belfast. About standing between those two forms of affront. So there's that element of self-accusation, which makes the poem personal in a fairly acute way. Its concerns are immediate and contemporary, but for some reason I couldn't bring army barracks or police barracks or Bogside street life into the language and topography of the poem. I found it more convincing to write about the bodies in the bog and the vision of Iron Age punishment. Pressure seemed to drain away from the writing if I shifted my focus from those images; . . . (Cole)

In this eloquently dense statement, Heaney gives voice to the epistemological difficulty of understanding and representing violence, which is the single most important cornerstone of the collection *North*. Although the Italian translation is unlikely to stand out as an empathic statement with the "standing in-between" Heaney is mentioning in the interview, it does keep an important dimension of the poem: the poet's guilt at his admitted complicity. Italian readers are also expected to condone the *voyeur*'s silence, as shown by Mussapi's decision to maintain "the stones of silence" as a plural, although in Italian a more conventional translation inspired by the biblical episode would rather be *la pietra del silenzio*, a singular. Yet this would have turned an anonymous deed into a more individual, conscious, and therefore culpable action. *Le pietre* instead becomes a marked expression that highlights the poetic voice's simultaneous separateness and belonging to the plurality of the crowd. This is important to make the poem relevant to Italian readers as a reflection about *omertà*, a topical concept within Italian society, still highly affected by organized crime especially in particular regions, where most of the population is accustomed to "cast the stones of silence."

All things considered, the Italian translator, has ended up creating his own poet's version anyway, as it constructs a reception quite far removed from Heaney's concern with the role of poetry in times of upheaval, unlikely to engender some of the conventional interpretations of *North* within the Irish context, accusing Heaney of endorsing the implicit statement that the violence of today can be read in the light of timeless violence, innate in human nature. Yet "Punishment's" re-signification is almost imperceptible, and no obvious re-contextualization occurred, especially within the translation proper.

The overall economy of a collection as craftily structured as *North* is nonetheless significantly affected even by such apparently negligible changes on a single poem's micro-level, as the internal resonances, the complementarity and the progress that Heaney's poems – in their entirety and mutual relations – achieve, can be hardly replicated.

The concern with the effectiveness of poetry and the purpose of writing at all, for instance, timidly emerging from "Punishment", will come to the forefront in the second part of the book, where the urban reality becomes more prominent in the articulation of Heaney's personal, direct response to violence. A view of the Bogside in Derry replaces the metaphor of the bog, so to speak. Heaney's own concerns with his poetic of ambivalence also remains central, and the poem "Whatever You Say, Say Nothing" displays some powerful lines that encapsulate Heaney's exasperated pledge to remove himself from a journalistic account of events and be able to communicate something through a poetic diction that can simultaneously accommodate two oppositional truths:

> . . . while I sit here with a pestering
> Drouth for words at once both gaff and bait
> To lure the tribal shoals to epigram
> And order. I believe any of us
> Could draw the line through bigotry and sham
> Given the right line, *aere perennius*.

Once again, Heaney is metaliterary generating reconciliation through language, in particular with the expression "at once both gaff and bait," which contains an adverb expressing simultaneousness as well as "both" does as a conjunction, thus achieving the impression of a disjunctive and adjunctive linguistic charge at the same time. Once again, the Italian text has to play down the fervent richness of meaning of the source text, so clearly stressed by the comprehensiveness implied by "at once both." The target text simply reads: *"mentre siedo qui in una seccante/sete di parole che suonina da esca e da uncino/ per attirare le masse tribali all'epigramma e all'ordine."* The adverbial expression "at once" is totally omitted, and the conjunction linking the two nouns is simply *e*, meaning "and." A more akin disjunctive/adjunctive impression would have been achieved by the introduction of "sia (da esca) che (uncino)," but this would have further increased the syllable count of an already long line, all the more if *allo stesso tempo*, translation of "at once," would have also been introduced.

The concept of words failing to capture the multifaceted complexity of reality is important for this poem, as it creates a direct counterpoint to its title: "Whatever You Say, Say Nothing." This expression is a colloquialism particularly favoured by Catholics in Ulster, which describes a way of "getting by" by renouncing to make any statement that might fuel additional tensions in the sectarian environment of the North. A high level of locality, both in the diction and the themes, imbues this poem in particular, that chiefly constitutes a reflection on "the famous Northern reticence," and whether this has dented Heaney's art as a poet.

The translation expectedly evens out the markedness of the language in expressions such as "Prod," or "sure-fire pape," becoming respectively *protestante* and *di sicuro papista* (107). More importantly, the central line 'Of the "wee six" I sing' becomes *di sei piccolo contee io canto*, which suppresses the determinate article that identified Ulster as something familiar in the source text. Mussapi explicitates for Italian readers that Heaney is referring to six counties, but those remain distant and undetermined. The very expression "Northern reticence" is translated as *reticenza nordica* that, while does not erase the source text meaning, does nothing to highlight that Ulster is the central subject of the poem. *Nordico/a*, indeed, is an adjective more often used in Italian to refer to Northern regions in Italy or else the Scandinavian countries, known in Italy as *Paesi Nordici*. Northern Ireland is instead normally referred to as *Irlanda del Nord*, not *Irlanda Nordica*, so that the web of connections inherent to canonical linguistic utterances is somewhat altered. The original referent can nonetheless be easily recovered by informed Italian readers. The translator's endeavour rather consists in avoiding restricting the poem's interpretation to one closely relying on the knowledge of contextual elements.

It is interesting to note how Mussapi's linguistic re-elaboration of the poem is also still acutely aware of the critical framework he has posited in the introduction. This is particularly evident in the following passage:

> . . . The liberal papist note sounds hollow
>
> When amplified and mixed in with the bangs
> That shake all hearts and windows day and night.
> (It's tempting here to rhyme on "labour pangs"
> And diagnose a rebirth of our plight . . .
>
> . . . la nota liberal papista suona vuota
>
> Se amplificata e mescolata ai rimbombi
> Che scuotono cuori e finestre come foglie
> (vorrei far rima con "parto, e le sue "doglie",
> diagnosticando una rinascita dal buio . . .

The source text in this case presents a double-challenge for the translation, as it not only rhymes, as most of the stanzas in this poem do, but it metaliterary refers to rhyming. This means that the translator cannot opt to completely ignore the rhyme scheme, which is Mussapi's preferred choice in his attempt to recreate Heaney's conversational tone and loose syntactical arrangements throughout the second part of the collection. In order to create a rhyme with *doglie* – an important element of the metaphor of giving birth underpinning the collection and carefully reproduced by Mussapi as a unifying element whenever possible – the Italian text introduces the term *foglie*. This, however, slightly alters the image of the windows banging day and night, as it turns it into windows banging "like leaves."

The atmosphere of darkness evoked by the term night is therefore compensated by the translator in the last line, which literally reads "diagnosing a rebirth from darkness." In this way the translator is also shifting the focus away from "our plight," whose unspoken intricacies might be unfamiliar to many Italian readers – and would not be *their* plight anyway, thus lacking the same emotional resonance of the source text. The translator's solution, moreover, is recuperating a layer of meaning made explicit in the introduction, which gave *North* a more metaphysical scope and created a more direct progression from the collection *Door into the Dark* that, was published in a translation by Mussapi himself only two years before *North* was released by Mondadori.

Overall, although the act of translation unavoidably affected the dynamics of *North*, in regards to its relations to other literary works by Heaney himself or others, and especially as a self-contained volume, the translator undertook a skilful re-inscription within the Italian discursive representation of Seamus Heaney. The poems' explorations of the instability and questionability of authentic representation was also often displaced by translation, and some of the poems' significance might have been transformed in some of the readers' eyes; but that does not mean they have been lessened. Perhaps Heaney's statement of artistic detachment as a way to resist dogmatism, propaganda, and a journalistic account of events could not ring equally "true to life if subversive to common sense" (Heaney 1995) in Italy, because "life" conditions and what is considered "common sense" are different within this receiving context. Poems therefore have been deliberately crafted to be looked at from a distance. And yet, even from this brief illustration, emerges that – despite connections lost due to the different sequence in which poems have been presented to readers – Heaney's contours are still recognizable in the "poet's versions" of the committed scholars who performed the translations, his literary posture is still imposing. The alternative would be admitting that poetry is what is lost in translation. He preferred to believe that it is what is found instead, "because for word of poetry without translation, we would be nowhere" (Bray).

Works Cited

Bray, Allison. "Early Birthday Gift for 'Lucky' Heaney at Reading." *Independent* 12 April 2013. 2 Feb. 2015. <http://www.independent.ie/entertainment/books/early-birthday- gift-for-lucky-heaney-at-reading-29191176.html>.

Heaney, Seamus, and Erminia Passannanti. *Terra di Palude*. Salisbury: Brindin Press, 1995.

Heaney, Seamus, and Henri Cole. "Seamus Heaney, The Art of Poetry n. 75." *The Paris Review* 1995. 4 April 2014. <http://www.theparisreview.org/interviews/1217/the-art- of-poetry-no-75-seamus-heaney>.

Heaney, Seamus, and Roberto Mussapi. *North*. Milano: Mondadori, 1998.

Heaney, Seamus, and James Randall. "James Randall: From the Archive: An Interview with Seamus Heaney." *Ploughshares* 37.1 (2011): 173-88.

Heaney, Seamus. *Preoccupations: Selected Prose, 1968-1978*. Farrar, Straus and Giroux, 2014.

—. "Nobel Lecture: Crediting Poetry." *Nobelprize.org*. Nobel Media AB 2014. 2 Aug 2015. <http://www.nobelprize.org/nobel_prizes/literature/laureates/1995/heaney-lecture.html>.

Venuti, Lawrence. "The Poet's version; or, an Ethics of Translation." *Translation Changes Everything: Theory and Practice*. Routledge, 2013. 173-192.

Mark Ó Fionnáin

"The Future's Bright, the Future's Orange!" On the Translation of the Colour *Orange* into Irish

Abstract: Irish is one of two of Ireland's official languages, but English syntax and vocabulary is constantly influencing the language. One such development can be seen in the recent acceptance of "orange" as a Basic Colour Term at the expense of the more native colour term *buí* "yellow". This paper traces this development in Irish over recent years.

Keywords: colour terms, Irish language, English language, translation

1. Introduction

The Irish language has been one of the two official languages of Ireland, along with English, ever since the founding of the Irish Free State in 1922. However, Irish is very much the minority one. Ever since the defeat of the native Gaelic order in the early 1600s, Irish speakers were, at various times, dispossessed, excluded from the realms of business, education and politics, and had their language linked with poverty and illiteracy. Furthermore, approximately half the number of Irish speakers either perished in the Great Famine (1845–1852) or were forced to emigrate, and the mass emigration that followed the Famine saw the number of speakers plummet. The generally accepted number of Irish speakers before the Famine was approximately four million out of a population of eight million. By 1891 this figure had been reduced to just under 665,000, with less than 40,000 monoglots and only about 31,000 children under the age of ten being raised as Irish speakers. This decline has continued, albeit to a lesser degree, into modern times, and the language has thus been reduced to being a minority community language on the Western seaboard of the country, and spoken nowadays throughout the whole country by as little as 20,000 people or as many as 150,000, depending on how optimistic or pessimistic one's outlook is.

In essence, this means that the only place it is possible to be an L1 speaker of Irish surrounded by other L1 speakers are in those small, isolated, rural communities on the coast. If you live anywhere else in the country, you are surrounded by English or, if you can find other Irish speakers, the chances are that they are L2 speakers, and thus, to a greater or lesser degree, influenced by English. As Ó Béarra puts it (265), in a very general sense:

> In 1893, when *Conradh na Gaeilge* [The Gaelic League] was founded [with the aim of preserving the language], native Irish speakers made up over 90% of the Irish speaking population with the remaining 10% coming from the rest of the population. Today, the situation is the opposite with 90% non-native speakers and 10% native.

Ó Béarra draws a distinction between the types of Irish today (261–2), between that of the older generation, who, for the most part, have been uninfluenced by any English, and the younger generations who are much more exposed to the sea of English that surrounds them:

> By Traditional Late Modern Irish, I mean that language which was not only *spoken* in the Gaeltacht [Irish-speaking areas] by both young and old up until about the 1960s, but that was also *passed on* to the next generation. This language, while still spoken, is now mainly limited to those who are in their 50s or older … The influence of English on this type of Irish is minimal and is limited to lexicon. There is little, if any, English influence on the phonology, morphology or syntax. It is as if English never existed. The same cannot be said of the type of Irish spoken today.

Ó Béarra wrote that almost a decade ago, so such traditional speakers are now into their 60s or older. As such, Modern Irish, or, to use Ó Béarra's coining, Traditional Late Modern Irish, is constantly under pressure from the ubiquitousness of English, and the exposure that the younger generations have to it in their daily lives, and this exposure is influencing more and more the development (or possible decline) of the language. One way that this can be seen is the development of the word for the colour *orange* in the language, which this article looks at.

2. The Colour *Orange*

Traditionally, in many European languages the colour orange had either been described in terms of red or yellow, or else as a mixture of the two. For example, in English the original term was *ġeolurēad*, German had *gelbrot*, Welsh had *melyngoch* and so forth, all of which meant 'yellow-red'. However, as the fruit of that colour became more widespread, the name of the fruit itself came to be associated with the colour and so, in many languages, the fruit and the colour eventually became synonymous. Thus, for example, we get pairs of fruit/colour such as those below:

Fruit	Colour
orange	orange (English/ French)
pomarańcza	pomarańczowy (Polish)
naranjo	naranja (Spanish)
oren	oren (Welsh)
orange	orange (German)
sinaasappel/ appelsien	oranje (Dutch)
апельсин	оранжевый цвет (Russian)

As can be seen from that small representative sample, even in those cases where the fruit differs from the colour, as in the case of Dutch, the colour is still represented by a variant of *orange*. Russian is an interesting example, in that the name of the fruit seems to have come in from German or Dutch, but the colour from English or French, thus giving a unique pairing.

3. The Colour *Orange* in Irish

As with other languages, Irish also took in the name of the fruit as a loan word – usually *oráiste*, but sometimes given as *óráiste* or *óraiste* – Irishising both its phonetics and orthography. However, Irish speakers tended to refer to the colour itself by seeing it in terms of a darker shade of yellow or a lighter shade of red, and thus by using either *buí* 'yellow' or *dearg* 'red'. Therefore, for example, in Traditional Irish the Northern Ireland political grouping the Orangemen was referred to as *fir bhuí* 'yellow men', whilst the traditional word for the carrot was *meacan dearg*, lit. red tuberous root, even though both of these would fall under the colour 'orange' in English and other languages.

This division of orange into yellow or red was more or less the situation up until the writing of the 1937 Irish Constitution, and the need for an Irish version of the text and, furthermore, one that had the exact precision of the English. Article 7 of the English text of *Bunreacht na hÉireann* (8) states that "The national flag is the tricolour of green, white and orange." There thus arose the need for an exact equivalent of the colour orange to describe the national flag, seeing as how similar – but imprecise – words like *buí* 'yellow' or *órga* 'golden' would not do. In his study of the Irish version of the constitution, Ó Cearúil (3) notes that the translators went through several versions for the word 'orange' in Irish before coming upon one that seemed to be satisfactory. He says:

> We see in the drafts contained in the Archives how, for example, 'cróchda' was altered to 'órdha', finally appearing as 'flannbhuí', expressing 'orange', in Article 7 of the Constitution, where 'The national flag is the tricolour of green, white and orange' is expressed in the Irish text as 'An bhratach trí dhath .i. uaine, bán, agus flannbhuí, an suaitheantas náisiúnta'.

Cróchda means 'saffron', whilst *órdha* means 'golden'. *Flannbhuí* itself would seem to be an invention, a combination of *flann* '[blood-]red', and *buí* 'yellow', therefore giving a meaning of '[blood-]red-yellow'. Thus, as late as 1937 there was clearly no one, universal, word in Irish to describe the colour orange. In the following years *flannbhuí* seems to have garnered a large measure of acceptance. De Bhaldraithe, in his *English-Irish Dictionary* from the late 1950s, offers only *flannbhuí* as the colour orange (496), as does Ó Dónaill in his *Foclóir Gaeilge-Béarla* from twenty years later (552). Ó Dónaill does, however, give the term *dath oráiste* 'orange colour' under the heading of *oráiste* itself (932), but this is akin to saying something is the colour of grass or of the sky, and not the actual green or blue colour itself. It is also of interest to note that as late as 1991, in *An Foclóir Beag*, the small Irish-Irish dictionary published by the Irish Government, and which ironically has an orange cover, the orange fruit is described as follows (301): *toradh súmhar milis agus craiceann buí air a fhásann i dtíortha teo* 'a sweet juicy fruit with a yellow skin which grows in hot countries'.

To a speaker of Ó Béarra's Traditional Late Modern Irish this would, of course, make sense, but to the 90% of Irish speakers who are an English speaker first and foremost this would appear to be quite the opposite, as how could an orange not have an orange skin? After all, there is a big difference between the colour of a banana and that of an orange. But the editors of *An Foclóir Beag* stuck to the Traditional Irish colour scheme in referring to the 'orange' colour in terms of 'yellow'.

And there were other ways of dealing with this problematic English colour. Ciarán Ó Duibhín, in his discussion of *buí* v. *oráiste*, entitled "An dath é oráiste?" 'Is orange a colour?', gives the following example of how one native speaker – Séamus Mac Grianna – dealt with the problem:

> Tá sé suimeil fosta a fheiceáil mar rinne Séamus 'ac Grianna an cás a láimhdeachas ar lch 277 de "Faoi Chrann Smola", áit a rabh trácht sa Fhrainncis ar léarscáil "où les deux Amériques réunies par leur ithsme, dessinées d'un trait jaune orange, ressemblaient à une paire de grosses besicles". Scríobh sé: "bhí léar-sgáil den dá Mheiriceá ar an duilleoig seo, iad daithte buidhe ar dhath an oráiste agus cuing eatorra, nó go dtabharfadh siad péire de spéaclóirí móra i gceann duine."

> 'It is also interesting to see how Séamus 'ac Grianna dealt with the case on page 277 of "Faoi Chrann Smola", where there is a reference in the French to a map "où les deux Amériques réunies par leur ithsme, dessinées d'un trait jaune orange, ressemblaient à une paire de grosses besicles". He wrote: "there was a map of the two Americas on this page, coloured yellow of the colour of an orange with a yoke between them, so that they reminded you of a big pair of spectacles."'

4. *Orange* Before 1937

None of this means, of course, that the concept of orange as a colour was not totally unknown in Irish before 1937. As noted previously, the idea of a colour between yellow and red did exist, mostly, though, expressed either by *buí* or by variations of 'red-yellow', if it was considered worth mentioning at all, and a quick look at various dictionaries illustrates the authors' varying approaches. In the early 1700s Lhuyd, for example, gave *ruadh bhoidhe* as meaning 'of a reddish yellow' (404). Ó Beaglaoich and Mac Cruitín (516) give the fruit as *oraíste* and even offer 'an orange woman' as "bean dhíolas oráistíghe" 'a woman who sells oranges', but they make no mention of the colour. Connellan (75) again only gives the fruit. O'Neill Lane in 1904 also only mentions the fruit, but by 1917 he has added 'colour of an orange: ruadh-bhuidhe' (1121). Dinneen's first edition in 1904 only has the fruit, although he does classify *órdha* 'golden' as also having the sub-meaning of orange. He also gives *ruadh-bhuidhe* as meaning orange and 'reddish-yellow' (533). In his major second edition from 1927, orange as a colour gets grouped under *órga, cróchda* and also *óráiste*, but, like Ó Dónaill fifty years later, this is given in the sense of *dath óráiste*, 'colour of an orange'. McKenna in his 1911 phrase book, and in his dictionary from 1935, just offers the fruit.

As for dictionaries aimed at students, i.e. those people who would most likely want or need an Irish equivalent, Ó Duirinne and Ó Dálaigh merely give the fruit (117). Uí Chanainn, in turn, first defines *oráiste* as 'food, forage' and only then as an orange, but *flannbhuí* she defines specifically as the orange colour (123, 75). Ó Siochfhradha, in his dictionary from the late 1950s – and which has been regularly reprinted ever since – gives the fruit as *oráiste* (73), but then the colour as *odharbhuí* ('light brown-yellow'), some twenty years after the authoritative Constitution gave *flannbhuí*, but which isn't given in Ó Dónaill's major Irish-English dictionary from a mere decade later.

There are two dictionaries which are of interest, though. Foley, in 1855, in giving the fruit offers *oráisde* and *ór-úbhall* 'gold-apple' (261), and, when describing the colour, states 'orange *adj* dearg-bhuídhe, buídhe, oráisdeach', i.e. red-yellow, yellow, orange. Unfortunately, he gives no explanation as to where *oráisdeach* might be encountered, i.e. in the north of Ireland, where there would have been dealings with the political Orange Order, for example, or whether it is more an everyday word than a political one, or whether it is used in reference to the colour or some other aspect of 'orangeness'. Dwelly's Scottish Gaelic dictionary (711) explains *òraisteach* as meaning 'Full of oranges' or 'Like an orange', with no mention of the colour. Of further interest is Fournier d'Albe who gives *óráiste* as the fruit (206), but under the adjective gives both *deargbhuidhe* and *óráiste*, signifying that the fruit was possibly moving into the semantic field of the colour. However, it does not have an adjectival ending, unlike Foley's *oráisdeach*, and might thus be expected to be used in the sense of *dath oráiste* 'colour of an orange', as used by both Dinneen and Ó Dónaill, or else as an adjective in relation to the fruit, as in, for example, *sú oráiste* 'orange juice'. In either case, it is worth noting the appearance of *oráiste/oráisdeach* on its own to mean the adjective orange.

Roslyn Blyn-LaDrew, in her article on Irish words for orange, makes reference to "almost" thirty school- and text-books she consulted for her research, books that were published between 1922 (the year of the founding of the Irish Free State, and fifteen years before the Irish-language constitution introduced the world to *flannbhuí*) and 2005, and claims that not one of them mentions the colour *flannbhuí* (19). Up until 1937 this is to be expected, since *flannbhuí* only really came into existence with the Constitution. Unfortunately, Blyn-LaDrew does not mention whether they give an Irish for orange at all, nor does she give a list of the titles she consulted. She does, though, mention the earliest book she used, namely *Irish at Home* by Máire Ní Cheallacháin from 1922, which actually contains no list of colours at all for the student. However, in another book from the same year and by the same author – *Irish at School* – Ní Cheallacháin gives the following colour scheme for school-children (78): *white, black, red,* two *greens,* two *greys, purple, yellow, red (of hair), auburn, fair-haired, pink, blue* and *navy*. It is interesting to note that, for English-speaking school-going children, orange was not worthy of an Irish equivalent, but *auburn, pink, navy* and *fair-haired* were deemed more important.

Blyn-LaDrew does make the valid point, however, of asking how the word *flannbhuí* is ever going to become widespread seeing as how it is so rarely encountered in books for learners, and thus it is to be naturally expected that *oráiste* will move in to take over the sense of colour as well, since learners, with no exposure to anything other than *oráiste*, will simply use it for the colour too, just as they do in English. The paucity of a lack of a native one-to-one equivalent for orange and the influence of the English way of seeing the colour can be seen in Irish's sister languages. In the case of Scottish Gaelic, none of Dwelly, McBain or MacLennan, for example, give an equivalent for the orange colour, although, as is to be expected, the fruit makes an appearance. Even earlier, in Munro's list of colours from 1828 (34) we get *white, black, blue, green, grey, red, yellow, brown, purple* and *scarlet*. No orange. It is therefore no surprise that the Gaelicised word *orain[d]s* now exists in the language. Manx is no better, with Kelly, Cregeen and Kneen all avoiding the adjective, and only Fargher (538) giving a Manx version which is, unsurprisingly, *oranje*, the same as the fruit.

5. *Orange* in Recent Times

In the 1980s, the Irish Government's *Foclóir Póca*, under the headword 'orange' gives *oráiste* as the noun and *flannbhuí* as the adjective, and in the Irish-English sections classifies *flannbhuí* as being the colour (158, 365). *An Foclóir Beag* itself defines *flannbhuí* as being *ar dhath an oráiste* 'the colour of an orange' (182), and *buí* as *ar dhath buíocáin nó óir nó arbhair aibí* 'the colour of a yolk or of gold or of ripe corn' but without mentioning oranges (56). However, change was beginning to set in. The *Collins Gem Dictionary* by Mac Mathúna and Ó Corráin gives both *oráiste* and *flannbhuí* as adjectives (218), although they are more precise in the Irish-English section, where *flannbhuí* is described as 'of colour', and *oráiste* is only given as a noun, with no adjectival meaning (110, 177). *Oxford*'s Ó Cróinín, a few years later, totally dispenses in his English-Irish section with the word *flannbhuí*, giving *oráiste* as meaning both noun and adjective (208). He redeems the situation somewhat, by offering *flannbhuí* in his Irish-English section, but he still qualifies *oráiste* as being both a noun and an adjective (491, 581). There seems to be no reason, however, for him not to have offered *flannbhuí* under the English heading of orange.

6. Conclusion

As such, it can be seen that the colour orange has had many variations over the years, from *ruadh-bhuidhe*, *dearg-bhuidhe*, *flannbhuí* and even *órga* – and, with no context given, by *oráisdeach* and *oráiste* itself – but even as late as Ó Siochfhradha's school dictionary, which was still in use into the 1990s, *flannbhuí* was not always given as the Irish equivalent and is not mentioned in books for learners. It is thus to be expected that, not only is the 'original' Irish for *orange* an artificial one-to-one construct anyway, but with no exposure to *flannbhuí* the use of *oráiste* is spreading, and the result is a more literal equivalent. Final proof of this can be found on both the website of the official new English-Irish dictionary (www.focloir.ie) and that of *An Coiste Téarmaíochta* (www.tearma.ie), the Irish language terminology board. On both of these websites *oráiste* is now classified, along with the much-invisible *flannbhuí*, as an adjective meaning the colour *orange*, although, unlike Foley, no attempt has been made to give it an adjectival ending.

Indeed, the well-known Irish-language translator Antain Mac Lochlainn, in commenting on the recent 'official' acceptance of 'oráiste' to mean the colour orange, makes fun of *lucht cosanta na glan-Ghaeilge* 'the defenders of pure Irish' for insisting on *flannbhuí* to describe the colour, even though it is a very rarely used word outside of legal documents. He goes on to sympathise with the poor writer who, having to describe the colour orange, has to rely on *buí* 'yellow' instead, and gives the abovementioned quote from *An Foclóir Beag* regarding the fruit as having a yellow skin as an example of the ridiculousness of the situation. He does deign to allow the defenders of pure Irish, jokingly referred to as *na póilíní teanga* 'the language police', to *flannbhuí* away to their hearts' content if they don't like *oráiste*, or even to use *ar dhath an oráiste* 'the colour of an orange' if they so wish. He does accept that this was not the way it was traditionally, but, as he philosophically notes, "d'imigh sin is tháinig seo" 'this went and that came', i.e. things have changed.

However, all is not yet lost amongst older native speakers of Ó Béarra's Traditional Late Modern Irish. In the book *Rocky Ros Muc*, there is given a song written in the 1980s by Ciarán Ó Fátharta in praise of the boxer Seán Ó Mainnín who hailed from the Conamara *Gaeltacht*. The last verse describes Ó Mainnín fighting for the green, white and orange – the colours of the Irish flag – and the last line is as follows (Mac an Iomaire, 14):

> Ó, ghnóthaigh sé an cath ag troid do na datha uaine, bán is buí
>
> 'Oh, he won the battle fighting for the colours green, white and yellow'

But this would seem to be no longer so amongst the younger, English-influenced generations, amongst whom the universal English use of the word orange has worked its way into Irish. On a Website discussion board, where the topic of conversation was "Dathanna as Gaeilge" 'Colours in Irish' and, in particular, the 'correct' Irish word for 'orange', one user noted:

> Around Teach Mór and Lochán Beag in the 40's and 50's the orange colour was always referred to as flannbhuí . . .

In response to this, another user, a young native speaker from Conamara said:

> Yes, Oráiste is an introduced word. Flannbhuí was used more often before that, and still used for the national flag. But today most people use "oráiste" for the colour too.

As such, it would seem that, despite Irish surviving into recent years without any need for an exact equivalent for the colour orange, we are now witnessing a small portion of the language's uniqueness fading into oblivion, with the younger generations of speakers consciously imitating the English colour scheme, and thus losing some of the Irish language's authenticity in the process.

Works Cited

An Foclóir Beag. Baile Átha Cliath: An Gúm, 1991.

Blyn-LaDrew, Roslyn. "What Color Is an Orange? Carrots? The Flag of Ireland? or, "Ye Could Be Murd(h)ered for [Teaching] That!" *The Proceedings of the Barra Ó Donnabháin Symposium, 2007*. 17–26. 18 August 2015. <irelandhouse.fas.nyu.edu/docs/CP/4172/0017-0026_WhatColorIsAnOrange.pdf>.

Bunreacht na hÉireann. Baile Átha Cliath: Oifig an tSoláthair. 2012.

Connellan, Thaddeus. *An English Irish Dictionary*. Dublin: Graisberry & Campbell, 1814.

Cregeen, Archibald. *Fockleyr na Gaelgey*. Douglas: J. Quiggan, 1835.

Dathanna as Gaeilge. 21 September 2015. <www.irishlanguageforum.com/viewtopic. php?f=28&t=995&start=10>.

De Bhaldraithe, Tomás. *English-Irish Dictionary*. Baile Átha Cliath: Oifig an tSoláthair, 1959.

Dinneen, Patrick. *Foclóir Gaedhilge agus Béarla*. Dublin: The Irish Texts Society, 1904

—. *Foclóir Gaedhilge agus Béarla*. Dublin: The Irish Texts Society, 1927.

Dwelly, Edward. *The Illustrated Gaelic Dictionary*. Fleet, Hants: Dwelly, 1918.

Fargher, Douglas. *Fargher's English-Manx Dictionary*. Douglas: Shearwater Press, 1979.

Foclóir Póca. Baile Átha Cliath: An Gúm, 1986.

Foley, Daniel. *An English-Irish Dictionary*. Dublin: William Curry and Company, 1855.

Fournier d'Albe, Edmund Edward. *An English-Irish Dictionary and Phrase Book*. Dublin: Celtic Association, 1903.

Kelly, John. *Fockleyr Manninagh as Baarlagh*. Douglas: The Manx Society, 1866.

Kneen, John Joseph. *English-Manx Dictionary*. Castletown: Yn Cheshaght Ghailckagh, 1938.

Lhuyd, Edward. *Archæologia Britannica. Vol. 1. Glossography*. Oxford: at the Theater, 1707.

Mac Con Iomaire, Ruairí. *Rocky Ros Muc*. Indreabhán: Cló Iar-Chonnachta, 2014.

Mac Lochlainn, Antain. *Geansaithe oráiste is léinte pinc*. 18 August 2015. <http://tuairisc.ie/geansaithe-oraiste-is-leinte-pinc/>.

Mac Mathúna, Séamas, and Ailbhe Ó Corráin. *Collins Gem Irish Dictionary*. Glasgow: HarperCollins, 1996.

MacLennan, Malcolm. *Gaelic Dictionary*. Aberdeen: Acair, 1925.

McBain, Alexander. *An Etymological Dictionary of the Gaelic Language*. Stirling: Eneas Mackay, 1911.

McKenna, Lambert. *English Irish Phrase Dictionary*. Dublin: M.H. Gill and Son, 1911.

—. Lambert. *Foclóir Béarla agus Gaedhilge*. Baile Átha Cliath: Oifig Díolta Foillseacháin Rialtais, 1935.

Munro, James. *A Gaelic Primer*. Glasgow: John Wylie & Co, 1828.

Ní Cheallacháin, Máire. *Irish at Home or Gaedhilg sa mBaile*. Dublin: The Educational Company of Ireland, 1922.

—. *Irish at School or Gaedhilg sa Scoil*. Dublin: M.H. Gill and Son, Ltd., 1922.

Ó Beaglaoich, Conchubhar, and Aodh Buidhe Mac Cruitín. *The English-Irish Dictionary: An Foclóir Béarla Gaoidheilge*. Paris: Seamus Guerin, 1732.

Ó Béarra, Feargal. "Late Modern Irish and the Dynamics of Language Change and Language Health." *The Celtic Languages in Contact: Papers from the Workshop within the Framework of the XIII International Congress of Celtic Studies, Bonn, 26–27 July 2007*. Ed. Hildegard L.C. Tristram. Potsdam: Potsdam University Press, 2007. 260–69.

Ó Cearúil, Micheál. *Bunreacht na hÉireann: A Study of the Irish Text*. Baile Átha Cliath: Oifig an tSoláthair, 1999.

Ó Cróinín, Breandán. *Oxford Irish Minidictionary*. Oxford: Oxford University Press, 1999.

Ó Dónaill, Niall. *Foclóir Gaeilge-Béarla*. Baile Átha Cliath: Oifig an tSoláthair, 1977.

Ó Duibhín, Ciarán. *An dath é 'oráiste'?* 2013. 18 August 2015. <http://www.smo.uhi.ac.uk/ ~oduibhin/cruinneas/oraiste.htm>.

Ó Duirinne, Séamus. and Pádraig Ó Dálaigh. *The Educational Pronouncing Dictionary of the Irish Language*. Dublin: The Educational Company of Ireland Limited, 1922.

Ó Siochfhradha, Pádraig. *Learner's English Irish Dictionary*. Dublin: Educational Company of Ireland, Ltd, 1957.

O'Neill Lane, Timothy. *Lane's English-Irish Dictionary*. Dublin: Sealy, Bryers and Walker, 1904.

—. *Larger English-Irish Dictionary*. Dublin: Funk and Wagnalls, 1917.

Uí Chanainn, Eibhlín. *Foclóir an Mhic Léinn*. Baile Átha Cliath: An Press Náisiúnta, 1962.

Contributors' Notes

Debora Biancheri is an Irish Research Council post-doctoral research fellow, currently working on a project about Seamus Heaney's Italian translations. Her research interests include literary translation theory, linguistics and comparative literature. She is also lecturing on Italian and Translation Theory for the School of Languages Literatures and Cultures in the National University of Ireland, Galway. Amongst her more recent publications are "Translating Táin Bó Cuailgne for modern and foreign audiences: strategies and challenges", published in *Australasian Journal of Irish Studies* and "Translating Irish Literature into Italian: The Challenges of Decoding the Unfamiliar", included in *Authorial and Editorial Voices in Translation*.

Eliza Borkowska is assistant professor at the Department of English at the University of Social Sciences and Humanities in Warsaw. She is the author of *But He Talked of the Temple of Man's Body. Blake's Revelation Un-Locked* (2009) and a number of publications concerning British Romanticism that appeared, among other things, in *Blake/ An Illustrated Quarterly* and *Romanticism*. Since 2008, she has been a member of Wordsworth-Coleridge Association. Currently, she is completing work on her second book, *The Presence of the Absence: Wordsworth's Discourses on God*, whose focus is the treatment of religion in the work of William Wordsworth.

Said M. Faiq, FRSA, is Professor of intercultural studies and translation at the American University of Sharjah (UAE), where he was chair of department (2003–07, 2009–10), and director of the graduate program in translation and interpreting (2002–11). He is a visiting professor at Exeter University (UK). Prior to his current position, he worked in Africa, the Middle East and the United Kingdom (Salford University, (1990–2003), where he was director of studies for undergraduate and graduate programs in Arabic/English translation and interpreting; and Leeds University, (1996–1998), where he was visiting lecturer in applied linguistics). He has served as consultant to private and public organizations for educational and related sectors and serves on a number of academic editorial and consultancy boards/agencies. He is an established figure in intercultural and translation studies and allied areas and has directed and examined graduate research (Cambridge, McGill). His publications include *Agency and Patronage in Eastern Translatology* (co-edited with Ahmed Ankit, 2015), *Culguage in/of translation from Arabic* (co-edited with Ovidi Carbonnel and Ali AlManaa, 2014*), Beyond*

Denotation in Arabic Translation (co-edited with Allen Clark, 2010), *Cultures in dialogue: A translational perspective* (2010), *Trans-lated: Translation and Cultural Manipulation* (2007), *Identity and Representation in Intercultural Communication* (2006), *Cultural Encounters in Translation from Arabic* (2004).

Joanna Gładyga graduated from English Studies at University of Social Sciences and Humanities in Warsaw. She wrote her M.A. thesis on the works of Raymond Carver. She also graduated from B.A. studies in Journalism. Currently, she is a Ph.D. student of Cultural Studies at University of Social Sciences and Humanities where she is preparing a dissertation about approaches to creativity in culture, analyzing the notions of originality and authenticity. Her areas of interests include literature, with the focus on the relation between writers and their editors, Polish cinematography and folk culture.

Prof. Dr. **Nafize Sibel Güzel** has mainly a literary background. Her master dissertation is entitled "Major Barbara a Linguistic Study in Intentionality Acceptability and Informativity" (1991). Her doctoral dissertation is on "The Teaching of Literature in EFL classes: *Of Mice & Men* in the Light of Stylistics Structuralism and Semiotics" (1996). Her main interests lie in Stylistics, Modern Literary Theories, 18th Century Women Writers. Her book on the long 18th Century foregrounds some women writers of the period who are excluded in the anthologies of the time. She worked at Selçuk University, Konya; Celal Bayar University, Manisa as the founder of the English Language and Literature department there respectively and has been working as a professor at the department of Translation and Interpretation at Dokuz Eylul University, İzmir since 2014.

Natalia Kamovnikova, Ph.D., has been teaching languages, literature, translation, and interpreting since1998 at different universities in Russia and Bulgaria. Now an independent researcher, she has recently finished her book *Made under Pressure: Literary Translation in the Soviet Union, 1960–1991* devoted to the issues of censorship, manipulation, and the role of translated literature in the Soviet Union. Her recent publications have mainly been focused on the issues of censorship and manipulation in translation, as well as the problem of time and space modifications in literary translations. Natalia Kamovnikova is also a practicing conference interpreter and translator.

Lada Kolomiyets is Chairperson of the Department of Theory and Practice of Translation from the English Language, Institute of Philology at the Taras Shevchenko National University of Kyiv, Ukraine. Her research interests include: history, sociology and theoretical issues of translation in Ukraine and other Slavic countries, literary translation through the prism of postcolonial studies, cultural and gender issues of translation, eco-translation.

Wojciech Kozak is Associate Professor in Centre for Conrad Studies in the Department of English at Maria Curie-Skłodowska Univeristy, Lublin, and Lecturer in the Humanities Department at Szymon Szymonowic State School of Higher Education, Zamość. He has written a monograph of Joseph Conrad's usage of myth and a number of articles on various aspects of his fiction. He is also a translator for the series on Conrad published in Polish and edited by Prof. Wiesław Krajka (2 volumes to date). His academic interests include the literature of British modernism, postcolonial writing, literary and cultural theory, as well as the methodology of literary interpretation.

Abdullah Küçük received his B.A. degree in English Translation and Interpreting at Hacettepe University. He worked in various fields in the private sector as a manager, private English teacher, freelance translator; and as an English instructor at Ardahan University, Ardahan for almost a year. He is now an M.A. student in Translation Studies and working as a research assistant at the Department of Translation and Interpreting of Dokuz Eylül University, İzmir. He is busy with writing his dissertation at the moment, the subject matter of which is the reflection of thought and belief systems on literary works. His main interests are pseudo-translations, technical translations, translation theories, postcolonial translation.

Yulia Nanyak (b. 1986) is teaching English, Translation and Interpreting at the Hryhoriy Kochur Department of Translation Studies and Contrastive Linguistics at the Ivan Franko National University in Lviv, Ukraine. In 2007 received a Master's Degree in Philology (specialized in English-Ukrainian Translation/Interpreting). She is currently working on the candidate thesis Individualized speech as a problem for translation as based on the tragedy *Faust* by J. W. Goethe and its Anglophone and Ukrainian translations. This project is closely connected with Translation Studies, Cognitive linguistics and Pragmatics. Apart from that, her main areas of research and publications include Translation Historiography, Literary Translation Theories, Ethnolinguistics and Literature.

Mark Ó Fionnáin teaches classes in Irish language and culture and English at the John Paul II Catholic University of Lublin. He has translated from both Russian and Polish into Irish, and is the author of *Translating in Times of Turmoil*, on the translations into Irish by Liam Ó Rinn of Adam Mickiewicz. He is a qualified Irish language translator and his main areas of interest and research include Irish, Scottish Gaelic and Manx, their literatures, and related issues of translation. He is currently researching the traditional Irish colour scheme and how it is changing under the influence of English.

Agnieszka Podruczna is a Ph.D. student and a lecturer at the University of Silesia (Poland) at the Department of Postcolonial Studies and Travel Writing, and she is currently in the process of writing her Ph.D. dissertation on the subject of the body in postcolonial science fiction. Her academic interests include first and foremost postcolonial studies, gender studies and the theory of science fiction, but she is also interested in popular culture, queer studies and the theory of postmodernism.

Hanna C. Rückl is a doctoral candidate at the Institute of English and American Studies at TU Dortmund University (Germany) and part of the RuhrCenter of American Studies' PhD program. Her dissertation project deals with the role and position of the literary translator. In 2012, Ms. Rückl received her degree (Mag. phil.) in English and American studies from the University of Graz (Austria). She teaches classes in American cultural and literary studies as well as classes in which translation is used as a tool to critically engage with poetry. In her spare time she produces a bi-weekly one-hour program focusing on music, literature, and linguistics, which is aired on Radio Helsinki, a community radio station based in Graz.

Eriko Sato is Assistant Professor in the Department of Asian and Asian American Studies at Stony Brook University (State University of New York), where she earned her PhD in Linguistics. Sato teaches Japanese language and linguistics courses at Stony Brook University. Her research interests include Japanese linguistics and pedagogy, translation studies, and second language acquisition. In addition to several journal articles in these research areas, Sato has published a number of Japanese textbooks and grammar/kanji reference books including *Contemporary Japanese* (Tuttle Publishing) and *Complete Japanese Grammar* (McGraw-Hill). Sato serves as the advisor for Teacher Education Program for Japanese at Stony Brook University and the Director of the Pre-College Japanese Program.

Piotr Skurowski was founder and longtime director of the Institute of English Studies at SWPS. Currently Dean of the Faculty of Humanities and Social Sciences. Has also taught at the University of Warsaw and University of Łódź, and worked as a visiting professor at the universities of East Texas State, Kent State and Notre Dame. His main professional interests lie in the area of U.S. Cultural History and Cultural Studies. His publications include monographs on Henry Adams and on American intellectual history in the Progressive Era, as well as a Polish translation of Mark Twain's Autobiography.

Jerzy Sobieraj is Associate Professor of American Literature at the University of Social Sciences and Humanities (SWPS), Warsaw, Poland. He also taught Southern fiction at the Universitat Jaume I in Spain. His research focuses on Southern literature and history of the 19th and 20th centuries. He has published his articles and reviews in Poland, Great Britain, and the USA. As a recipient of several academic grants, he did research at Brown University, University of Tennessee at Knoxville, and Vanderbilt University. The first Polish monograph about the Ku Klux Klan is among his books. Professor Sobieraj has recently published *Collisions of Conflict: Studies in American History and Culture, 1820–1920* and is currently at work on a book-length study of the American Civil War.

Jacek Wiśniewski is a professor of English, teaching history of English literature, British Civilization and History of Britain at SWPS University in Warsaw since 2010. Before, he lectured at University of Warsaw for many years, where he served as Head of Institute of English Studies, and Dean of Faculty of Modern Languages and Oriental Studies at University of Warsaw. His main fields of interest include British poetry from the Romantics to the present moment; British and American attitudes to war and peace in the 20th c., as they are expressed in literature and culture (this produced three books and c. 50 scholarly essays which appeared between 1988 and 2009); most recently, the poetry of John Clare: the next project is a critical study of Clare's life and work.

Cultures in Translation
Interdisciplinary Studies in Language, Translation, Culture and Literature

Edited by
Elżbieta Muskat-Tabakowska and Agnieszka Pantuchowicz

Volume 1 Agnieszka Pantuchowicz / Anna Warso (eds.): Culture(s) and Authenticity. The Politics of Translation and the Poetics of Imitation. 2017.

Volume 2 Agnieszka Pantuchowicz / Anna Warso (eds.): Interpreting Authenticity. Translation and Its Others. 2017.

www.peterlang.com